Exploring the Tomato

Exploring the Tomato
Transformations of Nature, Society and Economy

Mark Harvey
University of Manchester, UK

Steve Quilley
University College Dublin, Ireland

Huw Beynon
Cardiff University, UK

Edward Elgar
Cheltenham, UK · Northampton, MA, USA

Published by
Edward Elgar Publishing Limited
Glensanda House
Montpellier Parade
Cheltenham
Glos GL50 1UA
UK

Edward Elgar Publishing, Inc.
136 West Street
Suite 202
Northampton
Massachusetts 01060
USA

A catalogue record for this book
is available from the British Library

Library of Congress Cataloguing in Publication Data

Harvey, Mark.
  Exploring the tomato : transformations of nature, society and economy / Mark Harvey, Steve Quilley, Huw Beynon.
    p. cm.
  Includes index.
  1. Economics—Sociological aspects. 2. Technological innovations. 3. Agricultural innovations. I. Quilley, Stephen. II. Beynon, Huw. III. Title.

HM548 .H37 2003
306.3—dc21

2002029839

ISBN 1 84376 189 0

Printed and bound in Great Britain by Bookcraft, Bath

Contents

Figures

Tables

Diagrams

Acknowledgements

The authors would like to express their great appreciation for the support and encouragement given to the 'tomato project' and the resulting book to all colleagues within the ESRC Centre for Research in Innovation and Competition. Many have been assailed with an endless stream of tomato stories and gossip, enduring them with remarkable indulgence. Serious critical comment and discussion have also greatly improved the arguments and development of the book. Much is due to the broadly stimulating atmosphere within which this project could breathe. A great deal of gratitude goes to Sharon Hammond as the Centre's Administrator for all the expert help and assistance that are so important for undertaking effective research. Her thoughtfulness and unstinting dedication have contributed enormously. Warmest thanks are expressed to Angie Lewis for preparing the text for publication with great patience and good humour, and admiration too for overcoming the many wicked obstacles raised by Microsoft.

The authors are deeply indebted to all the interviewees (listed in the Appendix), many of whom tolerated a level of ignorance from the social science invaders into their very different worlds. Thanks to them for sharing their knowledge and expertise and for giving their valuable time. Their diverse and passionate enthusiasms for, and professional interest in, the tomato were infectious, and this is hopefully reflected in the book. Especial gratitude is due to those who facilitated further interviews beyond their own, Nigel Scopes and Alan Parker for many contacts within the tomato growers' community, and Alun Beynon for his help in arranging a suite of interviews on working patterns in retail distribution. Marian Garcia of Wye College provided invaluable assistance by conducting interviews in and related to Spain.

Needless to say, although this book could not have been written but for all the contributions, stimulation and support from others, the authors are entirely responsible for the views expressed in the book.

1. The Human Tomato

The human tomato is the tomato that has grown up symbiotically with human beings. Since it was fully domesticated, possibly by around 5000 BC,[1] the tomato has never been quite the same. Nor, it can be argued, have humans.

From the time that human societies developed an intermediate world of cultivated nature, a new ecology, populated by a range of new varieties of flora and fauna, formed their most intimate natural environment. Even hunter-gatherer societies have produced major ecological transformations,[2] as did indigenous peoples in Australia, changing tropical rainforest into bush by means of an 'agriculture' of back-burning. But settled agricultural societies that domesticated animals and plants began a constructive intervention to create species whose characteristics and existence depended to a greater or lesser extent on human societies. For many millennia, therefore, the character of the planet earth is and has been persistently and inadequately represented by a bipolar antithesis of Man versus Nature. We inhabit a triangular world of society (including human biological existence), cultivated nature and non-cultivated nature. Interactions between them are also triangular. Impacts occur (in either direction) between non-cultivated nature and cultivated nature, between society (pollution, construction, irrigation) and non-cultivated nature (earthquakes, tornadoes, viruses and so on) and between human biological and social existence and both cultivated and non-cultivated nature.

One thread of the story of the human tomato is that, along with many other domesticated species, the process of its transformation and cultivation has been continuous and is ongoing. As human society has changed, so has the human tomato. Diamond (1999) has argued that the original geographical bio-availability of different species of flora and fauna for domestication was decisive in shaping broad geopolitical divisions of wealth and civilisation to this day. In his view, material constraints of climate and land mass subsequently facilitated latitudinal rather than longitudinal diffusion. If Diamond undervalues social, cultural and economic variation in favour of these basic material factors, nonetheless production and appropriation of agricultural surplus, possible only through the ongoing development of cultivated nature, have certainly shaped human history. Varieties of cultivated species have consequently inhabited cultivated ecologies, which in turn have been developed in relation to varieties of human society, culture and economy.

Within cultivated nature, there has been no 'natural' natural selection for many millennia, if by natural is meant 'that which occurs naturally', without human intervention. Species – such as, familiarly, the dog or the cat – selected for and hybridised by various techniques or technologies resting on historically different scientific and pre-scientific understandings, owe their existence to humans and their survival to modified and continuously maintained environments. On the one hand, therefore, they are distinctively and historically developing *socio-economic* species. But that does not mean that they cease to be biological species, or that human intervention or cultivation can in any way modify nature to the extent of changing the operation of natural laws, inventing species that defy gravity and exist without oxygen, or fabricating physiologies. One thing that humans are unable to do is to 'change the nature of nature' (Teitel and Wilson, 2000). So, on the other hand, they are *bio*-socio-economic species – as, indeed, in this historically developing symbiotic relation, are humans. For, as cultivated species, both humans and non-humans can maintain biological existence only within certain given, naturally occurring, physical and ecological parameters. Urban pollution, to take a most non-natural environment, has concentrated naturally occurring gases and minerals to levels which kill people in large numbers. Some things are immediately and lethally toxic if digested as food[3] (the tomato was long thought to be as poisonous as its close relation, deadly nightshade); and modes of cultivation or ecological modification need to be biologically appropriate for the cultivated species, and may be so in ways that are deleterious or disastrous to the surrounding non-cultivated species (forest clearance, for example).

SOME TOMATO ANTIPASTO

The cultivated species chosen in this book is the tomato and its attendant humans. Tomatoes, growing wild in the Andes, were first domesticated by the humans of that region. As twentieth and twenty-first century social scientists, encounters with the tomato provoked probably almost as much astonishment that experienced by the first Spaniards when, arriving in the Aztec city of Tenochtitlán in the valley of Mexico, they entered its markets:

> Customers plunged immediately into a bewildering maze of colours, shapes, smells, and sounds. Vendors spread gardens of greens over white cotton blankets on the ground. They offered piles of red plump tomatoes, purple sweet potatoes, brown jicama routes, and green cactus paddles. The merchants not

content with their colourful displays, sliced open samples and shoved them
under the noses of passing shoppers. (Pilcher, 1998, 8)

For, tomatoes, along with many other edible and cultivated flora and
fauna, were unknown in Europe before 1492, and it is likely that both the
word 'tomato'[4] and the first salsa were brought back to Spain following
these early crossings of the Atlantic and Hernán Cortés' conquest of Mexico
in 1519 (Smith, 1994, 1996). In 1998, at the United Kingdom Tomato
Growers Association, a scientist from Novartis (a large biotechnology and
agro-chemical company) explained how a team of their researchers had
been sent to scour the Andes for wild varieties of tomato, resistant to certain
diseases, whose beneficial traits could then be bred back into cultivated
species, using the latest recombinant DNA hybridisation technology. This
'return to the origin', another transatlantic passage, seemed to create a
strange loop in history, bringing together the ultra-modern with pre-
civilisation.

$$\sum\square\!\!\!\!\!\big]\big[$$

In the course of a visit to a tomato seed company, the historical appreciation
of the value of seed was revealed to have been given a bizarre new twist.
The Netherlands is a world centre for development of new seed varieties,
based on its horticultural tradition going back beyond the great
'tulipomania' of the seventeenth century. Seed manufacture is itself now a
global operation, the high-tech and scientific parts of the operation being
undertaken in Europe, whilst labour-intensive hand pollination is performed
by cheap labour in Thailand, Chile, Malaysia, Taiwan and elsewhere. Seed
weighs very little and, once treated, is transported across the world by air.
So by a peculiar combination of circumstances, the seed company is
situated very close to Schiphol airport. Its seed, and especially its 'portfolio'
of varieties, is banked in a 3-metre thick concrete bunker in case of an
aircraft accident. This somehow illustrates the difference between a natural
gene pool and a commercial seed portfolio.

$$\sum\square\!\!\!\!\!\big]\big[$$

Some encounters unavoidably leave questions hanging in the air. The
production manager responsible for sourcing tomatoes for Marks &
Spencer's fresh Tomato and Basil Soup described a trip into Turkey,
crossing the Bosphorus and heading off into the wilderness, in the middle of
which was an ultra-modern factory containing the very latest technology for
processing tomatoes. There was a way of extracting juice without heat

treatment or evaporation, known as 'reverse osmosis'. For him personally, the taste was the ultimate, the Holy Grail of tomato juice. The factory was owned by a Japanese company who gave permission for use of the juice in Europe, but only in soups, not in tomato drink for which the technology was intended in Japan. This seemed a strange contemporary way of dividing the world into different taste zones. But why Japan? Why in Turkey? How does fit this into understandings of the global and the local?

An encounter with the historical tomato dating from the beginning of the twentieth century jolted some preconceptions for different reasons. New York's first ever large neon advertising sign was a six-storey high illuminated apparition of bottle of Heinz Tomato Ketchup. It appeared in 1900. Advertisements for Campbell's Tomato Soup, subsequently mimicked (plagiarised?) by Andy Warhol who made the tins a twentieth-century American icon, began appearing across the United States at around the same time. Tomato ketchup and soup were pioneering the mass production of food. It was Fordism before Ford. Tomatoes before cars.

Then, entering a state-of-the-art greenhouse in Northern Europe, one encountered an unbelievable sight. The vines towered over humans, as in a tropical jungle, and grew to 5 metres in height, 15 metres long. The greenhouses stretched into the far distance, and tomato workers travelled down the rows on mobile platforms running on tramlines of pipework. But an important proportion of the labour had been taken over by insects. Bees did the pollinating. Wasps did the policing. Tiny wasps (*encarsia formosa*), 0.6 mm long and scarcely visible, zipped around vigilantly looking for whitefly. This was astonishing in itself, and became more so on discovering how these wasps were mass produced and provided with special ecologies to encourage them to work more effectively. Similarly bemusing were bumble-bees, a solitary insect, naturally evolved to reproduce once yearly. Yet, within the glasshouses, there were yellow cardboard boxes, distributed regularly between the rows of tomatoes, with pictures of bumble-bees and labels in seven major world languages (for humans, it can be presumed). These delivered bumble-bees for as long as need be, pollinating tomato flowers more efficiently than any human or mechanical means and on unpaid overtime. A technological breakthrough was required for their commercial mass and artificially accelerated reproduction. And, at the time of the research, Europe was witnessing a rather spiteful bumble-bee price war between the major bumble-bee producers, of the order, 'Buy our wasps, and get your bumble-bees free'. Meanwhile, supermarkets in the UK were advertising their tomatoes produced under this insect work regime as the most natural tomatoes in the world. It helped to distinguish between a marvel of nature and a natural marvel.

Then, taking an anthropological stance towards humans in order to see ourselves as strange as those first tomatoes were to the Spanish, there are 'cultures of production' which are quite specific to different societies. The Dutch industry faced a crisis in the mid-1980s, producing ever more tomatoes which were ever more tasteless. They decided to do something about it, and to cultivate something different from the standard 'commodity tomato'. Their production system is based on associations of small family units, so they determined that each association would only be allowed to grow one variety of tomato and every association's tomato had to be different from the others. The social identity of the association was thereby derived from the variety of tomato they grew, and any member not growing that variety was banished from the association. Product (including taste) differentiation was achieved, and the social organisation was built round it. A strange symbiosis between tomato variety and social identity.

People have long fantasised about discovering the secrets of everlasting life. So a further surprise arose when a scientist engaged in the genetic modification of the tomato declared that, for the tomato, the problem had been cracked. Without inserting any genetic material foreign to the tomato, a gene can be switched off (the one that controls the production of ethylene), and a tomato will sit unchanging on a desk for a lot longer than any human is ever likely work at one. And then, if one so chooses, ethylene can be switched back on for the tomato to die like the rest of us. So the tomato, it turned out, was one of the first organisms to be understood in terms of how its ageing process was genetically programmed to happen (collapse of cell walls, ripening, wrinkling, changing the colour of its skin, and so on), rather than resulting from natural decay, degeneration or being 'worn out'. In an issue of the *Financial Times* (23/4 January 1999), on one side of a page a scientist was proclaiming a miraculous breakthrough whereby it would soon be possible to trigger a 'Methuselah gene' and delay human ageing indefinitely, and on the other there was a report of protests on the dire consequences of genetic manipulation of plants. Interactions between humans and tomatoes occur even at the most fundamental biological level – which, *at the same time*, is profoundly social.

⟩⃤⟨

It is difficult now to imagine a European cuisine, either Mediterranean or Northern, without the tomato or the potato (Santich, 1995). Some cuisines are particularly difficult to imagine. After all, an English cooked breakfast could not survive without a fried tomato (Rhodes, 1999). And Italian cuisine or Greek salads? Looking at current consumption and patterns of trade in tomato, there remain considerable differences in national cuisines, which are, as many have noted (Appadurai, 1988; Goody, 1982), an important constituent of national identity. On the basis of the present, one tends to make assumptions about the past. To digress for a moment, an English person might be entitled to think that small independent greengrocers, where one imagines the tastiest tomatoes were always available, enjoyed a hallowed tradition that stretched back at least to the Napoleonic stereotypical view of the nation. Not so. Greengrocers were almost the last independent shop to emerge, in the early twentieth century, *after* the first multiple retail chains had appeared. A similar illusion could be held about Italian cooking, and, from a position of ignorance, it is nonetheless a surprise to discover that three centuries after the introduction of tomatoes to Europe, the tomato was still generally absent as a sauce for pasta or topping for pizza. The first published recipe for spaghetti and tomato sauce appeared in a Neapolitan cookery book in 1837 (Coe, 1994). From available sources, it seems that it was only after Italian unification at the earliest that the tomato spread and became a widely used feature of Italian cuisines (Grewe, 1987). Garibaldi's triumphal march in 1870 was when the tomato began first to be heralded as an essential ingredient of national identity, aided by the appearance in 1891 of the Italian equivalent of Mrs Beeton, Artusi's *Science of Cooking and Art of Eating Well* (Camporesi, 1993).[5] Before then, there is little evidence that the tomato was widely cultivated in Italy, and certainly not industrially so (Sereni, 1974). Yet maize, another novelty from the New World, rapidly became adopted and cultivated for making dishes with polenta, certainly by the eighteenth century. In Italy, maize thus became a human food, whereas in France it was recognised only as animal fodder. Reading the list of the wares available in the markets of Tenochtitlán (and there were many more than those cited above), there is a curious question, relating to cuisine and agriculture, about what items entered into national cuisines, when and why, which were 'blocked' and why. For the reverse migrations (wheat, pork, beef) from Europe to the Americas similar questions can be asked.

THE TOMATO AS PROBE AND OBJECT

These small tomato foretastes give a suggestion of things to come, an obsession to be shared. Triangular traffic between societies, cultivated nature, and 'natural' nature; new forms of mass production and consumption; cuisines and cultures; shops; construction of the global, refraction in the local; fundamental science as social process. How much of a changing world can be viewed through the lens of a changing tomato?

The tomato has been engaged with in two ways: as an empirical probe into the ways of the world and as an object of fascination in its own right. As a probe, many of the contexts and preconditions which sustain and support the many shapes and forms of tomato have been explored, along with other (mostly food) commodities. As an object of fascination, the tomato, fresh, processed, cooked and displayed, has been tracked from seed to supermarket shelf. There have been a number of similar studies, which have adopted other items of human diet,[6] of which Sydney Mintz's study of sugar stands pre-eminent (Mintz, 1986, 1996). Mintz traces the history of how 'sweetness' has been related to 'power', through regimes of production and consumption of sugar, derived from sugar cane. Domesticated in New Guinea in about 8000 BC, sugar cane migrated first westwards, and penetrated Europe primarily through the Muslim conquest of the Mediterranean. As a quasi-industrial crop from a very early period, the cultivation and milling of sugar was very labour intensive and relied on slave labour, a form of production that also migrated westwards with it, eventually reaching the Atlantic islands of Portugal and Spain (the Azores and Canaries), before crossing the Atlantic to introduce sugar cane to the Caribbean, the reverse passage from the tomato or potato. It then formed a central pivot in the triangular trade of slaves and sugar between Europe, Africa and the Americas. In Mintz's account, sugar was always socially coded by those who consumed it, at first as an aristocratic luxury subject to sumptuary laws and as a vehicle for conspicuous display in sugar confectionary, then as a cheap form of calorie intake for the newly urbanising English proletariat of the industrial revolution, when combined with tea as a stimulant. In so doing sugar subverted a fundamental characteristic of diet that had hitherto been almost universal in human societies, the meal consisting of a central carbohydrate staple accompanied by a taste-contrasting complement. For Mintz, the social coding for consumption, which became embedded in the habits of aristocratic luxury or working-class necessity, constituted the 'inner meaning' of sugar. This 'inner meaning', however, was historically transformed by changes in its 'outer', political meaning, its links with the power structures of the day, such as the emergence of a connection between a mercantile slaving elite and new industrial capital. Historically, therefore, there is a continuous interplay between 'inner meanings' and 'outer meanings' traced by the history of sugar.

The great strengths of Mintz's study were to link production with consumption, cultural change with economic and material change, and in a broad historical vision, to grasp major structural or configurational changes in what sugar is in human society. Sugar was also a particularly good candidate precisely because of its multi-layered connections between major power structures and common everyday consumption. The tomato or the potato (Zuckerman, 1999) are less elevated by virtue of being less 'well-connected', even though in their own ways, and inevitably, they enter into different patterns of power and inequality. However, if there is a weakness in adopting an object such as sugar as the organising principle of a research process and narrative, it is that the object is also embedded in linkages which overflow it, and yet which are essential to its understanding. So, for example, the central figure of the latter part of Mintz's story is the sweetened cup of tea. Tea has a quite distinctive historical trajectory, and is linked to a different aspects of power in the English Empire, as well as (eventually) a plantation system of growing involving forms of bonded and waged labour substantially different from Caribbean slavery (Griffiths, 1967; Guha, 1977; John, 1999). The example of fish and chips parallels that of sugar and tea. Zuckerman has provided an illuminating account of how the potato entered into different national agricultural and culinary regimes, and in so doing how new varieties, some more vulnerable to disease, were bred and cultivated with disastrous consequences for the people of Ireland. Kurlansky (1999) has written a more journalistic and gripping account of how cod changed the world, linked also to the slave trade, but latterly with the industrial revolution in iron and steam ships, as well as refrigeration. But one needs to put these two trajectories together in a UK context to arrive at fish *and* chips (Walton, 1992).

There are good reasons for containing a study by restricting its scope through the device of choosing a singular object. But the procedure also tends to focus on one aspect, in the case of sugar its central core functionality of sweetening, rather than explore all its varied manifestations in objects of consumption. Indeed, this has led some types of analysis to take each particular food item, including the twentieth-century development of sugar and sugar beet production, as a distinct 'system of provision' (Fine et al., 1996). With the tomato, this type of analysis seems quite inadequate, and for two main reasons.

Firstly, in thinking about how the tomato enters into different cuisines, which are always being historically transformed, it seems critical to be aware of linkages and complementarities between tomatoes and other foods.

Moreover, the diverse trajectories of fresh and processed tomato have to be considered. It is difficult to appreciate the significance of ketchup without the rise of the hamburger in US cuisine, for example (Hogan, 1997). The tomato is something that *usually* shares its life with others.

Secondly, departing furthest from the rather linear view of 'systems of provision' or food (and other) supply chains (Gereffi, 1996; Gereffi and Korzeniewicz, 1994), the tomato cannot be allowed to bear the full weight of the world it finds itself in. In the current world, new varieties and forms of tomato find their distinctive habitats on the supermarket shelf, or in new convenience foods. Pizzas and sandwiches provide it with new vehicles. Yet, it would be absurd to assume that these habitats and vehicles were created just for the tomato. It is here that the tomato therefore changes from being taken as object in its own right, and becomes a probe, one amongst many alternative candidates, for exploring the new habitats, new forms of food and eating. A wholesale market, for instance, is a place of exchange and a distribution centre for a host of foods, and wholesale markets came and went with particular forms of tomato production, varieties of tomato and retail outlets. To understand the tomato, it is necessary to step outside single and linear analysis to grasp this general context, its appearance and disappearance, and not to crush the tomato by attributing to it too great a burden of explanation. Barrientos's inspiring work (Barrientos et al., 1999 Barrientos and Perrons, 1999) on Thompson seedless grapes, or Dixon's (2000) fascinating study of the evolution of chicken production and consumption in Australia, exemplify the use of an object as a probe. The grape is used to explore gender dimensions of harvesting in diverse Southern climates, and the enmeshing of peasant agricultures with global counter-seasonal food distribution. The chicken is deployed to analyse particular power relations between retailers and farmers, morals of healthy eating and deep-fried fried chicken fast food outlets, and household structures and shopping patterns. As with this research on the tomato, the food item in question reveals multifaceted changes in contemporary society, but only as one food amongst many, subject to similar changes and in analogous contexts.

So, by adopting the tomato both as an object in its own right and as empirical probe, the aim is to achieve the best of both worlds. Directly, the tomato has undergone a process of proliferation and variation, assuming multiple forms, processed and fresh, in ways that make it an object of fascination. Cultures of production and consumption have appeared and disappeared. Even when treating the tomato as an object in its own right the attempt has been made to go beyond the analysis of the 'social life of a thing' (Appadurai, 1986),[7] especially if conceived of in terms of a 'biography of a commodity' (Kopytoff, 1986), and as something that exists only insofar as it is exchanged. Then, as a probe, the tomato, an extremely ordinary and commonplace object, has indirectly provided new perspectives and insights into the nature of change and variation in contemporary capitalism. It has provided a thread through a maze of contemporary and passing institutions: markets and supermarkets, pizza factories and scientific laboratories, seed manufacturers and satellite tracked trucks, glasshouses and cookery books. And it has also left many loose ends, a host of unanswered questions.

THE TOMATO, SOCIETY AND 'INSTITUTED ECONOMIC PROCESS'

If one thinks of a breed of cattle or of cat – Jersey or Burmese – they may have existed for centuries in conjunction with human beings, even though it is quite likely that there have been modifications along the way. In that sense, these breeds can be seen as social and economic *institutions* – with their own distinctive characteristics. Likewise the tomato: different distinct varieties have been developed, and often lasted for quite long periods of time. A peculiar example, if only for its name, is the common variety Moneymaker, a favourite amongst amateur gardeners, with small-scale greenhouses and grow-bags. It has a particular socio-economic existence, as a plant bred for the purpose. The peculiarity of its name is that it should, if anything, be called Moneysaver, insofar as it is not a major commercial variety, and is mainly grown for self-subsistence as a DIY extension of the allotment culture.

This view of breeds of tomato, indeed of the multitude of hybridised varieties of plants and animals, as bio-socio-economic institutions, leads to a much broader perspective which underpins the analysis of many aspects of this book. It is possible to see cans, such as cans of baked beans in tomato sauce, as socio-economic institutions. The ketchup bottle is an almost global institution. By extension, the supermarkets in which these items appear, or the horticultural production culture characteristic of Northern Europe, can also be understood as socio-economic institutions, essential to the tomato's existence. As already suggested, different national cuisines, and their development over time, are cultural, social and economic institutions.

The concept of 'instituted economic process' was first sketched by the anthropologist and historian, Karl Polanyi (1944, 1957), and an attempt has been made here to develop its radical potential for analysing the economic, cultural and societal in quite novel ways. Working on the tomato, conceptually and as a process of empirical research, is challenging to ways of thinking the biological, the economic and the societal. So, the empirical investigation of the tomato and the conceptual means of analysis have developed in interaction. This theoretical approach has been interwoven with the tomato narrative, and theoretical debates deliberately remain largely implicit, although sufficiently signposted for those familiar with them.

Most interpretations of Polanyi have taken the cosier concept of 'embeddedness' to suggest ways in which 'the economic' is enmeshed in social contexts and, at the micro level, interpersonal relationships and networks (Granovetter, 1985, 1992a, 1992b; Granovetter and McGuire, 1998; Callon, 1998a, 1998b). This approach tends to contextualise the economic, rather than analyse central economic processes directly. It gives economics a softer edge, whilst leaving the hard centre more or less intact, as something with which economists proper can continue to preoccupy themselves. There is a strong argument, however, that Polanyi's intention was quite different, and comes closer to Swedberg's (1998) recent appeal to economic sociology,[8] that it should concern itself with the central features of the economy: markets, price, competition and so on.

For, Polanyi was suggesting two things. First, that economic institutions are specifically economic, and have to be treated as such. There are historically different and various ways of instituting 'the economic'. Second, that the place and degree of differentiation of economic institutions differ in different societies: there is a shifting boundary between the distinctly economic and societal, legal, political and cultural processes, and that the boundary is itself therefore 'instituted' variably.[9] The consequences of this view are profound, both in terms of what 'the economy' is and how one goes about studying it. For, unlike classical political economy and its analysis of capitalism, or modern neo-classical economics, it means there are no fundamental axiomatic starting points on the basis of which an economy can be more or less constructed as a mechanical model, an abstract representation of flows and circuits, or static equilibria. The economy, rather, is essentially an historically and socially variable configuration of instituted processes, and *how* they are instituted (and de-instituted) as economic becomes the focus of study. It leads to a view of capitalism as a fundamentally multiple and diverse phenomenon, although not in terms of contextualised departures from a theoretically pure 'economic' form. It means that it is possible more coherently to pass from the study of the instituted economic to other distinctly instituted social, political, legal or cultural processes, and to explore their boundaries and articulations.

Take an apparently trivial example of the kind that stimulates thinking the economy differently: a can of tomato soup. To become a distinctively 'economic' institution within a capitalist society, tomato soup had to become an exchangeable commodity. In the US and the UK it did so under emergent mass production, which in turn entailed standardisation of the size of cans, quality of contents including regulation over use of chemicals, a pricing structure which applied to a whole range of canned goods and mass-produced foods, new modes of marketing and distribution, and so on. But, in Germany today it seems that in general not much canned soup is consumed, and if it is, it is sold mostly in much larger 2-kilogram cans. It does not make much sense to think of this difference in terms of divergence from optimal capitalist modes of production (as found in the USA). It makes more sense to analyse such differences in terms of how the 'economics' of food production and consumption is instituted differently in Germany (including unpaid work performed in the household, different retail markets, different patterns of agricultural production), and then how these 'economic' processes might be related to differently instituted cultural aspects, such as national cuisines.

In this analysis of the tomato as a bio-socio-economic object, a range of instituted economic processes, and how different tomato objects have become instituted and de-instituted, have been explored. The ways different markets through which tomatoes pass are formed, and how this affects the kinds of commodities they are, have been analysed. There are different types of industrial organisation, and different cultures of production. Although the main focus of the research has been on Europe and the UK, the appearance of cans of genetically modified *Californian* tomatoes in the UK made it necessary to examine differences between the USA and the European cultures of production. In the USA, most production is open-field and mechanically harvested, and Friedland and Barton provided a crucial understanding of how mechanical harvesting arose in the context of immigration laws restricting the flow of Mexican *braceros* into the Californian agricultural industry. Scientists at the University of Davis consequently hybridised a tomato that could be mechanically picked without damaging the fruit. New machines replacing human labour were matched by new varieties of tomato suited to machines. The study was called *De-stalking the Wily Tomato* (Friedland and Barton, 1975, 1976). And this historical turn can be aligned with a contemporary account of the tomato industry in Mexico, partly introduced by American capital and much of it dedicated to export to America, where open-field production employs thousands of seasonally migrant workers who continue to pick tomatoes manually (Torres, 1997).

Looking at these different cultures or regimes of production meant paying especial attention to the North European glasshouse horticultural regime, and this in turn stimulated an analysis of instituted competitive processes at various scales: between this regime and the Southern European open-field regime; between Dutch and UK growers within the Northern regime; and then finally between different groups of growers within the UK. Thus competition, so often addressed as a universal, global and anonymous market force, was seen to be variously instituted, in different markets, at different geographical scales. Competition, as instituted, can produce variety as much as homogeneity. Indeed, the way markets and competitive processes are established at different scales suggests that scale itself is an instituted phenomenon, leading to a more nuanced view of 'globalisation'. To be sure, there is a process of development of a global scale, and even of a global tomato (Busch et al., 1991; Bonanno et al., 1994; Friedland, 1994), although there have also been previous 'global' scales, such as the gold standard or the British *imperium*. But at the same time different scales, local, national and regional, are continually being constituted and reconstituted, providing new sources of variation.

Innovation, too, whether in new technologies of hybridisation, ecological transformation, or in the production of pizzas for Tesco's or Sainsbury's, as one of the major sources of variation can itself be seen as an instituted economic processes. Radically different modes and styles of innovation, and different ways of coordination in innovation processes between different agents (primary producers, manufacturers, biotechnology companies and retailers) have been central to developing an understanding of 'the tomato'. In the UK, the role of supermarkets as significant players in the innovation process, across almost the full range of tomato products and at all phases from seed to supermarket shelf, has been unique and distinctive: their presence, in the foreground or background, is pervasive. This stimulated an analysis of how shifts in the relative balance of power and power asymmetries between different economic agents (manufacturers, retailers, consumers), might have contributed to this distinctive role and new styles of innovation.

Thus, ways of analysing the process of variation of the tomato in capitalism led to new ways of thinking the economic, social and cultural. But an instituted economic process analysis, it should be emphasised, is not an exercise in descriptive relativism, in which varieties of capitalism are so many *sui generis* cases, each a law unto themselves. Explanations of what produces variety, and ways of understanding processes of variation, are developed. A key feature of the analysis has been in terms of different historical configurations of four interrelated processes: production, distribution, (market) exchange and consumption (see Diagram 1.1). These four elementary processes, it should be stressed, are not necessarily separate institutional spheres, and indeed, the argument is that they are differently instituted in different historical configurations.

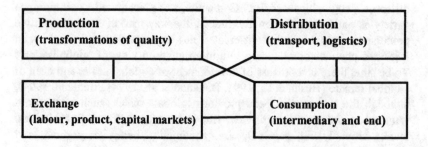

Diagram 1.1 Four interrelated economic processes

In the current historical capitalist period, these processes may be in both distinct *and* economic institutions (for example factories /offices and related firms; trucks and logistics companies; job centres, supermarkets and stock exchanges; intermediate producers and cinemas, sports stadia). But this was and is by no means always the case. The household, although arguably now a prime social space for end consumption, is neither a locus dedicated to consumption alone nor an exclusively economic institution.[10] The way 'the tomato' is instituted through each of these four elementary processes is examined, especially in Part II. It is argued that how these elementary processes are institutionally configured on different geographical scales and over historical time is fundamental to variations within capitalism. Of course, the tomato is but one probe. There would have been many other routes, and indeed methodologies, which would not necessarily take an object and look at it under this fourfold prism. It would, for example, be equally possible to take the labour-capital relation and analyse that in terms of instituted economic process, across the four elementary processes; or the changing institutions of final exchanges across a range of contrasting products (houses, cars, clothes).

There is one further point concerning this configurational analysis: in historical societies these four processes form a *relational complex*, and are to be found in some instituted combination. There is no original point in time when production was independent from consumption, exchange from distribution. Nor does it make sense to treat any of the four elementary processes *analytically* as in some way primary or as a process which could exist independently of a relation with the other three. Each process is *both* specific *and* defined by its relations with the other three processes in a relational complex. Consequently, the focus for an explanation of change and variation is primarily the change in *relations between* the four processes, as these are manifest in historically instituted configurations.

For example, the relations between early twentieth-century mass production, systems of distribution, wholesale markets, retail outlets and patterns of consumption, are analysed. Then the ways in which these relations have been transformed in the contemporary epoch, along with the institutions of supermarkets, product differentiation, logistics and new patterns of consumption, are examined in order to understand configurational change. Likewise, key differences in this relational complex are used to understand the difference, say, between the Netherlands tomato and the United Kingdom tomato.

'FOLLOWING OUR NOSES'

The methodology in pursuit of the tomato could be described simply as 'following one's nose'. No attempt is made to undertake a comprehensive and exhaustive world history of the tomato in all its past and present manifestations. Indeed, this is *not* a social history of the tomato – although history, as a means of exploring variation, remains central to the empirical method. So, as a measure of economy, critical moments or aspects of tomato history have been chosen, partly with a view to understanding the contemporary forms the tomato has assumed. Tracing the historical tomato involved looking at early cookery books, and original texts on tomato growing and culture from the nineteenth century, but mostly secondary sources were relied on. In seeking out critical historical moments, the Guernsey, Blackpool and Lancashire tomato industry were explored to see how the virtual disappearance of a once flourishing production–distribution–retail–consumption system threw light on much broader and general historical change. The development of the genetically modified tomato over a 25-year period has been researched in depth, because that too seems to be a critical moment in the historical life of the tomato.

For the contemporary tomato, a wide range of people were interviewed and a spectrum of organisations and sites visited, mostly in the UK, but also in the Netherlands, Spain and Italy (see the Appendix for a list of interviews and institutions). The tomato was traced across all its phases from seed to supermarket shelf, and in each phase key or strategically placed informants were interviewed. Although much of the eventual range of investigation was far from pre-planned, and wasps or laser bar-code readers proved irresistible distractions, there was an element of controlled serendipity. It was a question of tracking down what appeared to be the important connections and comparisons. The idea was to get an overview of the overall trajectory of the tomato, and although there are aspects not properly covered (packaging, for example), the research itinerary was far from random. Seed manufacturers, wasp and bumble-bee producers, import distributors, warehouse operatives and managers, tomato growers (a wide cross-section), soup, sandwich, pizza and salad manufacturers, scientists in public and private sector biotechnology, were engaged with during the enquiry.

To complement interview material, statistical data from Eurostat of the overall production and trade of the tomato in Europe was used to provide a big picture of differences and patterns within Europe. This comparative perspective was then supplemented, within limited research resources, by looking at the critical differences between the Netherlands, the UK and Spain as primary suppliers to the UK market. The aim was therefore to look for contrasts and differences, rather than to give comprehensive accounts of each of these countries.

Whether investigating the production of fresh tomatoes for salads or genetically modified tomatoes for purée, it has been important to acquire enough understanding of the biology of the tomato in order to grasp it as a biological institution, as much as a socio-economic one. When talking to growers, it is clear that their understanding, care and often passion for the plant and its attendant insects are essential aspects to the production process. In this sense, as social scientists there is a particular obligation to respect the tomato as tomato, and not to treat it as social construction, either scientific or economic-productive. It is not reducible to a social invention, inviting sociologists to reaffirm themselves within their own discipline or discourse. It is necessary to take full account of its – and our related – biological existence and reality.

The core of the approach of engaging the tomato as both object and probe thus brings together many different resources and methods, but necessarily has some arbitrary and whimsical aspects to it, as well as leaving many loose ends. The result of researching in this way means that the book can be seen as being made up of a series of closely interrelated case studies, of fresh tomato production, supermarket retailing, genetic modification, of wholesale markets and distribution centres. This is reflected in the structure and organisation of the book.

THE NARRATIVE VINE

The book is divided into two main narrative branches. Part I traces the trajectory of the tomato from its first domestication through to its genetic modification in the late twentieth century. This Part asks how and in what socio-economic contexts the tomato has been biologically transformed at critical moments in its long association with humans. Part II explores major and revolutionary twentieth-century changes in production, distribution, retailing and consumption. The aim of this second part is to analyse more systematically the four elementary processes and their interrelation, as preparation for a synthesis and analytical conclusion.

Part I opens with a broad historical chapter describing the transformation of the tomato from an exotic, possibly poisonous and aphrodisiac,[11] fruit into an ordinary object of consumption (Chapter 2). An overview is gained of how the tomato came to be cultivated on a mass scale, rather than as a small-scale, marginal element of production and consumption. Scientific breeding and the application of science to processing and canning under capitalism transformed the tomato from the irregular and erratic plant and fruit first encountered by the Spanish. The production of plate glass and new methods of horticulture, particularly for the control of disease, saw the beginnings of the creation of an entirely artificial ecology which the tomato was eventually to inhabit.

There follows a case study of the rise and fall of Guernsey as a once major tomato-producing economy for the United Kingdom (Chapter 3). Its rise involved the development of specific varieties of tomato that could endure the systems of transport and distribution, but which were also suited to the small-scale, non-capital-intensive production systems on the island. The collapse of the industry reveals the contingent and many-faceted process of change from a small-scale horticultural economy to an offshore financial services centre, involving the rise of supermarkets, international competition from Holland and the Canaries, fuel crises and other interlocking features. These combined, however, in a contingent manner to reveal a major shift and change in configuration for tomato production and consumption across Europe.

From the particular case of Guernsey, the overall patterns of production, trade and consumption of fresh and processed tomatoes in Europe over a 30-year period is examined (Chapter 4). This revealed the extraordinary growth in productivity of the North European horticultural regime (the Netherlands and to a lesser extent the UK), but also the very distinctively instituted patterns of trade, with Italy consuming a lot of 'fresh' tomato and exporting almost exclusively processed tomato and on a major scale, and Spain eating considerably less fresh tomato, but rapidly increasing its exports, and almost exclusively of fresh tomato. In terms of what 'fresh' means, however, there are two quite distinct regimes in Northern and Southern Europe. The different ways that 'freshness' is economically and socially instituted are explored. The chapter then explores in depth the export-oriented Dutch horticultural regime, serving especially the German discount market, its crisis of the tasteless tomato in the mid-1980s, and its subsequent reorientation and reorganisation.

The development of the latent potential of these glasshouse forms of cultivation to create and 'fabricate' a total ecology through multiple

technological innovations, in which every aspect is subject to human
transformation, is described (Chapter 5). And yet, such an ecology is a
natural ecology sustaining organic life, so constituting a 'fabricated nature'
– not a contradiction in terms. As an innovation process taking place over
two decades or more, many different types of firms, public research stations
and supermarkets were involved, as were many interlocking innovations
across the different dimensions of plant and ecology. It is a prime example
of a 'distributed innovation process'. For reasons which are explored, the
most technologically advanced and ecologically sustainable forms of
cultivation, computer controlled and capital intensive, were developed in
the UK very much in conjunction with the rise of the UK supermarkets. The
different forms of producing variety in the UK and the Netherlands are
analysed.

The transition from a high-tech hybridisation and ecology to the
emergence of the genetically modified, commercially successful tomato
product (Chapter 6) provides a critical moment in the history of the human
tomato. But why did the *tomato* become the first, and until now only,
example of genetic modification undertaken for the purpose of enhancing
processing and food quality, as against for purposes related to agricultural
cultivation and use of agrochemicals? The process involved both
fundamental advances in the understanding of the tomato *and* the
emergence of a particular commercial product at the end of a long and
tortuous history. At the beginning of the story, none of the participants had a
clue about the eventual outcome. The complex dynamics leading to the final
emergence of a can of genetically modified tomato purée on supermarket
shelves, its subsequent disappearance and the consequences for shaping the
future of biotechnology, are described and analysed. The process of
institution and de-institution of a market for genetically modified products
thus demonstrates broader social, political and economic forces involved in
the development of science, technology and markets. This moment in the
tomato's history stimulated fundamental questions about science and
technology as social practice, and the multiple causal strands that shape the
human interaction with nature.

Part II begins the more systematic analysis of changing configurations of
production, distribution, exchange and consumption with an account of a
revolutionary change in mass production and consumption at the turn of the
twentieth century, within which the tomato figures as a significant pioneer.
The astonishing emergence of mass-produced ketchup (Heinz) and tomato
soup (Campbell's), destined to become world super-brands, is examined
along with how mass markets were created. In the late twentieth century,
however, development of powerful supermarket chains, disrupted the
previous power relations, and introduced a radically different configuration

(Chapter 8). A growing conflict between these manufacturer-branded goods and the new range of supermarket-branded goods in chill and convenience foods, in which tomatoes play a prominent role, is seen to be critical in the dynamic of change. The role of TV chefs and trend-setting restaurants in generating innovations on supermarket shelves allows foods to become items of mass fashion in distinctive ways. New patterns of innovation are shown to develop, together with the new configuration of the relation between manufacturing, retailing and consumption. Considerable tension and instability marks the conflict between these two configurations, played out differently in different countries and at different scales. Different and conflicting models of retailing in the US (Wal-Mart), the UK (Tesco or Sainsbury) and continental Europe (Carrefour) suggest a far from stable institutional future.

Then, turning the focus to distribution (Chapter 9), the emergence over many centuries of the wholesale market as an intermediary between producers and, eventually, independent retail outlets, is traced. The history of Covent Garden, partly because of its dominant role in the UK and partly because of a salience in popular imagination (earning the sobriquet of 'Mud Salad Market' at the end of the nineteenth century), is examined as an example of transformation in market institutions. It reached its apogee in the early 1970s when, after a long travail, it moved to a modern and expanded location. But within the space of a couple of decades this whole configuration collapsed, to be replaced by an information technology-driven distribution system developed by supermarkets, which has created entirely new and strategic workforces. New temporalities of working to meet new demands of freshness and shopping in a 24-hour society form an intrinsic aspect of this generally hidden side of the supermarket shopfront. The 'fresh' tomato under this regime is quite different from the 'fresh' tomato of the wholesale distribution system, along with new forms of 'fresh' processed foods, from sandwiches to chill ready meals.

To complete this analysis, the transformation of retail outlets is analysed (Chapter 10), signalling 'two revolutions' in exchange configurations, the first occurring with the emergence of independent greengrocer and multiple grocery chains at the beginning of the twentieth century, the second heralded by the supermarket revolution of the 1970s to 1990s. Retailing institutions are seen as facing two ways: towards growers and producers, and towards consumers. This latter relationship forms the central focus of this chapter, suggesting ways in which the activity of shopping, the nature of the products that can be bought, and the social shaping of consumer demand are transformed in the reconfiguration of this relationship. Different retail outlets, situated in different urban socio-economic settings, market different ranges of tomato, sourced from different parts of the world. But in turn,

there is a relational spiral of new temporal patterns of consumption inducing
new patterns of working inducing new patterns of consumption.

The concluding chapter draws together this analysis to suggest how these
different relational aspects of production, distribution, exchange and
consumption combine to explain the remarkable transformation of the
'ordinary' tomato during the course of the twentieth century. The story is
one of dislocation, destruction and reconfiguration, as well as of
extraordinary dynamism and innovation, where changes in one relation
create disturbances and tensions for the others. There is no harmonious state
of rest for a contented tomato, but rather a continuous process of variation
and differentiation, producing ever new metamorphoses as the human
tomato develops with human society. The varieties in forms and
manifestations of the tomato thus stand at once as an aspect of, and a
metaphor for, the varieties within and between different manifestations of
capitalism.

NOTES

[1] According to Stark B. L. (1981)

[2] It is important to avoid romanticisation of such societies as being in some
way closer to a pristine nature. To be sure, their survival depended on the
ability to understand nature – as does ours – and their means to devastate
nature were certainly less developed. Nonetheless, their human
interventions were capable of dramatically affecting their surrounding
biodiversity and ecology.

[3] Some foods, such as almonds, were 'naturally' toxic to humans prior to
domestication and hybridisation, when the toxic trait (cyanide) was bred
out of the bio-socio-economic species (Diamond, 1999). Other common
cultural   foods with carcinogenic properties may have longer-term
deleterious effects   whose characteristics become manifest only with
demographic increases in   longevity.

[4] From the Aztec Indian word *xitomatl*, a large variety of the *tomatl*
(Smith, 1994, 15).

[5] 'After the March of the Thousand the tomato triumphantly spread through
the whole peninsula .... The tomato had long been neglected in culinary
practice, viewed almost with suspicion and relegated to a negligible role.
Now, much more than the potato, it became a revolutionary new element
that broke the mould of eighteenth-century Italian cooking' (Camporesi,
1993, 127).

[6] For a fuller comparison of these see Harvey (2002).

[7] Appadurai contrasts the social history and cultural history of things, the
latter being internal to a given culture, the former the trajectories of things
over the long term (Appadurai, 1986, 35–6). Although the approach is

both historical   and comparative, by looking at processes which produce variation, it is   hoped to avoid a 'methodological fetishism' of the object which treats it as   having a life of its own.

8 'The main thrust of economic sociology should be to analyse economic phenomena, with less emphasis on phenomena at the intersection of the economy and other parts of society ... [It] should address problems situated at   the centre of the economy, such as prices and different types of markets' (Swedberg, 1998, 166). For discussion see pp. 162–72.

9 'The instituting of the economic process vests that process with unity and stability; it produces a structure with a definite function in society; it shifts the place of the process in society, thus adding significance to its history; it   centres interest on values, motives and policy. The study of the shifting place occupied by the economy in society is therefore no other than the study of the manner in which the economic process is instituted at different   times and places' (Polanyi, 1957, 250).

10 Of course, it can be argued that not even factories are exclusively economic institutions, inasmuch as they contain main cultural and social aspects. Likewise, one pays to go into a cinema to see films, which is what sustains cinemas, whatever else might go on in the back rows. The conditions for their existence, however, are economic, as evidenced either by the bankruptcy of individual firms, or the economic obsolescence of whole classes of firms. The changing relationality of the household with other institutions has certainly shifted its economic function, but as an institution it has many other 'core' functions as conditions of its existence, such as the reproduction of emotionality, transmission of culture and so on.

11 An interesting example of how fear of the unknown combined positive and   negative properties in a single object, undecided as to whether it was poisonous and aphrodisiac, or poisonous, or aphrodisiac.

PART I

From Domestication to Genetic Modification

2. From Nature into Culture and Economy

INTRODUCTION

Over the last 450 years the tomato has emerged from obscure origins in South America to become one of the most ubiquitous components of diet and food culture on the planet. It belongs to a family of plants (potato, pepper, aubergine, tobacco and petunia), which appear to have an almost in-built propensity for domestication and subsequent hybridisation[1] (Nevins and Jones, 1987, 3–6). Domestication and adaptation to human agriculture created the conditions for this global extension in the plant's range. Association with people has proved a supremely successful evolutionary trajectory. There is not a country or region on the planet where tomatoes are not eaten in some form or other, and few where it is not cultivated.[2] But unlike the definitively global Coca Cola, the tomato has in nearly every case 'gone native', and been assimilated into 'localised' horticultural-culinary traditions. One only has to consider its role in the 'traditional' cuisine of India or the Middle East to appreciate the extent to which the tomato has become an agri-cultural polymorph.

The tomato has come to occupy a central and varied place within contemporary diet through major geopolitical events beginning with the early modern 'discovery' of the Americas by Europeans. The tomato's emergence onto the world stage and its subsequent diffusion was then intertwined with the development of global capitalism and the world market. From the first tentative processes of internationalisation associated with early mercantile capitalism, followed by the growth of industrial capitalism and the consolidation of the Victorian liberal economy of the nineteenth century, right through to contemporary processes of globalisation, the history of the tomato can be seen to coincide with the history of capitalism.

EARLY TOMATO ENGAGEMENTS

'Peru – Mexico – Spain – Italy – Provence; This was the route followed by the plant' (Hyam, 1954, 39)

25

Probably first domesticated in the Andean *alto plano* by neolithic peoples around 5000 BC (Stark, 1981), the tomato spread in untraced and untraceable ways from South to Central America during succeeding centuries. The (cherry) tomato originated in the coastal highlands of western South America. Hyam (1954) argues that the plant was domesticated under the ancient Peruvian civilisation around Lake Titicaca, with domesticated varieties subsequently diffusing north, through Guatamala, and into Mexico. It followed cultural pathways similar to domesticated maize (Manglesdorf and Reeves, 1939). In the years before the arrival of the Spanish, some unknown process of cultural migration had caused the plant to move up to central America where Mayan and other Meso-American peoples domesticated it and used it in their cookery. Much later, the Aztecs inherited tomato husbandry and consumption from these early Mayan farmers. Following Dressler (1953) and Rose (1899), Smith (1994) argues that the Aztecs adopted the plant readily because of its superficial similarity to the *tomatl* or Husk Tomato (*Physalis ixocarpa*) with which they were already familiar. The *tomatl* was small, green or yellow, sour and covered by a paper-thin membrane. Their name for the tomato – *xitomatl* – meant 'large *tomatl*'. By the time of Cortés' invasion of Mexico in 1519, Hernandez had documented how the tomato was a significant aspect of Aztec culture (Hyam, 1954, Coe, 1994). The famous Franciscan friar Bernadino de Sahagún, a precursor of later colonial anthropologists, explored and described many aspects of Aztec life within a decade of the Conquest, including their national cuisine. Following the capture of the capital Tenochtitlan, he observed the city's market:

> The tomato seller sells large tomatoes, small tomatoes, leaf tomatoes, thin tomatoes, sweet tomatoes, large serpent tomatoes, nipple-shaped tomatoes, serpent tomatoes. Also he sells coyote tomatoes, sand tomatoes, those which are yellow, very yellow, quite yellow, red, very red, quite ruddy, bright red, rosy dawn coloured. (Sahagún, 1950–82, retranslated Coe, 1994, 93)

This evidence of tomato variety puts even the contemporary top-of-the-range supermarket store to shame, although Sahagún also encountered the 'bad tomato seller' who sold:

> spoiled tomatoes, bruised tomatoes, those which cause diarrhoea; the sour, the very sour. Also he sells the green, the hard ones, those which scratch one's throat, which disturb – trouble one; which make one's saliva smack, make one's saliva flow; the harsh ones, those which burn the throat. (cit. Coe, 1994, 93)

Tomatoes were then used in a variety of culinary ways, in chicken or shrimp casseroles with red chillis, and in various salsas with different kinds of chilli. These sauces were often used to accompany tortillas, commonly sold on stalls by street sellers:

He sells foods, sauces, hot sauces; fried food ... juices, sauces of juices, shredded food with chilli, with squash seeds, with tomatoes, with smoked chilli, with hot chilli, with yellow chilli .... He sells toasted beans, cooked beans, with mushroom sauce, sauce of small squash, sauce of large tomatoes, sauce of ordinary tomatoes, sauce of various kinds of sour herbs, avocado sauce. (Sahagún cit. Coe, 1994, 117)

From this hotbed of culinary culture, which anticipated many of its contemporary usages, the tomato spread around the world and can perhaps be seen as a most significant yet little recognised legacy of the Aztecs to the modern world.

The cultural priorities and European hegemony of the Spanish Empire provided the first step in the internationalisation of the tomato during the sixteenth century. The Spanish adopted many of the plants and fruits used in the agriculture of their conquered territories. Desirable fruits were not only taken back to Spain but spread throughout the Spanish-speaking world as a matter of deliberate policy (Smith, 1994, 16). In this way the tomato was not only introduced to the Caribbean and the Philippines (where it has subsequently become a major cash crop), but also reintroduced as a food crop back to Peru and Northern Chile.

Although the tomato was not the only transplant, it was certainly one of the most successful, proving easily cultivated in climatic regions far removed from its lofty Andean origins. The hardy nature of the plant, self-pollination and genetic variability made the tomato readily adaptable to the wide range of environmental and socio-cultural circumstances it encountered on its travels. However, after being introduced to the Spanish court in the early sixteenth century, its insinuation into the cultural universe of Europe was a slow process. Coe (1994, 28–9) classifies New World produce into four categories: those that meshed well with existing cuisines and agriculture (maize, beans); those that travelled well and attracted immediate appeal (pineapples); those that lacked instant appeal but were cheap to produce and rich in calories (potatoes, manioc); and finally, 'sleepers' which encountered much suspicion, and were unsuited to many temperate climates, and took a long time to establish themselves in European cultivation and cuisine. The tomato exemplified this last category. Extraneous processes of cultural association invariably influenced the manner in which it was received and accommodated. Although the fruit was radically foreign to epistemic codes existing beforehand, European culture managed to locate the plant in terms of ancient Greek systems of cultural and scientific classification, as well as diffuse Biblical associations.   Thus in 1554 the Venetian herbalist Pietro Andrae Matthioloi made one of the first references to tomatoes:

> We have recently become acquainted with another species of love apple, which are flat and round like apples and divided into segments like melons; their colour is at first green, and then later when they are mature, they are golden in some plants and red in others.   They are commonly known as Pomi d'oro, that is, Golden Apples.   They are eaten in the same manner as the others. (cit. Luckwill, 1943, 120)

The term 'Golden Apples' was widely used throughout Europe, including Britain, well into the seventeenth century. Matthioli classified Golden Apples alongside the poisonous mandrakes and nightshades, an association which carried over into Anglo-Saxon culture well into the nineteenth century. However, the mandrake was also associated with aphrodisiac qualities. This was partly because of the Biblical association with the Genesis story of Rachel and Leah who make a love potion from its roots. But it also related to the influence of the Greek doctrine of signatures whereby medical qualities of plants were associated with external appearance: mandrake roots were held to look like entwined lovers. Smith points out that the Hebrew term for mandrake is *dudaïm* – which translates as 'love plant'.

From the sixteenth century the Renaissance witnessed a flourishing interest in horticulture and systems of botanical classification.   The widespread circulation, plagiarism and translation of 'herbals' was evidence that this was a genuinely European phenomenon. Second-hand references were copied and passed around between experts, and their publications were reproduced with little by way of verification. Thus Henry Lyte's herbal, which went on sale in London in 1578, was a translation of a work by Frenchman Charles de L'Ecluse, itself a translation and elaboration of a work by his Flemish colleague Rembert Dodoens.   In his version, L'Ecluse cites the Greek myth of the Hesperidies, who were the guardians of the golden apples given to Hera at her wedding to Zeus.   The apples were tokens of eternal life and divine fertility.   The Hesperidies were assisted in guarding the apples by a dragon, later slain by Hercules who then carried off the apples (Smith, 1994, 14). This mythic derivation of the term 'Golden Apples' and also the associations with love and fertility were later repeated by Gerard in his famous *Herball* first published 1597 (Gerard, 1636).   The precise derivation of the English 'love apple' is uncertain. It may simply relate to these mythic aphrodisiac associations or to a direct translation of the French *pomme d'amour*. The term 'love apple' remained dominant in the British scientific literature until the end of the eighteenth century, and in the parochial spoken language even into the early twentieth century. The term was still familiar today on the island of Guernsey where old growers remembered it being in common usage.

Gradually, however, the 'love apple' is displaced by 'tomato', derived from the Spanish conversion of the Aztec *tomatl* into *tomate*. In successive volumes of the *Gardener's Magazine* between 1826 and 1842, edited by J.C. Loudon, both terms are listed, with an editorial preference for 'tomato'. Whereas Robert Sweet (1830, 1839) persists with the older, poetic term, Johnson's *History of English Gardening* (1829) mentions both love apple and tomato. Likewise, by 1850 Loudon was using both terms interchangeably. *The Cottage Gardener,* also edited by Johnson, switched terms from 1850.[3]

CULTIVATION AND CUISINE

The tomato was being cultivated and consumed in Southern Europe from the mid-sixteenth century, but only gradually became an important culinary ingredient. Rudolf Grewe (1987) notes that it was absent from the most comprehensive account by a physician from Seville – the centre of trade for the Spanish West Indies – in 1569. Nicolás Monardes's *De todas las cosas que traen de nuestras Indias* (All the things we have brought from our Indies) ignored the tomato. Matthioloi (1544) indicated that golden apples were cooked in the same manner as aubergines, recently imported from South Asia that is, fried in oil with salt and pepper. At the end of the century Gerard reported that:

> in Spain and those hot regions …. [they]do eat apples with oil vinegar and pepper mixed together for a sauce to their meat, even as we in these cold countries do mustard. (Gerard, 1636)

But evidence from both Spain and Italy suggested that even innovatory cooks were slow to adopt the tomato, which remained marginal to their cuisines from the sixteenth to the eighteenth century (Grewe, 1987). In Italy, Antonio Latini's *Lo Scalco alla moderna* (The Modern Household Manager, 1692/94) there were a handful of tomato recipes including one for tomato sauce. In Spain, Juan Altimiras' much later volume (1745) included a recipe for salt cod and tomatoes, a truly Spanish combination derived from its colonial and slave trade, but his *Nuevo Arte de la Cucina, sacado de la escuela de la experiencia económica* (The New Art of Cookery, Based on the School of Economic Experience) contained only 13 recipes out of 200 that used tomato as an ingredient. This work was reprinted as a standard text into the nineteenth century.

However, whilst in Britain it was clearly well known that tomatoes could be and were eaten elsewhere in Europe, and Salmon (1688) mentions consumption in Africa, Egypt, Spain and Italy, the fruit continued to be looked on with a great deal of suspicion. The reasons for this are not clear, other than a general conservatism in relation to food. For instance, Gervase Markham (*The English HusWife,* 1615) talks about the value of home, grown and familiar food rather than that which was 'the furniture of markets ... [esteemed] for the strangeness and rarity it bringeth from other countries' (quoted in Mennell 1985, 84). The tomato's exotic provenance was compounded by its odour and perceived botanical associations with deadly nightshade, which was known to be toxic. Gerard famously referred to the plant being of a

> rank and stinking flavour [yielding] little nourishment to the body and the same naught and corrupt (Gerard, 1936)

For this reason, in Britain the tomato was cultivated for many years only as an ornamental curiosity, valued for the prettiness of its small red fruit. This attitude persisted into the late eighteenth century and was periodically reinforced by pronouncements from people such as Richard Bradley, Professor of Botany at Cambridge University, who deemed the tomato to be positively dangerous (Bradley, 1728)[4]. The proliferating popular literature on gardening and horticulture provides a useful index to the changing status of the tomato. Initially, northern publications such as *The Scots Gardeners Director* (Edinburgh, 1754) tended to be less likely to mention the tomato. During the eighteenth century the tomato was usually listed not under the comprehensive sections dealing with kitchen gardens, but under ornamentals and flowers (Justice, 1765). This cultural resistance to the idea of tomato as a possible food also seems to have carried over into Anglo-Saxon American culture. Thus whilst Thomas Jefferson wrote about cultivating the tomato as an ornamental, it did not appear to find a place at his table (Jefferson, 1944, 55).

Gradually this prejudice began to subside and the tomato began to appear at the metropolitan fringes of English cuisine. By the mid-eighteenth century, Hill (1755) was reporting that many British people were eating the tomato on a regular basis. Likewise the *Encyclopaedia Britannica* (1771, 752) referred to their daily use:

> being used either boiled in soups or browths, or served up as garnishes to flesh meats.

Similarly, Miller (1748) noted the cultivation of both yellow and red cherry varieties and a larger red-fruited variety with 'furrowed sides'. He claimed that it was the larger, furrowed tomato that was used in sauces and salads by the Spanish, Italians and Portuguese. Though noting their cultivation for ornamental purposes and their disagreeable odour he also commented that the same tomatoes were widely used in England for soups. Similar references are found in Garton's writings (1770, 87). Meader's detailed description of the plant implies that the reader was possibly unaware of the culinary possibilities (1771, 108). By 1820, Joseph Sabine wrote in the *Transactions of the Horticultural Society of London* of:

> the great use which has been made of the tomato of late years for culinary purposes has occasioned it not only to be regularly grown in private gardens but has also rendered it an object of cultivation for the market of the metropolis. It appears to be used when fresh in a variety of ways in soups and sauces; and its juice is preserved for winter use in the manner of ketchup (Sabine, 1820, 342)

By 1842, in a letter to the *Gardeners Magazine* (vol. 28, 272) one "C.B." reports extensive cultivation around the capital, commenting that there was scarcely a gentleman's garden in which love apples are not to be found.

However, this insinuation of the tomato into British eating habits was a long drawn-out and uneven process. It is not mentioned by successive editions of Briggs's summation of *The English Art of Cookery* (1788) or Farley's *London Art of Cookery* (1789). This absence is probably more indicative of more general cultural practices than the letter in the *Gardener's Magazine*. Unlike the gentleman gardeners and culinary aficionados mentioned above,[5] Briggs was for many years the cook at the Globe Tavern on Fleet Street, the White Hart Tavern in Holborn and subsequently the Temple Coffee House in London. Even as late as 1822 Henry Phillips did not see fit to mention the tomato in his extensive history of cultivated vegetables, although in this same volume, there is a long entry for the potato, including notes on its distillation (Phillips, 1822). Likewise, the tomato is not mentioned in Loudon's *Encyclopaedia of Agriculture* (1831).

In the eighteenth century, horticultural knowledge and culinary use of the tomato was limited to a largely metropolitan elite centring on London. Here there is some evidence of the role played by religious trading minorities in spreading tomato culture. John Hill (1755) reports that among Jewish families in particular, tomatoes were eaten both stewed and raw. At this time many Jews were involved in trade with the Caribbean and the Americas.

Many were of Spanish or Portuguese descent and had migrated from or maintained contact with Jewish communities in the New World. At the same time at least one Jewish physician introduced tomatoes into Virginia in the mid-eighteenth century (Smith, 1994, 18). Similarly, the Quaker merchant Peter Collinson returned from Italy in 1742 reporting that:

> apples of love [are] much used to putt when ripe into their brooths and soops giving it a pretty tart taste (cit. Coates et al., 1970)

The wider social and geographical diffusion of 'tomato culture' from the mid-eighteenth century was related to what Keith Thomas has called a 'gardening revolution' (1983). Alongside the systematisation of botanical knowledge that accompanied Renaissance science, he points to the importance of the massive influx of exotic plants and the commercialisation and professionalisation of horticulture. The exotic imports were initially cultured in private collections and scientific-botanical gardens, which were established in large numbers from the sixteenth century. This development provided the impetus for the consolidation of a significant base in knowledge and expertise acquired by the hired hands and professional gardeners retained to look after the collections (Harvey, 1974, 24). Gradually, however, there emerged a class of professional nurserymen and commercial nurseries providing seeds and plants for general sale. The first such commercial operations dated back to the sixteenth century and particularly the dissolution of the monasteries and the loss of the specialist horticultural function. Harvey points to the existence by 1800 of 200 such specialist firms operating across the country (ibid.,: 7)

> The few known firms of the seventeenth century became after 1700 a widening flood, and after 1800 a torrent – where it is difficult to discover the names of nurserymen before 1650, the difficulty by 1850 is to see the wood for the trees. (ibid., x).

As Harvey underlines, the influx of exotica was an offshoot of the age of discovery, exploration, world trade, colonial expansion and imperialism. The utilitarian importance of plant exploration and cultivation was only one factor among many stimulating the trade. At least as important were aesthetic factors in garden design and appreciation, cycles of fashion and the growing preoccupation with 'collecting'. The fashion for hothouses and hothouse cultivation of ornamental tomatoes was to be understood in this context. One of the earliest references to the tomato in the context of these professional nurserymen is found in the late seventeenth-century catalogue of William Lucas. In his study, John Harvey describes a shop called the Three Crowns and Naked Boy – owned by one Edward Fuller. Fuller's complete plant and seed list of 1688 was carried over directly from that of William Lucas. The shop provided the focus for several generations of professional seedsmen. Harvey refers to a handwritten list from 1677, of 18 herbs and flowers including the 'love apple'. He speculates that the list was probably a special collection for a country vicarage garden or suchlike. Lucas's catalogue confirms that New World introductions had already taken root in English gardening culture, listing the love apple alongside potato, capsicum, aubergine and sweetcorn. Another typical example is the catalogue of Stephen Garraway, seedsman and netmaker at the Rose, near the Globe Tavern in Fleet Street – which lists love apple seeds along with the flowers, underlining their ornamental status.

Although such seedsmen operated primarily to supply large private and semi-private gardens, there were also growing numbers of commercial market gardeners. This was especially the case in the Thames valley, where a rich alluvial soil, and water for irrigation and transport, created a fertile production environment in close proximity to a relatively enormous metropolitan market. However, despite this growth in commercial market gardening, the tomato remained a novelty and was not grown for sale on a large scale until well into the nineteenth century when gardeners experimented with open-air varieties (Webber, 1972, 32). This was partly due to technological barriers, namely the absence of commercial-scale hothouses. However, it also reflected an absence of a consumer market for the fruit.

Although commercial production was a long time in coming, over the course of the nineteenth century popular awareness of the tomato and its culinary possibilities rose steadily. An important medium for this growing appreciation was the printed press in the form of books, but also specialist horticultural and gardening magazines and journals. Rising levels of literacy and the increasing production of relatively cheap printed matter meant that such sources of information were increasingly available across the social classes including the lower middle classes and in some cases working-class enthusiasts.

The terminological shift from 'love apple' to 'tomato' also paralleled a growing recognition of the plant's culinary possibilities. This was reflected in a number of very obvious ways, not least the section heading under which it was listed. Thus gradually the tomato loses its place among the flowers and hothouse ornamentals and is found in 'the kitchen garden'. Over the decades, more space is devoted to a discussion of recipes and techniques for ripening, preserving and pickling and so on. Initially these are indicative of a fairly elitist social context for tomato consumption. For instance in 1826 in a section called 'domestic economy' in *the Gardener's Magazine* (vol. 1, 353) there are recipes sent in from one John Anderson – Fellow of the Horticultural Society and gardener to the Earl of Essex at Cassiobury. An eminent French cook lately in the Earl's service apparently passed on the recipes. In 1837 in the same journal (vol. 7) a Mr Murtie, head gardener to Lord Anson of Shugborough in Staffordshire, wrote in with a recipe for tomato sauce. He noted in passing that annual consumption in Lord Anson's house was about two bushels a day, produced from around eight plants. We know from Francatelli (1841(1973)) that Queen Victoria was offered 'Tomata [sic] or Love Apple Sauce' as well as 'Tomatas a Là Provencale'. Over the next three decades such correspondence indicates a diffusion of tomato consumption throughout the social scale.

There is also evidence of wider influences of Empire in the way in which tomatoes were cooked and consumed. Thus, in the *Gardeners Magazine* in 1832, 'BB' writes that the tomato deserves more attention, particularly in relation to the excellent sauce which can be prepared – similar but superior to 'Bengal Chutney'. Over the next decades the tomato becomes a defining ingredient in a variety of ketchups, catsups, chutneys and pickles. This partly reflects the importance of domestic food preservation techniques and the use of sauces made from fruit and vegetables over the winter months. By 1861 Mrs Beeton's popular *Book of Household Management* provides a recipe for a tomato and anchovy sauce 'intended for keeping' (595).

It is noticeable that throughout the century tomatoes were used only in cooking and not for salads. Although popular acceptance was growing, there was still some uncertainty as to whether the tomato was a fruit or a vegetable.[6] The resulting suspicions mitigated against eating the raw fruit in a salad (MacKendry, 1973, 187). Somewhat overstating his case, Shewell-Cooper makes the same point:

> As late as 1860 and 1870s those who ate tomatoes were considered heroes or martyres[7] and plants were usually grown in greenhouses for decorative purposes. Even books published just before the 1914 war almost treated the tomato as medicine. (Shewell-Cooper, 1979)

However the allusions to a perceived medicinal function are not misplaced. In a section entitled 'Analysis of the Tomato' Mrs Beeton says:

> The fruit of the love-apple is the only part used as an esculent, and it has been found to contain a particular acid, a volatile oil, a brown, very fragrant extracto-resinous matter, a vegetable-mineral matter, muco-saccharine, some salts and in all probability, an alkaloid. The whole plant has a disagreeable odour and its juice, subjected to the action of the fire,

emits a vapour so powerful as to cause vertigo and vomiting. (Beeton, 1861, 596)

And under the heading 'Tomato Medicinal', she notes that:

to many persons there is something unpleasant not to say offensive in the flavour of this excellent fruit. It has however been used for culinary purposes in various countries of Europe.

She then cites Dr Bennett as to its positive medicinal properties:

a more effective substitute for calomel . ... and one of the most powerful de obstruents of the materia medica ... He has successfully treated diarrhoea with this article [i.e. tomato extract] alone .... in the diet it is a sovereign remedy for dyspepsia and indigestion. (ibid.,1096).

During the 1830s in America these perceived medicinal qualities became the focus for what Smith calls 'the great tomato mania' – a fad generated largely by the preposterous claims of the same Dr John Cook Bennett referred to with approval by Mrs Beeton (Smith, 1994, 106–38). His claims of miracle cures for his patented tomato extract very quickly generated hundreds of articles in both the popular and specialist agricultural press. His pills were marketed under the slogan 'Tomato pills will cure all your ills'. By 1838 rival tomato extracts reached the market, prompting a 'tomato pill war' fought by way of thousands of acrimonious advertisements and newspaper articles, and by 1840 the market collapsed. However the 'tomato mania' did a great deal to raise the profile of the tomato and reverse the traditionally ambivalent and suspicious attitudes towards its consumption. In America sales of tomato seeds rose rapidly as a result of this episode and never went down, so that by mid-century tomatoes were being transported great distances from the Southern states to supply out-of-season Northern markets. In America, production and consumption more than quadrupled in the 1840s and 1850s (Smith, 1994, 142) and was so pervasive in American food culture that a British visitor remarked that the tomato had become the 'sine qua non of American existence' (ibid., 145). Although the effects of this tomato mania were less obvious in Britain, Dr Bennett's claims were aired widely in the popular press[8] and certainly fostered the general impression of the tomato as a healthy and nutritious food.

By the end of the nineteenth century pre-processed tomato products had become a regular feature of consumption across nearly all social classes, in the form of soups, sauces, chutneys and ketchups. The range of such products on the market is neatly illustrated by the Army & Navy Stores catalogue of 1907, which lists tomato chutneys (Heinz, Cross & Blackwell, A&N own brand, and 'imported from India'); tinned tomatoes (whole from France, peeled from Italy); tomato ketchup (Heinz and Gordon & Dilworth); bottled tomatoes; tomato conserve (from Paris and Lisbon); tomato puree; tomato soups (own-brand, and tomato and okra by Bishop's of California). Processed tomatoes were largely imported from America, and particularly the burgeoning industries of California.

This growth in tomato produce and in canned and bottled fruit fuelled an enormous expansion of tomato production in the USA. During the second half of the nineteenth century, there was a rapid transition between a labour-intensive handicraft canning industry to automated manufacture of cans (Philips, 1978). At the same time, whilst the basic technologies of preservation in sealed cans had been developed by Appert in 1812 to sustain Napoleonic armies (Appert, 1810; Shephard, 2000), industrial pressure cooking, notably through use of the Shriver's Retort from 1873, later transformed the process (Bitting, 1912, 1937). As a result the tomato canning industry in California developed rapidly. Canning for tomatoes was a critical step towards mass cultivation, and at the same time made it possible for the tomato to become available throughout the year in a truly national market, permeating every corner of the USA. The canneries, later merged to form Del Monte, began to establish their own farmers growing dedicated, process-specific, varieties of tomato from a massive horticultural hinterland. These tomatoes were grown outside as field crops. This expanding canned tomato industry forms the historical backdrop to the subsequent emergence of two icons of tomato mass consumption in the twentieth century, Heinz tomato ketchup and Campbell's condensed tomato soup (Chapter 7).

Strong links with English merchant wholesalers ensured that they were the main suppliers for the large British market. This production regime was of course predicated to a great extent on the extensive US rail system and transatlantic shipping. So almost from the beginning, processed tomato commodities were implicated in an international network of trade and distribution. This reliance on imports was largely responsible for the very late development of an indigenous canning industry in Britain (Johnston, 1976). But even as domestic food processing and can production began to take off during the inter-war period, pre-processed tomato ingredients continued to be sourced abroad.

THE EMERGENCE OF A TOMATO GLASSHOUSE INDUSTRY

Growing consumer familiarity with the processed commodity no doubt gradually enhanced the expanding urban markets for fresh tomatoes – markets initially served by regional growers operating in distinctive 'horticultural districts' such as the Lea Valley and later Guernsey. Domestic producers using glasshouse technology on the basis of small-scale, family production units, served the massive increase in domestic consumption of the fresh product during the early to mid twentieth century almost entirely. This division between fresh and processed tomato commodities became a fundamental one that saw different sides of the tomato industry developing with different dynamics and trajectories.

By the 1880s in the UK suburban gardeners were growing limited quantities of tomatoes in small greenhouses. At the end of the nineteenth century there was a proliferation of magazines to supplement the *Gardener's Chronicle* and the *Gardener's Magazine*: the *Horticultural Advertiser* in 1883, the *Nursery Man and Seedsman* in 1894, the *Greengrocer, Fruiterer and Market Gardener* in 1895 (Webber, 1972). New varieties were emerging, many aimed specifically at amateur gardeners. Advertisements in magazines such as the *Florist, Pomologist and Suburban Gardener* (Moore, 1880–85) frequently referred to first-class certification by the Royal Horticultural Society[9]. However, it was during the early twentieth century that the tomato became established as one of the most ubiquitous aspects of amateur vegetable gardening. One popular manual published in 1911 went through eight editions by 1932 (Castles, 1911). This reflected partly greater access to allotments by the increasingly affluent working classes, but also suburbanisation more generally. The practice of keeping a small greenhouse and growing tomatoes can be seen as a particular refraction of a more general cultural consolidation of a suburban lifestyle. It was also a reflection of the increasing availability of glasshouses and domestic-scale horticultural technologies for heating and soil sterilisation at affordable prices. By 1930 in a DIY book introducing the greenhouse to amateur growers, Macself was able to comment that:

> so much has been written about tomato culture that it seems almost superfluous to attempt to condense into the limited space available the routine principle of cultivation (247) ..... [and that] varieties of tomatoes are so numerous and ever changing that I make no attempt to give a list of names. Any good seedsman's catalogue supplies names in plenty (Dakers and Macself, 1930, 249)

Inevitably, such pervasive domestic production rapidly broke down any remaining prejudices in relation to consumption of the raw product as a salad vegetable. Middleton and Heath (1937, 89–97) include in their book many recipes including a Basque-style salad, tomato ice, green tomato jam and a pickle.

Although commercial marketing gardening supplying the London market goes back to the early seventeenth century, the commercial production of tomatoes did not emerge until well into the nineteenth century and was not carried out on a large scale until after the First World War. It may well be that, along with American canned tomatoes, fresh tomatoes from North Carolina in the 1880s also led the way in creating a mass market for salad tomatoes (Drummond and Wilbraham, 1939). The process of cultural accommodation of the tomato from ornamental decoration to commonplace food in England, as elsewhere, was a lengthy and tortuous one. This process was mediated partly by domestic production – firstly in the larger gardens and hot-houses of the upper classes, only later extending down the social scale to amateur (lower) middle-class gardeners.

But, there were also technical impediments relating to the cost and efficiency of glasshouse technologies.[10] A critical turning point arrived in 1833 with the invention of a process for the large-scale production of sheet glass in Birmingham (Webber, 1972, 78). Prior to this glasshouses had to be constructed from broad and crown glass, neither of which was ideal for horticulture. The new sheet glass was more transparent, allowing in more light. It was thicker than crown glass but available in 6 foot lengths. This created the technical possibility for a revolution in glasshouse construction.

In 1837 Sir Joseph Paxton built a conservatory at Chatsworth measuring 277 by 123 feet and clearly demonstrating the construction possibilities. He went on to design the glass for the Great Exhibition at Crystal Palace. Although the new glass was initially very expensive for a prospective grower, the repeal of glass taxes in 1845 reduced the prices by up to 600 per cent (Webber, *1972,* 78). Commercial applications followed fairly quickly. For instance George Beer built a large glasshouse in 1879 at Chenwood Gardens for the commercial cultivation of peaches and cucumbers. By 1898 the Worthing area had 70 acres of glass supplying the London market and this Sussex industry kick-started developments in the Lea Valley, the Channel Islands and even Belgium and Holland.[11] As well as the glass itself, horticultural technology moved on in other ways. By 1898 one F.E. Sparkes of Westcourt Nurseries in Worthing was using moveable lights, special boilers and skeleton houses with movable canvas and glass roofs. By the 1890s there were many big glasshouses – such as Seymour Cobley in Goff Oaks, Cheshunt – with significant sections devoted to tomato production. Webber refers to a grower called Larsen from Denmark, who set up an operation at Waltham Cross to grow tomatoes, peaches and nectarines. He built a 'street' of glass with 189 houses covering 25 acres:

Ninety boilers were need to heat the houses and a small railway was employed to carry produce from the glass houses to the packing shed (Webber, 1972, 84)

The distinct nature of glasshouse horticulture *vis-à-vis* agriculture became evident as early as 1896, when the Agricultural Rates Act excluded horticulture from the local tax dispensation accorded to agricultural land. The test case in 1899 was brought in relation to a horticultural operation in the Worthing area, where Robert Piper had constructed 57 glasshouses on two acres of land, growing tomatoes, cucumbers and grapes. This was deemed to be a non-agricultural use of land, and was subject to tax, because both the steam-treated soil and the heating systems were deemed to be 'artificial means' of cultivation.

Although Worthing and the Lea Valley led the way, other parts of the UK also began to develop small glasshouse industries which were to expand rapidly during the middle decades of the twentieth century. In Blackpool, benefiting from the climate influenced by the Gulf Stream, the industry started with small-scale lean-tos on the sides of houses. The first commercial tomato crop was reported in 1880. Into the twentieth century, previously distinct city-regional markets were gradually supplanted by an integrated national market serviced by an extensive distribution system based largely on the railways centralised in Covent Garden, and redistributed to secondary regional wholesale markets. In Lancashire and Guernsey especially, the trajectory of entire local economies became synonymous with the production of tomatoes. Here, and in stark contrast to the large-scale intensive agriculture that had become associated with the cultivation of the tomato in open fields in the USA, small-scale glasshouse horticulture emerged to serve the market for fresh produce. In place of vertically integrated capitalist corporations, the glasshouse industry developed with a strong local-regional dynamic on the basis of small family businesses. Both the organisation of the market and the logic of horticultural production seemed to impede the indefinite expansion of such familial forms. In the classic tomato horticultural regions such as Blackpool and Guernsey, the typical situation would be for a smallholding of a couple of acres of glass, managed by a husband and wife team, and supplemented by the limited employment of seasonal labour. Guernsey was to exemplify this era of tomato production, and its extraordinary rise and fall are explored in the next chapter.

Over subsequent decades a series of technological innovations, along with regulatory and market transformations, created the basis for a modern industry. The emerging horticultural sector served largely urban markets and developed in tandem with a rail and later road-based transport and distribution system organised around the wholesale markets. This system was subject to a continuous process of technological innovation and serviced by ancillary construction, manufacturing and service industries. These industries provided an enormous range of specialist inputs: the construction and maintenance of the glasshouse units themselves; dedicated heating and lighting equipment; specialist glasshouse machinery, chemical pesticides, fertilisers and herbicides; delivery systems, and, vitally, seeds for a rapidly expanding range of fruit and vegetable varieties.

Initially this process of technical innovation was haphazard and driven by the immediate practical concerns and problem-solving mentality of individual growers. However, horticultural research was institutionalised as government-funded, notably with the establishment in 1913 of the Cheshunt Experimental and Research Station, which subsequently moved to Littlehampton where it still plays a significant role for innovation in the industry. They orchestrated large-scale trials of new varieties, pest control and growing systems. The dominant sensibility nurtured by such institutions was very much a productionist faith in the application of science.[12] Writing in 1945, Richards, a former nursery manager at Cheshunt, was typical:

> Possibly in the future, by skilful breeding and selection, scientists may produce strains of tomatoes which will resist not only leaf mould but many other diseases. Who knows? (Richards, 1945, 27)

From 1953, the British Weed Control Council actively promoted the use of chemicals, including organochlorines and phosphates, as well as the now banned DDT.[13] This chemical regime of soil sterilisation and pest control became ubiquitous during the years that followed, providing a useful antidote to any indulgent nostalgia for tomatoes of bygone years. Horticulture and greenhouse cultivation were later to become the arena of an extraordinary scientific and technological development, pitting their closed ecological systems against the open-field production typical of California or the Mediterranean (Chapter 5). Closed ecologies enabled biological controls to replace the agrochemicals still relied on for open-field production.

MULTIPLE HISTORICAL TRAJECTORIES

Much of the focus of this historical account has been on how the tomato entered into English consumption, cultivation and production. The tomato, from being an 'unknown' went through various permutations, poisonous or aphrodisiac, disgustingly odorous or ornamentally decorative, cooked, raw and medicinal. It went from being grown as a dilettante aristocratic esoteric pastime, amateur enthusiast or small-scale household cultivation, to a mass -production, agrochemical-based agriculture. In all these transitions, the pathways were circuitous and often painfully slow. Even in those prime tomato cultures, Italy and the USA, themselves strongly contrasted, the emergence of the tomato as a salient feature of consumption and production took centuries from the first European encounter in the early sixteenth century. In Italy, for example, the tomato was not a national symbol of culinary culture or a major agricultural crop before the twentieth century. It required Italian unification and Garibaldi's triumphal march from Naples to extract the tomato from a previously limited and regionally circumscribed existence (Camporesi, 1993). The Italian equivalent to Mrs Beeton, Artusi, championed the tomato and gave it cultural respectability for bourgeois and aristocratic tables only in 1891 (Artusi, 1891). In the USA it gained a *mass* presence and acceptability only from the mid-nineteenth century.

This is not an attempt at reconstructing a comprehensive history of the multiple historical trajectories of the tomato. The diversity of routes, of resistances and assimilations, of climates and cuisines, has made the tomato both ubiquitous and polymorphous. There are different modalities of assimilation and development: how it is known, how it is grown, and how it is eaten. Its appropriation by pre-existing frames of knowledge in Europe was at least partly responsible for it being in turn poisonous and aphrodisiac by association. Diverse knowledges and technologies of cultivation and cooking – and of preserving – also transmuted the plant from its South American past. Gardening manuals and cookery books were vehicles of familiarisation, embedding the tomato in local and national routines of practice and technique.

The industrialisation of agriculture, both as precondition and consequence of the industrial revolution, afforded the tomato an entirely new and capitalist future, starting in the United States. The Californian tomato industry was built around that base from the mid-nineteenth century and remains to this day not only the overwhelmingly dominant producer in the USA, but almost equal to the whole production of processed tomatoes of the Mediterranean and North African basin (*Tomato News*, 2000). Here, the development of canning and the mass processing and preserving of tomato transformed it from being a local and seasonal fruit to a mass-consumption commodity, permeating national markets and transported across the globe. The tomato thus became global only by being diverse, locally and regionally intertwining different aspects of its existence, scientific, agricultural and culinary, in different cultures and climates.

Having engaged the tomato as a probe into aspects of its history, it is now pursued down its more contemporary English and continental European pathways, beginning with Guernsey, an island bridge between past and present.

NOTES

[1] During domestication, the tomato mutated to become self-pollinating; its pollen and seed have a long life and it naturally produces a high level of variation with distinct and particularistic phenotypic effects.

[2] See for instance Sexton for tomato culture in Papua New Guinea (1988).

[3] This journal was aimed at lower middle-class and petty bourgeois amateur gardeners, as well as respectable 'cottagers'. The subtitle changed to *A Practical Guide in Every Department of Horticulture.*

[4] Bradley was typical of the growth of scientific interest in agriculture and horticulture, providing a series of publications in the first half of the eightennth century for the *Gentleman and Gardeners* Calendar of activities, including in the glasshouse (Bradley, 1720).

[5] Gerard, for example, was a surgeon and for 20 years chief gardener to Lord Burghley, Minister to Queen Elizabeth I.

[6] Knowledgeable journals persisted in placing entries for the tomato under the fruit garden section, along with apples and apricots (Johnson, 1850).

[7] As Smith demonstrates at some length, there were many examples of self-styled tomato pioneers, publicly mocking popular prejudice as to the poisonous qualities of raw tomatoes and making very public demonstrations of its edibility. The story of a 'public eating' by Robert Gibbon Johnson who gathered a crowd on the town hall steps in Salem in 1820 was one of over 500 such tomato introduction stories (Smith, 1994, Chapter 1). In Europe, Coates (1973) cites an identical but much earlier story relating to the sixteenth century Swiss botanist and plant taster Konrad Gesner, who was credited with demonstrating the wholesomeness of tomatoes to incredulous Europeans.

[8] *Gardiner's Chronicle,* (1859, 19 November, 932).

[9] By this time, the Society had become the arbiter of national standards and parameters in relation to size, shape and colour (in much the same way as the Kennel Club was at the same time instituting standards for dog breeds).

[10] Having said that, there have been periodic experiments with outdoor production. The first took place in Evesham in 1884 which continued on a small scale until the very dry summer of 1887 when very high profits tempted other growers onto the market. Dedicated outdoor varieties were developed including Old Red and Early Evesham (Webber, 1972, 86). Webber reports larger-scale outdoor production during the second World War in Essex. However, the vagaries of the British climate meant that such outdoor production was always subsidiary and usually small scale.

[11] Webber claims that young men came in large numbers from Belgium and Holland to learn about the glasshouse industry in Sussex.

[12] See for instance Henry Spice (1959) on the development of polythene as a possible alternative to glass during the 1950s and 1960s. Spice was very ptimistic about the possibilities for horticulture in the age of plastic.

[13] 'The introduction of DDT closely followed by a whole range of systemic insecticides brought about important changes in the sphere of insect pest control' (Webber, 1972, 145).

3. Broken Glass

INTRODUCTION

In the post-war period, fresh tomatoes had come to form an important part of the summer diet of people in the UK. Mainly used in salads, the tomato was also served fried or grilled in the 'traditional English breakfast'. At this time, local greengrocers were usually supplied by their local wholesale markets. In the North of England, many of these tomatoes came from growers in the Blackpool area and became known, with some affection, as the 'Blackpool tomato'. More generally, however, British households received their tomatoes from the island of Guernsey. Situated off the French coast, the warm climate allowed the Guernsey growers to get their crop into the British market much earlier than their mainland competitors and they came to dominate the British market, with over 60 per cent of sales.

Marketed as the 'Guernsey Tom' and with a distinctive spherical shape, these tomatoes came to have a significant impact upon British domestic life. It was also completely central to the lives of the people who lived in Guernsey. For two decades and more, tomato production dominated the economy of the island. This was part of a complex production and marketing system built around the owner-producer and state-supported agricultural and marketing co-operative. As such in 1967 over 30 per cent of the male labour force was dependent indirectly or directly on horticulture. During the exporting season the infrastructure of the island was overwhelmed by the movement of the tomato crop from the greenhouses to the packing sheds and onto the ships. Thirty years later, in 1997, the industry had become part of memory. With only a handful of men working in the greenhouses, the industry had come to depend to a great extent on imported seasonal labour. The great packing sheds are no more and the island provides just 0.70 per cent of the UK market. The 'Guernsey Tom' has disappeared and as an official report summarises, Guernsey's position in relation to the British

44

market has changed dramatically. In the words of the Chair of the States of Guernsey Horticultural Committee:

Sales [are] focused on multiples with the need to sell a distinctive value-added product (Ogier, Interview)

The scale and dimension of this decline is quite remarkable (See Table 3.1). The 'Guernsey Tom', a specific bio-socio-economic species, had a meteoric rise followed by an equally rapid decline. The story serves as a relatively self-contained test-bed for exploring complex interactions between different institutions and process: geographical, economic, biological, legal and socio-cultural.

Table 3. 1 The decline of the 'Guernsey Tom'

Year	1966	1976	1986	1990	1994	1996
Crop area (ha)	298.3	221	36	19.4	8.3	5.4
Export volume (000kg)	57,000	47,595	9243	5424	2777	1850

Source: adapted from Ogier, 1997, 30

THE HISTORICAL ISLAND

Guernsey and the Channel Islands have occupied an anomalous position within the British State for several centuries (Duncan, 1841). Its historical links date back to the Norman Conquest (local historians will tell you, mockingly, that Britain is part of Guernsey and not the other way around) and have continued in different ways ever since. Suspended in a space (geographical, cultural and political) between Britain and France, its inhabitants speak English but they have also developed their own language (Guernsey French). Enjoying the pleasures of the Southern climate the island also (as a British dominion) benefited from the support of Empire and subsequently of Commonwealth Preference. Once the centre of licensed piracy, its merchants traded on the spoils of war. Subsequently, in a more prosaic mode, it became a centre of horticulture, growing grapes, then tomatoes and flowers in hothouses.

The processes that produced this change were slow and hesitant. Gillow has identified the emergence of the private hothouse as early as 1792 at a residence that now houses the Guernsey Museum. This example seems to have set a trend and with it the commercial production of grapes (Gillow, 1958). Girrard (1966) identified the building of the first glasshouse for profit in the 1840s. The export trade was given a huge stimulus in 1861 when a regular steamer service was introduced. Linked with the expansion of the railways in mainland Britain, the steamers provided a daily link with the mainland during the summer months. As a result, 277,400 packages of horticultural produce were exported in 1867. In 1830 under a domestic system there was only a surplus of 3474 lbs of grapes available for export. This trade increased incrementally until it reached a peak of 2514 tons in 1915. It was this trade that saw the hothouses emerging as commercial vineries; a term which survived long after the decline of the grape trade (Hill, 1874).

The Guernsey Tomato Growers Association was formed in 1894. By the beginning of the twentieth century it seems that the tomato was an integrated part of a domestic subsistence economy with occasional surpluses being turned to export. Tomatoes shared the fields and vineries of the islands with a variety of other market garden produce that included lettuce, radish, peas, potatoes, melons, beans and carrots. This horticultural regime was an appealing one to many people living in the South of England, especially in places like the Lea Valley in Kent. At the turn of the century, many families from this area moved and established themselves in the Guernsey countryside (Girrard, 1966). Fred Higgs, a tomato grower, remembers that his family came to the island at that time:

My uncle was growing tomatoes in Guernsey from ... 1898. He was growing strawberries and so on in Kent ... Uncle heard about growing in Guernsey and came over here ... Of course most of the growing then – which is why the greenhouses are called vineries – was for grapes. Then there was the changeover from grapes to tomatoes. (Higgs, Interview)

By the 1920s the tomato had overtaken the grape industry. Fred Gallienne's family was also involved in the early development of the industry and he reflects on patterns of development in the 1930s:

Growing tomatoes was the thing and everyone started growing tomatoes. There are still a few traditionalists who kept up with grapes but they were few and far between. During the 30s a lot of greenhouses were built. You had a lot of men who worked for large vineries and they started borrowing some money, build a greenhouse, they would work a full day and then in the evening and weekends and look after their greenhouse. Within about 7 or 8 years they'd probably got about 400 feet of glass, which was quite enough for man and wife to look after and it give a very comfortable living. That's how they became growers. That's why there were so many small family concerns in Guernsey. (Gallienne, Interview)

Expansion in the number of growers and in the tonnage produced, was associated with the rapid construction of new greenhouses (vineries). This drew upon the skills of carpenters who had increasingly found that their skills as boat-builders had been superseded by the emergence of iron ships. Many of them were looking for work and they turned their hand to the construction of vineries. As John Ogier expressed it:

What the island really did was turn the boat hulls upside down, knock out the wood and put some glass in between – and that's where you get the size and shape of the traditional Guernsey glasshouse. (Ogier, Interview)

This arrangement continued over several decades. One observer noted that at the beginning of the 1960s:

in the days when I came, the postman would have a glasshouse, and when he'd finished his letters he was in the glasshouse, the fisherman did, everybody had a glasshouse to produce tomatoes, and they followed the traditional techniques. (Moffat, Interview)

This was the arrangement that was turned into Britain's first tomato monopoly.

THE RISE OF GUERNSEY TOMATO ECONOMY

In exploring the rise of the Guernsey tomato economy, no one causal factor is suggested. At its heart was the growth of a relatively simple product. But in organising its production, distributing it and getting it into the kitchens of UK households it was supported by a set of refined rules, regulations and coordinated social relationships. A contingent and transitory combination of processes and institutions can be seen to be critical. These include: location, trade regulation, state institutions, a structure of production based on family holdings, related informal cooperative knowledge and technique sharing, and the articulation of the Guernsey tomato institutions with the then current mainland marketing institutions and rising demand.

Location

John Ogier's father was in the greengrocery business and he remembers that in the heyday of Guernsey's tomato industry 'there was still a seasonal trade in production, and there was definitely a premium for being the first on the market with the quality product' (Ogier, Interview). Seasonality combined with the nature of the fruit to give Guernsey an advantage over its neighbours in Jersey and those more widely afield. In Jersey, the land faced South, and the fields were much larger. As such, they went into outdoor production, saving the costs of building the glasshouses. The downside for them, is that they were never able to match the quality of the Guernsey fruit, its reliability and also its earliness in the season. Guernsey therefore developed as a powerful supplier and although there was some alternation between tomatoes and irises an essentially mono-crop form of agriculture developed in the island's glasshouses.

Trade regulation

Guernsey was bombed and then occupied during the Second World War. In the period after the war its economy was seriously weakened. However, the glasshouses had been maintained during the war as a source of food. In good condition, they were easily converted back to tomato production at a time when the British population was desperate for fresh fruit and vegetables. In these conditions tomato production took off and the crop came to make up about 49 per cent of the island's GDP. So central had the industry become to the local economy that the state became critically concerned to support it and to protect its position in the market place. In spite of its proximity to the French coast, almost all the Guernsey crop headed to the Portsmouth and Weymouth harbours. This concentration in the UK market was, in large part, a product of the system of Commonwealth Preference that had operated effectively until the UK joined the European Union. As John Ogier puts it:

> Because we were part of the British Isles, we were not subject to the levy (there is a levy prior to Britain entering the Common Market – a tariff barrier, for tomatoes) so that we had, if you like, an advantage, compared with the Dutch. (Ogier, Interview)

Commonwealth Preference was therefore important both for steering Guernsey tomatoes solely towards the UK and giving them special access to market – prior to joining the Common Market.

The formation of a distinctive state organisation

It was difficult to maximize this advantage, however, when the trade was fragmented by the presence of a large number of small producers. In the early post-war period, each of the growers had private marketing arrangements with particular wholesalers on the mainland. Under these arrangements every grower was responsible for harvesting his tomatoes, grading them on his property and then, when they were packaged, sending them down to the depot to be exported. Every grower had a number and was paid by the wholesaler on his number. Older growers on the island still remember their number and speak of it with a great firmness. It soon became clear that this arrangement was inadequate in securing real advantage within the UK market. As a consequence (and after much argument) the growers agreed to subordinate their independence to a cooperative organization based upon the Guernsey Tomato Marketing Board.

The GTMB was set up in 1952 and instituted a pivotal and *centralised* market channel for tomatoes. It would organise for all Guernsey produce to be distributed across the wholesale markets of the UK using a network of agents or 'panelists'. Produce was shipped to the UK via Portsmouth (serving the East) and Weymouth (serving the West) using two ships one of which *The Cora* was chartered by British Rail. Produce unloaded at ports early on Tuesday morning would usually be on sale at the markets on the Wednesday. On arrival at market a designated panellist would divide up the load among other GTMB agents. The same panellist would ensure pallets were returned to a central point for collection. The relationships between the GTMB and the panellists were close and personal and sustained over many years. Regular visits supplemented daily telephone conversations that relayed market information back to the GTMB in Guernsey. The subsequent day's delivery could then be matched with anticipated demand.

The GTMB worked by monitoring very closely the state of the wholesale markets and making constant adjustments in the volume and geographical fit of supplies of Guernsey tomatoes to demand in different parts of the UK. This required a sophisticated operation with many clerks, statisticians and analysts gathering the information, processing it and making distributional and logistical decisions, conveying these to the depot and hauliers. In practice this amounted to hundreds of telephone conversations every day. Whilst the relationship with panellists was close and sustained over long periods, it was not without tension or conflict and GTMB found it necessary to constantly monitor and regulate what their UK agents were doing. An important statistic was the deviation of the clearing price at any market against the national average. This was calculated daily and provided a detailed picture of the changing market.

Jim Le Garff, previously in change of the Guernsey Tomato Shipping Board, was the first General Manager of the Marketing Board and held the position until his retirement in 1972 when his Assistant Manager Bob Kimber replaced him.[1]

> our objective if we could achieve perfection would be to have every market in the country selling at the same price. This would indicate that we had adjusted quantities and allocations to meet varying demand very precisely …. If one wholesaler or market or one area is above or below the general values pertaining for the country as a whole we take the necessary steps to correct the matter.'[2] (Le Garff, Interveiw)

The nerve centre of the GTMB's marketing operation was the 'intelligence room' at the Board's St Sampson's headquarters which bore comparison to a military operations room, 'working against the clock on a continuous inflow of fresh information'.[3]

This hub of contractual relationships organised by the GTMB was indicative of a strongly producer-oriented system mediated by State institutions with a legal remit granting the GTMB a monopoly over tomato exports.[4] Although the constitution required that growers were represented and consulted over matters of policy, the institution effectively operated as a quasi-State organisation. It worked closely with the States Committee for Horticulture and often made joint representations to the States of Guernsey, over questions of financial aid for price support or modernisation programmes. GTMB was responsible for the store packers, the Guernsey hauliers who supplied the depot (operated on a three-year rolling tender), contracts with the shipping agents, the UK road hauliers and a wide network of panellists at the UK wholesale markets.

The central depot was in St Samson, occupying 40,000 square feet with six conveyer lines on each side and 20 bays. The GTMB always contracted out the local transport to local hauliers. At the height of the season the depot employed 100 people including 14 States Inspectors. Seasonal workers included in the mid-1970s a number of French workers who came in April to stay for around three months, being housed in a GTMB hostelry nearby. There were five sailings a week to Portsmouth (Commodore Shipping Ltd) dropping to four at either end of the season. Weymouth was served by British Rail.

The articulation with the mainland wholesale market

One of the most significant features of the Guernsey system lay in the ways in which it organised the marketing and distribution of the tomato to the mainland wholesale market. The efficiency of the system impressed many observers who noted how the tomatoes were dispatched:

> to the wholesale markets, Covent Garden, Leeds, Newcastle, Manchester – you name it, all the tomatoes went from here and were exported, by lorries, to all the big wholesale markets throughout the UK. And in those days it wasn't roll on, roll off, it was all craned on and off by pallets – terrific industry really. Every day …. That was the distribution system, and it went very well. (Gallienne, Interview)

The Guernsey Tomato Marketing Board had powers enforced by law, which accorded it the responsibility for collecting and grading all marketed tomatoes on the island, and distributing them to the wholesalers on the mainland. It emerged as a key institution in the island's economy. The Marketing Board, backed by the State, had significant powers:

> It was at a time when compulsory boards were thought the way ahead for the industry, and people who grew tomatoes, had to export their tomatoes through the board and they had to be inspected by the inspectors. Inspectors became both loved and hated by the industry, because if an inspector could look at your tomatoes and he could reject them, just on what they looked as they were going to leave the island – you can imagine the sort of rows that happened. And you had to send your tomatoes for him to inspect them. (Ogier, Interview)

The Board organised the marketing of the tomato throughout the UK via a complex system of agents and market information. Controlling 60 per cent of the UK fresh tomato supply meant that it exercised considerable monopoly power, and through its complex set of contacts and networks was able to influence price and maximize the revenues of the growers. In this it established, and protected, the brand name of the island's produce – the 'Guernsey Tom':

> It was a very big industry at that time. That time, in the 1960s, we were producing something like 50,000 tonnes. A tonne of tomatoes per inhabitant just about – the population was 50,000, so it was a tonne per

person, and one fifth of the local population were involved in the tomato industry. You wouldn't believe it, looking at it now, but it was incredible. (Gallienne, Interview)

State regulation

Guernsey is a small island with a unique set of political and institutional arrangements. One astute observer contrasted the political organisation of the States with those at Westminster:

> because the States here, they are not ministries, they just have a committee that looks after shall we say, health, or a committee for education, we have a committee for horticulture – they are local people, who are not professional politicians, they are simply elected by the parish of the island to represent their interests. (Moffat, Interview)

These policy-makers were therefore directly involved in the day-to-day life of the island and its economy. Many (perhaps all) of them had greenhouses of their own. Certainly they were members of families who earned income from horticulture. As such they were alert to the particular needs of the trade. They were also conscious of the need to promote a dynamic economy. Growth in the acreage of glasshouses could threaten to squeeze the physical space open to other activities. More importantly there was a labour market tension between the need for labour in the relatively stable but low-paid agricultural sector and development in other areas such as tourism, light industry and later the financial services. The development of these other sectors was often seen as problematic. The relatively higher wages could easily attract younger generations away from employment in the family horticultural business – possibly threatening its economic viability or at least stimulating the demand for 'imported labour' with attendant accommodation and welfare problems. Likewise, without a clear generational succession, family businesses were liable to underinvest creating a structural 'modernisation dilemma' which was indeed apparent from the early 1960s.

In short, horticulture was the island's economic mainstay responsible indirectly for more than a quarter of employment. But given the structure of thousands of small family firms, often with far less than an acre of glass, it also underwrote a definite pattern of social and cultural life on the island. In the broad regulation of the industry, policy-makers were (perhaps dimly) conscious of a much wider web of interdependencies and relationships that made the balance between growth and control difficult to maintain.

An economy of family holdings

Remarkably, the Guernsey production system was rooted in a system of family holdings. During its expansionary phase, this meant that up over 2500 smallholdings constituted the basic production units feeding into the GMTB distribution system. In this, the tomato crop was one part of the income generated by a family:

> The local grower grew a crop of tomatoes, and then when it got to July/August – tend to lose interest, because there were lots of other things to do like fishing, and going out in your boat and all these sorts of things. (Moffat, Interview)

There were a number of large producers and their role becomes increasingly important as producers and as determinants of the strategic development within the industry. However, in the period of the stable tomato monopoly the majority of the product came from the greenhouses of small family concerns, which were often semi-professional, providing an important supplemental income.

High levels of lay knowledge

A central feature of this 'traditional' economy lay in the ways in which expertise was developed through practical experience, haphazard processes of discovery and problem-solving. In this the communitarian nature of the island fostered informal discussion and knowledge-sharing. Within this context growers established a status through seniority and the practical demonstration of expertise. In the regular shows and competitions, men like Harold Naftel came to be revered across the island as excellent housemen and plant breeders:

> He was very traditional, had a very small unit of glass, probably knew all his tomato plants by name, you knew that sort of degree of intimacy. A very good grower, produced very good crops and had his own variety [the Naftel Discovery] which was his own selection. (Daly, interview)

The power of the Potentate

The industry was based upon the indigenous production of seed and a particular Guernsey breed – The Potentate:

> The Potentate is a very meaty tomato, something like the French tomato, but you could get them some of them were nice and round and some were just odd shapes but the odd shape ones which went in the white grade were very large sometimes. (Gallienne, Interview)

Moreover, this specific variety of tomato was tailor-made for the production and distribution system it inhabited. It had to be a tomato that travelled well, and was able to withstand the many stages of handling from grower to central hub on the island, from portside to ship, from ship to rail, from wholesale market to greengrocer, from greengrocer to consumer. It was also a variable product in terms of size and shape, as it came from the hundreds of smallholdings, and the GMTB grading system reflected and institutionalised that production-side variability. The whole fabric of Guernsey's interlocking socio-economic characteristics gave institutional power to The Potentate in its heyday.

CHANGING ECONOMIES: CHANGING RELATIONS

But the very source and nature of that power transpired to be also at the heart of its downfall. Each of the characteristics just analysed as being at the basis of comparative advantage, turned to disadvantage. Even in the period of its heyday, the signs were there. For what seems clear is that the instituted set of economic processes that supported the tomato monopoly for over 20 years was not replaced by others capable of dealing with dramatically changed circumstances. The old system, patterned into British Commonwealth Preference, enabled the island's economy to overcome the logistical handicap of its offshore location. This was exacerbated by a number of other important institutional factors: problems of modernization and innovation within a household production system, the loss of locational advantage, the intensification of competition with the ending of Commonwealth Preference and joining the European Common Market, the disappearance of the mainland distribution system and rise of supermarket supply chains – and the oil crisis.

Modernisation versus the household tomato economy

Between 1936 and 1968 the States erred on the side of caution, maintaining a policy of restricting new growth and limiting the size of greenhouses (established at 666 square feet in 1938). As such, in 1950, at the height of the industry's 'golden years', the total acreage under tomatoes (911 acres) was actually less than the pre-war figure. By the late 1960s, however, there was a growing awareness within the States Committee for Horticulture (SCH) and the Guernsey Tomato Marketing Board of the need to modernize the industry.[5]

In several respects, therefore, this push toward modernization was finding that features of the Guernsey system that were once strengths had become sources of weakness and obstacles to innovation and change. Fred Moffat[6] remembers the change:

> That was then 1960/62 and Guernsey wanted to upgrade their tomato industry and the States of Guernsey decided that they would establish a Horticultural Advisory Service, to provide scientific advice to growers – of which there were none at the time . .... We established an experimental station – persuaded the States to build glasshouses – so that we could do experiments and research – and ... looked at the horticulture industry and started doing some research and experiments to bring it up to date .... there was a long history of producing tomatoes in Guernsey, a long, long history. But it was all done on skill, tradition, [and] keen observation – but there was no real and technical, scientific input into the industry (Moffat, interview)

This development (involving a shift from lay knowledge to the application of science to production) was seen as an essential part of a reorientation of the industry with a view to improving yields and trialling the most modern types of greenhouse.[7]

In many ways, the modernisation policy was preoccupied with the problems of challenging and transforming the culture and economy of family holdings. The advisors were young men, new to the island, fresh from university and commercial laboratories and keen to change everything. To the old housemen they were upstarts: 'can you wheel and wheel-barrow?', they asked. However there were also a number of large growers on the island. These companies became enthusiastic supporters of the policy. One such was Kenilworth Vineries. This company with the support of Harold Daly (who was to become Managing Director) became the most innovative grower on the island, combining all the modern growing techniques with forms of scientific management based upon time study and a group bonus system. Kenilworth employed over 50 people in its greenhouses

These adjustments to the labour process and payment system saw Kenilworth emerge as the premier and most profitable tomato producer in Guernsey. It was the clearest exponent of the raft of scientifically based innovations[8] that had been introduced into the industry. As a consequence the company began to hold a critical position amongst the Guernsey tomato growers. As the production process was revolutionized, these scientific techniques extended further into the regulation of job tasks and the activities of human labour. Harold Daly had moved from the Horticultural Advisory Service to be Managing Director of Kenilworth Vineries. In his new position he quickly became a member of the Marketing Board (later he was elected as Chairman) and then of the Horticultural Committee. Through Daly, Kenilworth was placed at the very centre of the administrative and political apparatus of the industry. In this position Daly was able to intensify the modernization programme that he had helped to establish with the Advisory Service. Critically this involved the expansion of the company's greenhouse holdings and increasing investment into modern glass. All of the company's greenhouses were taken though a process of modernisation.

Throughout the 1960s and 1970s the Advisory Service maintained the momentum for change. These scientific developments led to significant changes in the organisation of the Guernsey tomato industry. They resulted in the production of a yet more durable tomato, large increases in yields, and laid the foundation for a highly innovative industry capable of competing in the European market.

Concentration of production and ownership

The next part of the strategy involved expansion. In its effort to build on the potential offered by Guernsey's comparative advantage in the UK market, and to prepare for competition with the Dutch, Kenilworth's greenhouse acreage increased eightfold (from 11 acres to 85) in the period between 1969 and 1980. The States also pressed this move toward concentration politically. In his position on the Horticultural Committee, Daly was a firm advocate of this as the only viable policy for the industry. In 1974 this was confirmed as its official policy for dealing with the industry's emerging problems. It emphasized the need for the consolidation and modernisation of glasshouse holdings as a prerequisite for future rationalisation.[9] Over the four years

1973–76 the total number of holdings came down from 2466 to 1921 with the steepest decline taking place in the smallest category. The small householder was retreating from the industry. By 1976, holdings in excess of 2000 square feet accounted for 33 per cent of the total. This process of contraction and consolidation around larger units was a critical development. In Harold Daly's view:

It was largely acquisition of existing units, not entirely, but largely it was acquisition – people going out of business and quite a lot of them were modern units of glass that people had built and then decided for whatever reason that they wanted to get out. (Daly, Interview)

Increasing competition and the oil crisis

In the 1970s, a tomato economy that had developed over the previous 50 years was dramatically altered. In this, changes beyond Guernsey played an important role in stimulating internal changes.

The Guernsey industry traditionally relied upon coal to fire its boilers. However in the 1960s, given the competitive price of oil, the large growers began to switch away from coal-based heating and steam systems. The rapid increases in oil prices in the early 1970s turned this logic upside down:

That was the beginning of the demise of the growing industry in Guernsey – of tomatoes certainly. They just simply could not compete with the Dutch (Moffat, Interview)

The oil crisis and the related consolidation of holdings therefore combined to accelerate the drive to modernize (Owen, 1974). By 1976 modern 24-inch glass accounted for 22 per cent of the total (rising from 14 per cent in 1972). Although the percentage of 'obsolete' greenhouses had fallen from its 1972 level (46 per cent) it still remained vulnerably high at 39 per cent of the entire tomato acreage. The area equipped with automatic ventilation had risen from 9 per cent in 1969 to 23 per cent in 1976. Likewise the percentage of cropped area equipped for CO_2 enhanced atmospheres had risen from 22 per cent in 1967 to 52 per cent in 1976.[10]

It is clear that many of the families resented the new directed approach to what had once been a simple life. Many of these (like Fred Gallienne) moved out of tomatoes and into flower cultivation to remain 'his own man'. Also (as with all small farming communities) the question of inheritance and continuity became a burning issue. Under the new conditions fewer children were interested in continuing with the family vineries; especially if this involved considerable debt. The emerging financial sector in St Peter Port was beginning to present opportunities for a very different way of life, which many people found attractive. As a consequence, while production of tomatoes remained at a high level, with improved yields and fewer producers the dynamic centre of the industry shifted from family-based producers to an organised capitalist form of agriculture. This involved the extensive employment of wage labour and the ongoing use of the kinds of management techniques that had been developed at Kenilworth at the end of the 1960s. Increasingly these workers were migrants employed on temporary contracts to cover the tomato growing season. They were young single women from Northern Ireland, and then Madeira and, more latterly, Latvia.

Processes of modernization and concentration, however, even had they overcome resistances, proved inadequate to develop a complex institutional fabric to sustain a tomato future for the island. In the first years of the 1980s, the tomato industry on the island virtually collapsed at a pace far quicker than anyone expected. The horticultural slump led to significant levels of unemployment appearing on the island for the first time since the war – up to 4 per cent during successive winters at the height of the recession. The years 1980–82 were particularly grim. Everywhere there was a sense of catastrophe. The political elite of the island attempted to pressure Westminster to obtain support and favourable treatment in the UK market.[11] They explained the problem as one of rising costs, low returns, and 'unfair competition from subsidised imports into the UK of horticultural produce form Holland and elsewhere'.[12] The States Committee for Horticulture, for example, made clear in its report that the 'competition is neither equitable nor fair'.[13] The subsidy for the Dutch tomato takes the form of 'a special low tariff for natural gas supplied to horticulture' which results in energy costs which are only 50 per cent of those of Guernsey growers – an effective subsidy of £10,000 per acre. Given these special conditions the report demanded a price support scheme for tomatoes. This was forthcoming and continued into the mid-1980s (see Table 3.2).[14]

State support allowed for a softer landing that would otherwise have been the case. Nevertheless the decline of the industry in the 1980s was pretty dramatic. By 1986 the area under tomato cultivation had fallen to 26 hectares compared with 221 just ten years earlier. What remained were highly productive greenhouses but their total output was just 20 per cent of the 1976 figure (see Table 3.3).

Table 3.2 The price squeeze

	1978	1980	1981	1982
Crop area (acres)	567	456	401	318
Crop value	£26,476,260	£24,659,128	£20,581,266	N/A
Break-even price per tray	N/A	£2.87	£3.38	£3.77
Actual price per tray ex. GTMB	£2.53	£2.75	£2.50	N/A

Source: States Committee of Horticulture (1982), 'Review of Guernsey Horticulture 1982 and Proposals for Support to 1993'.

Table 3.3 The investment squeeze

	1978	1979	1980	1981
% 24" Modern Glass of all glass	30%	35%	38%	39%
Acres of 24" glass	296	354	384	381
Acres of 24" glass for tomatoes	232	277	274	259
% of crop area	41%	51%	60%	65%

Source: States Committee of Horticulture (1982)

In the context of a sharp decline in acreage and holdings from 1978 it was observed that 'without the enormous increases in productivity over the last five years the reduction would have been more drastic'.[15]

Pulling the plug and loss of locational advantage

Several large firms made detailed commercial assessments of their interests and the future of the tomato market. Intriguingly, Kenilworth Vineries, the company that had become the key exemplar of the drive for modernization on the island, was the first to decide to get out of the business. The strategic eye that it had directed on the application of science to production was brought, all the more keenly, to an assessment of the industry's future in the 1980s. Harold Daly felt that:

after a year or two it became pretty apparent to me what was going to happen was production was going to move south. Guernsey had some of the advantages ... but had this tremendous disadvantage of the transportation of the produce at that stage which wasn't easy ... Having built the company up I felt that this process was going to happen and advised the other directors that we should now be getting out of it. (Daly, Interview)

Kenilworth's decision to divest itself of tomato acreage was made on the basis of assessments made of the UK tomato market. As a consequence of the reorganised production regime the crop was evenly spread across five or six months and was capable of being delivered in bulk in the early months of April and May. By the mid-1970s, however, it faced competitive pressure from a variety of different producers throughout the year (see Table 3.4).

What had seemed to be Guernsey's permanent geographical and climatic advantage now disappeared with new technologies that allowed the growing season to be extended elsewhere. The Canaries were also taking advantage of bypassing wholesale markets and supplying supermarkets directly. By contrast, Guernsey was encumbered by an obsolete distribution system, making the complexity of its transportation a positive disadvantage.

Thus, in its erstwhile premium months of April and May 'Guernsey Toms' faced severe competition from within the UK and elsewhere. Reflecting on these developments Fred Moffatt noted that even the neighbouring island of Jersey could turn its previous lack of a tomato industry to advantage:

Jersey is a very rich island and when they saw the tomato industry was going .. they then leap-frogged. They said we haven't got any glasshouses – so straight in with the new techniques to produce them without soil – hydroponics, nutrient film or rockwool – straight in, right at the top. And when they built glass, they built big glasshouses .... Jersey just did it. In Holland – they simply just built glass – straight in with modern techniques. So everybody was developing modern techniques, so where was our advantage? We were losing it. (Moffat, Interview)

Table 3.4 The 1970s: the structure of the seasons

Month	Guernsey % of Total	Sources of main competition
April	11	Canary Islands mainly, plus Dutch and Romanian, and the start of the UK grown and Jersey (indoor)
May	21	Canary Islands (finishing) Dutch, UK grown and Jersey
June	20	UK grown (inc. Scottish) Dutch and Jersey and Irish
July	18	UK, Jersey. Irish and fewer Dutch
August	14	UK, Jersey. Irish and fewer Dutch
September	9	UK grown Jersey (indoor) and Dutch – all declining. Jersey (outdoor) now in production
October	4	UK grown and Jersey finishing. Spanish mainland starting
November – March	3	Spanish until Xmas – otherwise almost entirely Canary Islands

Source: Year Book of Agricultural Co-operation (1977, 81)

From institutional vehicle to institutional obstacle.

Throughout the 1970s, the Guernsey Tomato Marketing Board used all of its accumulated skills and experience to deal with these changes in competitive circumstances. The GMTB had been the command centre of the Guernsey tomato economy, and all were reliant on its ability to adapt to circumstances. Yet these changed circumstances eroded the very type of the power it could exercise: control of supply and distribution. Determined to maintain the price of the crop it developed its sophisticated marketing acumen. At the start of the season Guernsey product was targeted at Scotland and the North and only as supplies increased did this extend southwards. Later in the season Guernsey tomatoes were withdrawn from the East of England and Lancashire in the face of strong competition from local producers and the Dutch. In this way, Guernsey sales were maintained (with only a slight reduction) through the decade. In 1979 sales figures were still little short of 50,000 tonnes (see

Table 3.5). However, by this time the UK market had expanded substantially and Guernsey's share had dropped to less than 15 per cent. The Canaries had become the market leader with the Dutch in third place.

Table 3.5. International competition for the UK tomato market: UK sales by country in 1979 in tonnes.

Country	Sales volume (tonnes)
Netherlands	43,927
Ireland	5,737
Spain	22,347
Canaries	73,832
Others	2,787
Guernsey	49,867
Jersey	11,375
UK	126,800
Total	336,672

Source: States of Guernsey Archive, HC3–8

It became progressively clear that the Board's capacity to maintain prices as competition increased could not be maintained. Its strength had lain in its monopoly power to control prices through its total control of the distribution system. Not only had it lost that power through emergent competition, it had lost it also as the distribution system itself became obsolete, and the supermarkets developed alternative routes.

UK supermarkets and supply-chain management

The multiples caused problem for the Guernsey system in a number of ways. Initially the supermarkets had already attempted to reduce intermediation by dealing directly with the Board, rather than with local wholesalers. This created considerable complications. As their capacities developed they became more and more concerned to have direct contact with producers and to be able to identify and supervise the whole chain of supply between the grower and the store. The supermarkets' capacity to interfere with the GTMB's monopoly pricing policy derived from the availability of alternative supplies and their enormous purchasing power:

When the multiples originally came into being, they had buyers. The buyer would go out to Convent Garden Market at five o'clock, or whatever it was in the morning, and he had in his hands the power to buy two thousand tomatoes. Or not, as the case maybe. All of these salesmen were sitting there and they wanted to serve him because he was the biggest customer. That was their initial power, on the markets. (LeGarff, Interview)

At first, therefore, the supermarkets developed their own distinct relationship with the Marketing Board through particular salesman at the wholesale markets. But this arrangement rapidly proved inadequate:

Eventually they said well you know we can't be doing with this as we don't want these middle men any longer, we are big, we are Sainsbury, we are Tesco, we want the fruit delivered directly to us into our depot and we will agree a price that is based on the market. (Le Garff, Interview)

This process began to further affect the capacity of the Marketing Board to protect the Guernsey grower through price maintenance. Once direct deliveries were agreed the multiples were in a strong position to bargain directly over price with the growers. Inexorably, this process led to the supermarkets placing greater and greater demands upon the grower. They employed their own horticultural experts, many of them familiar with (and to) the industry on Guernsey. Aware of the ways in which standards were developing, these men became innovators in their own right. Fred Moffat knew them all and observed how the modernising norms that he had fought for within the industry began to be inculcated from outside. He remembers how packaging and a new integrated cool chain was developed:

They wanted you to pack them with covers with, shall we say, Sainsbury's name. Then they had to be sent refrigerated, cool chain all the way through, so the grower then had to put cold-stores in, when he picked his tomatoes they had to go into cold store. Then it was put into a lorry which was taken to the depot – again in cold store – so the supermarkets started then to insist on certain standards. Then cool chain all the way to their depot – then at the depot they would test to see whether they were conditions that they would accept. (Moffat, Interview)

This process of change was incremental. Until well into the 1970s the policy of the Board was to actively resist change at its own loss of control by limiting direct sales to 20 per cent and for even these to physically go through the market, via the local panellist who would deal with receipts and paperwork. The GMTB's existence was based upon a view that the product of growers should be aggregated within specified grades and sold as from a single source with growers remunerated according to the weight of fruit supplied and the average price returned across all of the various regional UK markets.

But, the variability of the old Potentate tomato under the family holding system of production was no longer adequate for supermarket shelves, where supermarkets wanted to ensure uniformly high levels of standard products, week in, week out, across all their stores. To achieve this, supermarkets cut out intermediation. The new supermarket systems of 'traceability' and integrally managed supply chains ran counter to the very *modus vivendi* of the 'Guernsey Tom'. On the mainland, the wholesale market, and especially New Covent Garden,[16] was disappearing as the main conduit for tomatoes into the supermarkets. Guernsey, and specifically the GMTB, was no longer the institutional plug that fitted into the UK national tomato grid. The Potentate had been disempowered.

TRANSFORMED INSTITUTED ECONOMIC PROCESSES

To conclude, the complex interlocking processes of the Guernsey system (once a source of strength) were undermined by equally complex changes in the organisation of markets, competition and production in Western Europe. Perhaps the clearest expression of change was that by 1999 no standard round tomatoes were produced in Guernsey, and the island had become a net importer of tomatoes. On the island many of the people now work in the expanding financial services sector as banks have replaced vineries as the mainstay of the island's economy. Like the derelict windmills on Mallorca, the rotting vineries and broken glass of Guernsey testify to a very different past. In some ways, these dynamic processes of capitalist economies might appear to be captured in Schumpeter's notion of 'creative destruction'. And indeed, innovations behind glasshouse technology undermined Guernsey's early-seasonal advantage, as did those behind supermarket supply systems its distribution institutions. But the dynamic of change was much broader than that. A contingent and complex configuration of instituted economic processes, of State, trade regulation, markets and competition, as well as of property holding and production culture was dislocated. The very conditions that made the configuration viable prevented the emergence of a new one and, once dislocated, disintegration followed. In Guernsey, people's memories are dominated by the tomato economy and many feel deeply about its loss. The tomato, however, moved on.

NOTES

1   The following description of the operation of the GTMB is based on interviews with Jim Le Garff and upon readings of the Working Party on Tomato Marketing, *Minutes,* 7 March 1980
2   Bob Kimber quoted in 'Flexibility: The Key to the GTMB's Vital Role', *Supplement to Food Trades Journal* 9th May 1975, ix.
3   Ibid.
4   The Board was composed of ten members. The term of office was four years with half the board retiring every two years but with members allowed to stand for re-election. The growers were allocated one vote for every 500 packages exported the previous year. forty people were employed in the GTMB office with up to 140 in the depot at St Sampson, see *Year Book of Agricultural Co-operation,* (1977).
5   States Horticultural Committee *'Restrictions on Glass House building 1936–*
      1968, States of Guernsey Archive HC 8–2 7/2
6   Fred Moffat and Harold Daly arrived in Guernsey in 1962–63 to take up positions as scientific advisors, coming from Fison's Lemington Research Station in Ipswich.
7   States of Guernsey Horticultural Advisory Service, States of Guernsey Archive HC/AS42–15 and AP Mitchell (1964) – a general report comparing modernisation and investment in Holland with the failure to upgrade in Guernsey.
8   For the innovation process in glasshouses, see Chapter 5.
9   Letter from States Committee on Horticulture to President States of Guernsey, November 1974 Re: Policy for Guernsey Horticulture, States of Guernsey Archive – correspondence.
10   'A review of tomato experiments at the Guernsey Experimental Station', *States   of Guernsey Horticultural Committee Minutes,* States of Guernsey Archive HC/AS 43–45 See Chapter 5 for an explanation of the use of CO_2 in glasshouses.
11   In September 1981 the President of the States of Guernsey referred to a meeting with the Home Office the previous August which successfully sought a price support scheme for tomatoes.
12   *States Committee for Horticulture,* 30 July 1981 *Aid for Horticulture* States of Guernsey Archive HC016 – 03

[13] Ibid.

[14]The scheme came into operation in July 1980 (Billet d'Etat No. XI). It provided for a cash payment per tray sold by GTMB during the months of March, April, May and June. The payment varied with the price realised for tomatoes by GTMB. If the price was low then payments up to 10 per cent of the break-even price was paid. In March 1982 a full payment of 86p per tray was paid followed by 67p in April. There was a limit to the overall cost of the scheme such that in the same year there were no funds remaining to make payments in May and June.

[15] 'A review of tomato experiments at the Guernsey Experimental Station, *States, of Guernsey Horticultural Committee Minutes*, States of Guernsey Archive, HC/AS 43–45

[16] See Chapter 9 below.

4. The Round European Tomato

To walk into a supermarket in England is to be faced with a bewildering array of fresh and processed tomato goods from all over the world. One could be forgiven for thinking that we live in one global market and increasingly share a common global 'tomato experience' with similar-looking tomatoes produced in similar ways from wherever they come. But, even within Europe, the emergence of a single 'euro-tomato' is more distant than a common currency.

MAPPING THE EUROPEAN TOMATO

After decades of mass Mediterranean holidays, convergence towards a common European fresh tomato might be anticipated. What, if any, are the signs of harmonisation towards a single culinary tomato 'currency' within an integrated European market? To give an initial but rather striking response, a rough calculation can be made of how many fresh tomatoes[1] per capita were eaten per day throughout the year on average by the peoples of Germany, Belgium, Holland, France, Portugal, Italy, Spain, Greece and the UK (see Figure 4.1).

At the top is Greece where on average every individual eats over six fresh tomatoes every single day of the year. All those Greek salads? That level of consumption is roughly 20 times greater than in the UK or, perhaps paradoxically, the Netherlands which, as the lowest fresh tomato consumer of this whole group of countries, is the largest producer and exporter of fresh tomatoes amongst Northern countries. Lest one jumps to the conclusion that fresh tomato consumption is a straightforward effect of hot sunny climates, Spain has only a third of the consumption per capita of neighbouring Portugal. Yet of all Southern countries, as we shall see, Spain is also the largest exporter of fresh tomatoes.

So it can be said that on the basis of these first crude indicators common consumption patterns are a distant reality even within Europe. Equally, Europe is strongly divided in terms of different cultures of production and systems of distribution, reflected in strongly contrasting patterns of trade.

Broad divisions of consumption, production, and distribution through international trade, will be a central focus of this chapter, and justify a concept of different 'tomato regimes'. Different tomato regimes grow different varieties of tomato (cultivars), and these different cultivars are produced to satisfy different markets and consumption preferences. This patterning provides an example of how the tomato is bio-socio-economically 'instituted' within Europe.

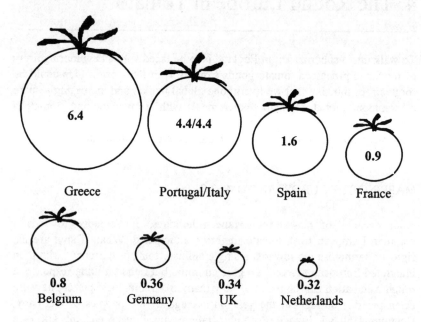

Source: Eurostat Bifrelega 1998 and Spanish Ministry of Agriculture 1998. Adapted from Tables of Total Domestic Use.

***Figure 4.1** Per capita consumption of number of fresh tomatoes eaten per day in various European countries, 1998*

In general terms, the scale of tomato regimes is still strongly regional for both fresh and processed tomato. Europe and the Mediterranean has its own distinctive configurations, and although there is a certain amount of transatlantic trade and transfer of especially Italian processing technology to the USA, most trade is still within the region. The USA, and especially the main tomato growing area in California, has developed a quite different system and variety of tomato production.[2] For Europe as a whole, there has been a steady increase in production and consumption of both processed and fresh tomatoes, reflecting general trends in food consumption of fruits and vegetables. The total amount consumed, whether in salads or in soups (fresh and chilled), pizzas, pasta sauces, or convenience foods has nearly doubled since 1970.

However, within this European regional scale, there is a 'great divide' between the North and South, the North being characterised by production under glass in highly controlled atmospheres, the South being either open-field or plastic-covered production. Then, shifting down a scale, within the Northern technological regime there are two distinct configurations, the Dutch and the UK; and within the Southern regimes there is an equally marked contrast between the two big tomato producers, Spain and Italy. In the next chapter, the focus will close down yet further to explore the variations within the UK national scale. These different scales of 'tomato regime' also constitute different scales of competition: North versus South; Dutch versus UK; UK versus UK, which can be read as battles for domination between different bio-socio-economic varieties of tomato, or processes of very un-natural selection. The regimes are far from stable, and there are degrees of complementarity and conflict, interpenetration and sharpening differentiation. As a result, there is a continuous process of emergence of new variety, whether of tomato configuration or of the tomato as biological species.

NORTH VERSUS SOUTH

In broad terms, the division between the tomato regimes of the North and South of Europe can be seen in terms of production systems, the horticultural regime of the North, and the open-field or semi- and plastic-covered regime of the South. However, this shorthand characterisation entails much more than a difference in the 'hardware' of production technologies. There are also profound centuries-old differences in the production cultures of horticultural traditions as against, for examples, patterns of Moorish irrigation systems along the Southern Spanish coastal fringe. These are certainly 'ways of life'.

But the difference also lies behind what is meant by 'fresh'[3] when speaking of fresh tomato. Northern horticultural regimes produce almost exclusively a salad tomato, a fresh sold tomato to be consumed fresh. Fresh means eaten fresh. In the South, fresh is almost as much a cooking ingredient, or a produce for further processing, as in the case of sun-dried tomatoes. Moreover, different varieties of fresh are used for different purposes – mainly plum for cooking, some round for eating fresh, and so on. But in the North, fresh bought midi-plums and even standard plum tomatoes, partly because of their higher price, are rarely used as a bulk cooking ingredient to be reduced in making sauces. Thus fresh plum tomatoes become appropriated into the Northern conception and use of 'fresh'. Canned and diced plum tomatoes are the preferred cooking ingredient, and so figure as consumption of processed tomatoes.

In speaking of a 'production culture' too, much more is involved than use of technique or equipment. As Friedland has said, it may be true that:

> All foods consumed by human beings in advanced industrial societies are products of thousands of years of human intervention: through the breeding of plants and animals, through the development of myriad forms of intervention in the production process, through the ways in which the product is handled after actual production has been accomplished. Indeed, to talk of 'nature' and 'natural' with respect to any foods presently consumed in advanced industrial societies is to ignore the fantastic levels of intervention by human beings that have transformed those foods from their original forms found in nature. (Friedland, 1994, 211)

A horticultural regime creates a special form of 'artificiality' in which *all* elements of cultivation process become the object of manipulation and experimentation to an extent that is not possible in open-field farming. This enables the development of new forms of 'naturalness' as well as the replacement of 'natural' elements such as soil and sun by 'artificial' substrates and generated heat. Horticulture is itself a technological culture, which requires development of skills of disease and pest recognition in order to counter the intensification of risks of crop infestation within closed environments, and to reflect the higher value placed on each and every plant.

Different tomato regimes also contest the 'naturalness' of the seasons in various ways. Whereas supermarkets attempt to ensure 'counterseasonality' by means of trade, and source from different parts of the globe whose 'natural' seasons are complementary, the competitive response of a horticultural regime is to find ways of achieving counterseasonality within the glasshouse by extending the growing season throughout the 12 months. As already shown, from at least the nineteenth century the very existence of glasshouse cultivation was predicated on achieving either exotic or counter-climatic production. Counterseasonality, in the sense of extending the time frames within which produce can be grown in a given location, is a very old agricultural concern.

The juxtaposition of deeply divergent tomato regimes provides some clues for interpreting the contemporary 'tomato map' of Europe. Tomato production, consumption, and the trade flows between regimes have contrasting and characteristic features, as do changes in the relative productivity of the two regimes. The difference between fresh and processed tomatoes across these dimensions also provides a critical contrast, as much as overall totals.

Italy is unquestionably the premier European tomato nation. Its total production of fresh and processed tomatoes exceeds that of all the other major tomato growing countries put together (Figure 4.2). It did so in 1965, and still did in 1996. In between, its own production had increased by more than double, the sharpest increase being between 1975 and 1995. Spain, as the next biggest overall producer, increased its total production by nearly three times from 1965 to 1996, but from a much lower base.

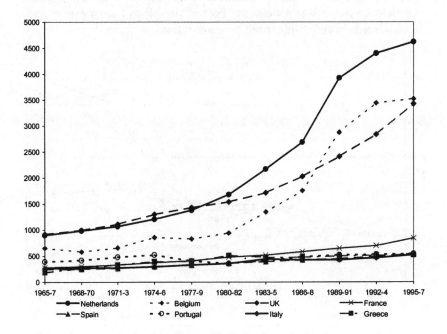

Figure 4.2 *Total production of fresh and processed tomatoes by principal European producing countries, 1965–96. Eurostat.*

During a period of growth, Italy has enhanced its domination for both processed and fresh tomatoes. But Greece has been the second most important producer of processed tomatoes since the early 1970s, whilst slipping to third rank below Spain for the production of fresh tomatoes in spite of its penchant for fresh tomato consumption.

Looking more closely at production growth in fresh tomatoes, the Netherlands and Italy, as leaders of the Northern and Southern regime respectively, can both be seen to have nearly doubled their production since 1965 whereas Belgium, as a new entrant in the Northern regime and starting from a much lower base, has witnessed the most spectacular growth of nearly 400 per cent over the period (Figure 4.3). The UK, partly reflected in the Guernsey story, is the only country to experience an overall decline in production over the period, losing nearly 40 per cent of its output from 1965 to 1990, with some signs of stabilisation thereafter. Of all the Northern regime countries, it was perhaps the most vulnerable to loss of market share to both Northern and Southern regime competitors.

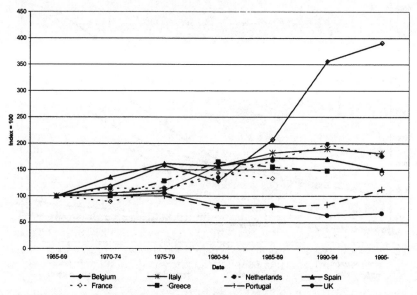

Figure 4.3. *Indexed production of fresh tomatoes, 1965 = 100* Eurostat

This then sets the broad production scene. But 'regime effects' become yet more conspicuous when turning to patterns of trade and consumption. The leading exporting country of fresh tomatoes, and by quite a margin until 1995, has been the Netherlands. Italy until 1990 scarcely exported any significant tonnage of fresh tomato and Greece, an even more negligible amount. Spain, as the other important exporter of fresh tomatoes, began its bid to become the leading European exporter of fresh tomatoes from the mid-1980s, when intensive, semi-covered production systems were introduced into Almeria, Murcia and the South-Eastern coastal strip (Figure 4.4).

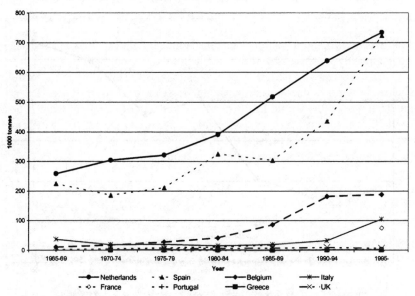

Figure 4.4 Export of fresh tomatoes by leading European producers, 1965–96. Eurostat.

By contrast, the positions are almost totally reversed for the export of processed tomatoes (see Figure 4.5). Here Italy and Greece are by far the dominant exporters, and, as might be anticipated from the difference in the configuration of 'fresh' within the Northern regime, the Netherlands, Belgium and the UK effectively export no home- or horticulturally-grown tomatoes. Any exports of processed tomatoes from these countries are almost certainly re-exported via the produce of companies like Campbell and Heinz.[4]

This articulation of Southern and Northern regimes around the different systems of production and their respective constitution of 'freshness' versus 'processed', is further reinforced by the nature of their export orientation – the extent to which their production is dedicated to export; and also, by the destination of those exports, the importing countries, and their patterns of consumption. Amongst Northern regime countries, the Netherlands, along with Belgium, have primarily export-driven production, with nearly of 90 per cent of their production going for export. Most of that, about 80 per cent, goes to the German market. UK production is dedicated to domestic consumption, with only about 2 per cent going for export. In other words, the Northern 'fresh' tomato circulates within the North. As a regime, it is 'inward looking'.

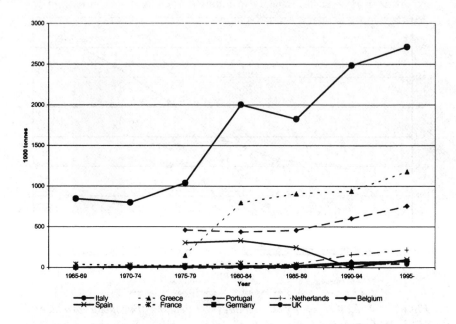

Figure 4.5 *Export of processed tomatoes from leading European producer countries, 1965-96. Eurostat.*

Turning to the Southern regime, the most striking contrast can be seen by its two leading exponents, Italy (paralleled by Greece) and Spain (Figure 4.6). For Italy, fresh tomato production is as much for domestic consumption as is the case in the UK: only 2 per cent is exported in 1995. Conversely, three-quarters of its production of processed tomato is exported. Spain, by contrast, only exports 10 per cent of its rather small-scale processed tomato production but exports a third of its total fresh production. From interviews in Spain and with importers in this country, one explanation of this contrast is that the growth of new, relatively high-tech, semi-covered systems in the South-Eastern coastal strip has been dedicated to the production of the typical North European 'commodity' tomato.[5] Almeria, the Canaries and Murcia have become export-oriented centres of production, and the regional map of Spanish fresh and processed tomatoes shows the clear distinction between these three areas producing 78 per cent of fresh tomatoes, and the Extramadura with 64 per cent, by far the dominant region for producing processed tomatoes. Whereas in Italy or Greece fresh tomatoes are not North European retailers, an export industry sufficiently regular, round and uniformly coloured to be acceptable to the North European retailers, an export industry with the capacity to mimic horticultural standardisation has been developed in Spain.

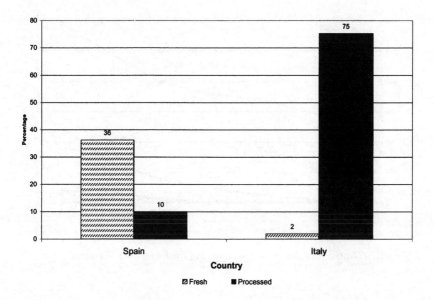

Figure 4.6 *Southern contrasts: patterns of export of fresh and processed tomatoes, Spain and Italy, 1995. Eurostat.*

As for the import side of the trade flows, Germany, with virtually no domestic production, is by far the leading importer of fresh tomatoes with almost double the level of France and more than double the level of UK (Figure 4.7). Moreover, the bulk of the German fresh imports comes from the Netherlands, forming the statistical backdrop to the interesting 'tale of the trading tango' between a yield-intensive production system and a discount retail industry, to be told later.

But, for processed tomatoes, the UK has overtaken Germany since 1985 to become the premier consuming nation of imported processed tomatoes in Europe, signalling the recent shift in cuisine that has occurred to buttress the traditional consumption of tomato soups and ketchup (Figure 4.8). Italy, too, has become a significant importer of processed tomato during this period, reinforcing its dominant role as a tomato processing and manufacturing country, for re-exporting 50 to 60 gallon drums of tomato pulp[6] from Greece, Turkey and the Middle East.

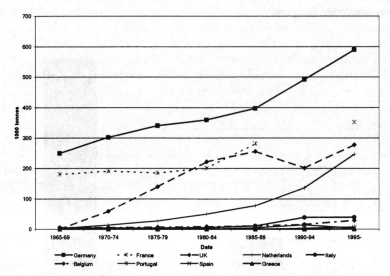

Figure 4.7. *The German dominance in importing fresh tomatoes. Eurostat*

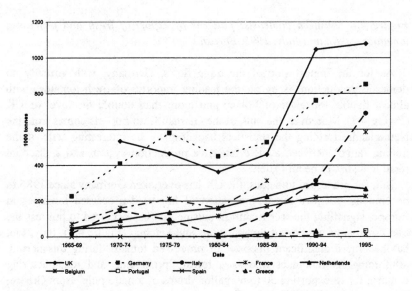

Figure 4.8. *The UK takes the lead in importing processed tomatoes, Eurostat*

From these patterns of production and trade, it is now possible to give a more discriminating picture of national patterns of tomato consumption, having also marked the difference between Northern 'fresh' and Southern 'fresh'. In terms of ranking the tomato–eating nations of Europe, the per capita picture remains similar to the consumption of fresh tomatoes in Figure 4.1. But, by virtue of higher consumption of processed tomatoes, there are a number of significant tomato 'leapfroggers': Italy overtakes Portugal amongst Southern regime countries, Belgium swaps ranks with France, and the UK makes a jump to clear Germany by a big margin (Figure 4.9).

The difference between the Northern and Southern regimes becomes much sharper (Figure 4.10) when looking at national preferences for fresh or processed tomatoes. For Spain, Greece, Portugal and Italy, at least two-thirds of their tomato consumption is of fresh tomatoes, with Greece and Portugal at levels of 90 per cent. Conversely, Belgium, Germany the Netherlands and the UK eat a markedly higher percentage of processed than fresh. The UK is the afficionado nation of processed tomato, with over 70 per cent of its total consumption.

There is a broad division in production processes and cultures, distribution patterns and consumption styles that together cohere to form distinctly Northern and Southern 'tomato regimes', each with their dominant spatial zone. To be sure, there are increasing signs of instability between the two regimes, above all demonstrated by the growth of purpose-made Northern–style 'fresh' tomato in Spain and to a lesser extent Italy. But the broad point remains. Consumption, production and distribution patterns are articulated with each other in distinctive patterns and have 'co-evolved' in the formation of their distinctive profiles and spatial zones. Even the points of instability in some ways suggest a reinforcement of the difference, with Northern techniques and skills producing the 'Northern tomato' in those export-oriented tomato-producing areas within the Southern regime. So which regime is destabilising which?

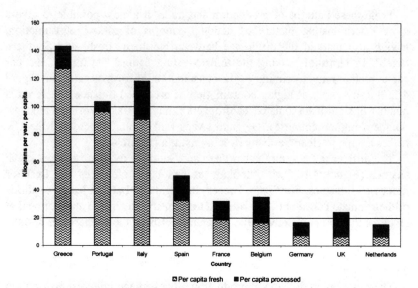

Figure 4.9 *Who eats the most tomatoes in Europe, processed and fresh? Per capita total domestic use, fresh and processed, 1995, kilos per year. Eurostat.*

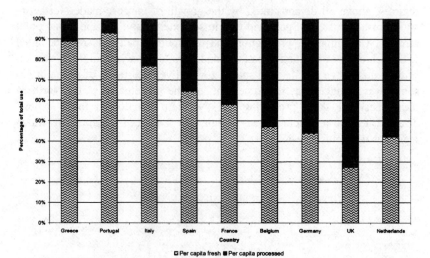

Figure 4.10 *Portugal versus England (UK): fresh versus processed. Per capita consumption, percentage of fresh and processed total use, 1995, Eurostat*

THE BATTLE OF TOMATO REGIMES: CONTENDING WAYS OF
ORGANISING THE TOMATO

Walking into a Tesco or a Sainsbury to purchase a weekly supply of fresh
salad tomatoes in mid-season, most consumers probably scarcely notice that
in the last couple of years, one week you might find a box labelled 'The
Greenery' for Dutch tomatoes, and the next a box with a logo of the UK
Tomato Growers Association. At turning points in the season, each of these
could vie for shelf space with Spanish tomatoes, Bonny or Bonyssa. But this
succession of labels, containing apparently identical fruit, is the outcome of a
continuing and complex power struggle. Having surveyed the grand European
scale, it is now time to look more closely at different national tomato regimes,
the different species of regime within the genus 'North' and the genus
'South'.

It might seem strange that a simple fruit is subject to complex and
intersecting power struggles as part of its journey from seed to mouth. There
are many stages, and different ways of organising them, for a tomato to come
to economic fruition. In current business language, the organisation of these
stages is characterised as 'supply chain management'. In this view, all the
stages of supply come under one integrated linear management control,
linking the different firms, or groups of firms, present at each supply stage.
The keyword is 'chain', each link locked to the next uninterruptedly, from
one end to the other. But this conception of a chain is just one conception of
the control and organisation of supply. There are different ways of organising
the interlocking of the stages of supply, and different patterns and loci of
control upstream or downstream. Moreover, these different organisational
modes are interacting with each other, in competition or conflict with each
other. Different modes of control are vying for supremacy in different markets
and in different parts of Europe. The bizarre outcome of this 'battle of the
models' is that it affects the nature of the tomato and what kind of tomato is
produced for sale in what market.

Three broad models for the control and organisation of supply can be
compared. These are not intended as exhaustive descriptions, rather as
schematic or stylised representations, to demonstrate contrasting patterns
present in Europe. It should also be stressed that the diagrams themselves
represent only a slice in time in a historical process of change. The three
diagrams picture the supply organisation for the Dutch; the Spanish, French
and Moroccan system; and the United Kingdom. Before engaging in a more
detailed discussion, their differences can be briefly summarised:

1. North European Tomato Regime: Mark 1. The Dutch organisation of
    supply (Diagram 4.1). A multitude of very small, family business

producers, typically with holdings of 2 to 4 hectares, supplied to a centrally organised daily auction, to be then distributed by a number of distributor companies to external markets, principally, as we have seen, to the German discount market. This is essentially a producer-led model, where the growers are seeking to prevent erosion of their power over the supply to either distributors or retailers.

2. South European Regime: Spain, Morocco, Southern France (Diagram 4.2). Typically, small producers are organised into marketing co-operatives, increasingly linked to major wholesale distributors. These co-operatives have strong local and national state support, with legal recognition. The export-led parts of the industry, especially the Canaries, and the South Eastern coastal strip, however, has witnessed the increasing role of major export-distributor companies.

3. North European Regime, Mark 2. The United Kingdom represents the clearest manifestation of supply chain management, with linear control exercised significantly by major retailers (Diagram 4.3). Amongst growers, there is a very wide range of production unit size, from one grower operating 120 hectares, supplying 35 per cent of the market, down to small family businesses with 2 to 3 hectares. There is effectively an absence of intermediaries between retailers and growers. For growers, the power balance here is therefore a lot to do with size, and with being an

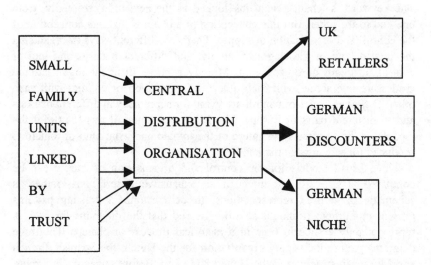

Diagram 4.1. The Netherlands: the modified central auction systems

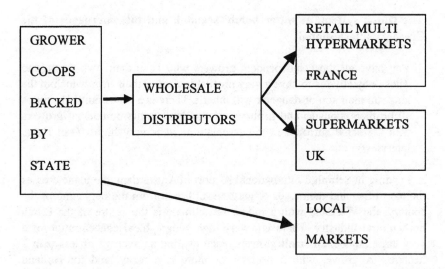

Diagram 4.2 Co-operative, State, export domestic market model (Spain, Morocco, France)

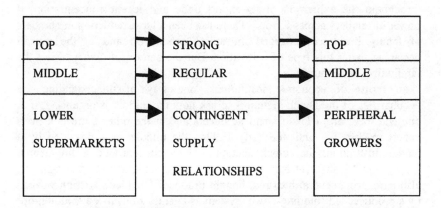

Diagram 4.3. The UK retail dominance model. 'Supply Chain Management'

'insider' or 'outsider' to a retailer supply chain. There is also a hierarchy, with top-of-the-range producers linked through strong supply chains to top-of-the-range supermarkets, with increasingly weak linkages and lower quality at the lower end of the hierarchy.

The Dutch system, a 'water bomb' scandal, and the emergence of the Greenery international

You have all those independent growers who have their own firms, and whose objective is to have a very profitable firm of their own, which in the long run their son or daughter will inherit. There is a lot of family business all brothers, cousins and nephews. If you look at the number of growers with the same surname in the associations, it is very high. (van Haan, Interview)

Landing in Schiphol International Airport in Amsterdam, the plane crosses the North Sea and then a sea of glass. Established from the beginning of the century, the Westland with a milder sea climate is the centre of the Dutch horticultural industry. There is a very high geographical concentration of a very large number of small growers, each owning an average of less than 2 hectares. A grower with 5 hectares or more is a rarity, and for Holland constitutes a 'large' grower.

In some ways, the story of Dutch horticulture must be a story of the tremendous resilience of this small family business and landholding throughout the expansion of its export trade and recent concentration of power of retailers across Europe. There has been a large reduction in numbers of family businesses engaged in tomato production and in the overall hectarage under this type of cultivation. But the pattern of ownership of the family firm has endured.

In terms of economic institutions, one way of understanding the peculiarities of the Dutch system is to ask how the middle is organised, if at one end there are a lot of small producers and at the other there is a mass export market. Up until the early 1990s, 'the middle' was provided by a market institution, the 'clock auction', which concentrated a fragmented supply into 15 different local outlets at which distributor-export companies, also numbering several hundred, bought produce. The clock auction worked by a producer-led 'bidding-down' system as against a buyer-led 'bidding-up' system, with literally or metaphorically the hands of a clock pointing at lower and lower prices, starting at the top until successive buyers are found and the market is eventually cleared:

In the Netherlands, everything was sold through the auction system, on a daily price basis, everything being brought to market on a daily basis. There were no contracts, whatever the price was for that day, everybody had to pay. (Barnet, Interview)

So the market was institutionally organised for 'arm's-length' trading, the producers bringing the product to market with no other project than to obtain best price. The auction itself was (and where it survives, still is) co-operatively owned by the growers, and although the auction also established norms of quality and actively engaged in seed development for quality improvements, the growers' representative ran the auction boards and through them controlled the auction manager:

They almost controlled him like a puppet on a string. (van Haan, Interview)

In describing this as a 'producer-led' trading system, it should be noted that producers control only up to the point of sale. There is then a 'black box', the clock auction where nobody knows who is buying from whom, or what other than standardised tomatoes. Whilst for the producers, the auction system was essential both for the concentration of supply and their control of the selling market, the 'black box' is nonetheless very much an institution, not just an empty space, or void. Moreover, during the course of the 1990s, the auction system itself became the focus of major institutional change.

Dutch horticulture suffered a 'traumatic episode', the Great German Water Bomb Scandal, triggering the development of new institutions. Scandals normally involve at least two parties, and normally only one of them gets the blame. In the case of this scandal at least, it is clear that Dutch producers, German retailers and consumers were all deeply involved. However, the object of the scandal *was* the tomato, and as producers of it, the growers were the natural scapegoats. From the mid-1980s to the beginning of the 1990s, the perception grew in their biggest market that Dutch tomatoes were completely tasteless:

They called them water bombs. They were things that looked good and were red and shiny. But they had no taste. They are just water bombs. It is red coloured water. So there was a lot of criticism from the German consumer organisations especially, from some cooks, famous German culinary writers. Until then, it was just 'the Dutch tomato'. Everybody delivered them in the same boxes, in the same packaging, blue boxes for Dutch tomatoes with the Dutch girl on it. (van Haan, Interview)

It is unclear how a tomato came to be thought of as a bomb, although perhaps it arose from the need to ironise the advertising hyperbole of things exploding with flavour. But it is certainly unfair to blame only the Dutch for a watery bombing campaign against hapless German consumers, although so successful was the victimology that even the Dutch appear to be suffering from undue war guilt. The story is essentially one of how the arm's-length auction trading system developed in tandem with German retailing discounting strategies. The Dutch concentrated on

> producing good volumes of good looking tomatoes, and taste well, it was number ten on the list. (van Haan, Interview)

The German consumer market is driven by

> Price. Germany is price. Britain is quality. To be simple about it. So, they are totally different markets. (Barnet, Interview)

Put a producing system concentrating on volume and cost yield ratios together with a consuming system concentrating on the lowest possible price and a constant switching of supply to obtain it, and a dance is choreographed of ever-decreasing circles terminating in the tasteless tomato. At that point, everybody realises that was not where they intended to go and seek to apportion responsibility for ending up in the wrong place. In the paradigm of demand being independent of supply, responsibility has to be allocated to one or the other. Clearly, under this view, the German consumer did not desire water bombs. So the supplier carries the can.

A different paradigm, in which institutions of supply and demand are related to each other via market institutions, suggests that a dynamic of competition channelled production and consumption towards an undesirable end that was mutually engendered. In this view, it is equally untrue either that the Germans got what they deserved or that the Dutch engaged in a water bombing campaign. The story is exemplary of how consumers may neither get what they want nor want whatever they get. Spirals of demand and supply are mutually conditioning and can occasionally, and hence revealingly, end up in dead ends. In this case, the dead end can be seen as an effect of the distinctive institutional relationship between a Dutch production and trading system (the clock auction), and the German retailing consumer orientation, where price overrides other considerations.[7]

This traumatic episode more or less coincided with two other important developments to which the auction system and the growers had to respond. On the one hand, there was the impact of the general, European-wide concentration of retailers and the growth of supermarkets and hypermarkets:

> In order to survive in the long run, the Dutch felt that they had to come together in one organisation, which could be weighty enough to face this concentration of the retail side. (van Haan, Interview)

On the other hand, some UK supermarkets had been circumventing the auction system because of their very different organisation of supply chains and, through distributors, had established long-term supply relationships with particular groups of growers. The Dutch growers overall felt that their market position was being eroded and that they were increasingly pulled in two different directions. They were in danger of doing the splits between German consumers that no longer wanted water bombs and UK supermarkets that were especially resistant to anonymous trading through auctions.

The confluence of these three major pressures has triggered a major reorganisation of the stages of supply into the different retail outlets, a reorganisation that from the current vantage point appears to be far from secure. Much as was the case with the Guernsey industry but here on a much grander scale, there was an imperative to adapt or sink. It must be stressed that peculiarly Dutch adaptations were made to the uniquely Dutch circumstance of being primarily an export industry, and to markets with very different requirements.

There have been two main aspects to the supply reorganisation:

- the emergence of grower associations,
- the replacement of the central auction system by The Greenery International.

Grower associations
An immediate response to the water bomb scandal was for growers to find ways of differentiating themselves from each other by differentiating the tomatoes they produced. The result exemplifies the emergence of new bio-socio-economic variety. Fifteen grower associations were established with between 20 and 50 member-growers each, and each association now produces one or occasionally two varieties of tomato in order to distinguish itself from the other 14. No two associations grow the same tomato variety. There are growers of Evident 'particularly well suited to the UK market',[8] growers of Prominent 'deep red, shiny and easy-to-slice with a long shelf-life and very well-suited to the US market'; growers of Cherita 'outstanding flavour and shelf life make it suitable for all quality oriented markets and distant export destinations' (including Japan and the US); or growers of Roma Vine 'plum tomatoes-on-the-vine with an attractive appearance, available in red and orange'; and so on.

There is a logic behind this social solidarity around a tomato variety. Members of an association run excursions to horticultural research stations and to other growers' associations, disseminate best practice amongst themselves, and collectively obtain technical or financial services support from outside agencies as required. But the bond between a growers' association and a particular variety of tomato is much more intimate than that:

It is a matter of scale, and of concentration on doing one thing right. Different varieties demand different growing regimes, different feeds, different everything. For reasons of efficiency and simplicity of working, most of the growers concentrate on growing one particular variety. (van Haan, Interview)

Each association is thus closely linked to the seed manufacturer that supplies their particular seed variety. There are also sanctions and splits. One of the growers' associations, Gartenfrisch, had opted for a high-tasting but marginally lower-yield variety. There was a move to change the association's variety identity, but alternative seed was not available. A section of growers in the association decided they wanted to grow a different variety anyway. But:

The other variety they wanted was not allowed in the Gartenfrisch Association. So some fifteen members left and started their own association with a different variety. (van Haan, Interview)

The shift from growers (nearly) all producing '*the* Dutch tomato' to 15 associations bonding around different varieties to create product differentiation is a process that is only intelligible within the context of the small family businesses of a couple of hectares each. This scale of production unit more or less prohibits extensive product differentiation *within* the unit, especially granted that cultivation regimes vary with tomato varieties. Equally, at the opposite end, the 700–900 tomato growers' co-operative structure would be unlikely to survive if each grower alone decided independently to grow a particular variety. Consequently, the old co-operative structure tied to 15 auctions was now broadly mapped onto product differentiation of 15 varieties. The prior organisational framework was adapted to new ends, to create a uniquely Dutch production organisation for the development of new markets.

The Greenery International
The second major institutional transformation had the goal of eliminating the 15 clock auctions and replacing them by a single new and unified marketing intermediary, The Greenery International. The 'super-co-operative' formed to undertake this in 1996 was the VTN,[9] which in turn set up The Greenery International as its marketing arm. It was thought that only a unified intermediary would be able to counterbalance the power of the new retailers

and prevent the danger of divide and rule, where distributors and retailers could pit one association against another.

The process of institution of new modes of supply and trading, however, is subject to a great deal of turbulence from other resistant or counter-acting organisations or from interaction with different institutional models of supply. As a new intermediary institution, The Greenery faced tensions both upstream and downstream. Upstream, there were growers who were unwilling to cede too much of their autonomy, and downstream distributors and retailers were vying to establish alternative ways of organising tomato supply to maximise their control and share of the value.

In the event, only nine of the 15 auctions initially decided to enter into The Greenery, which currently accounts for 60–70 per cent of the total vegetable and tomato production from glasshouses. The other auctions dealt directly with distributors, and yet other growers, those who are anachronistically called 'outside the auction' (BVO), deal directly with distributors or exporters and are not members of any co-operative structure. Yet others form groups of growers growing for UK supermarkets, but also for Albert Hein, the largest Dutch retailer, again intermediated by distributors in dedicated supply chains.

In 1998 The Greenery bought up two of the important distributors,[10] who have themselves been undergoing a rapid concentration from between 120 to 130, down to 20 key distributors for the business of supplying the major European multiples. The Greenery thus also threatened to destabilise some long-standing supply organisations, outside the auctions, that had adapted to the pattern of the UK supermarket supply chains, dedicated lines of supply with long-standing partnerships.

The Dutch tomato became an object of market-political struggle over who controls the supply and how that supply is organised, with growers, distributors and retailers each having different positions, visions and objectives. The current instability can be represented as one where four different modes of organising supply are contesting with each other (see Diagram 4.8).

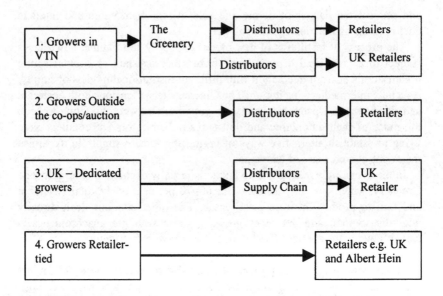

Diagram 4.4 Four competing modes of organising supply

From this diagram it can be seen that although The Greenery's organisation of supply is the dominant one, the growers are divided into potentially mutually competing groups. The distributors, as already mentioned, have also been amalgamating to enhance their power and subsume the organisation of supply under their aegis:

> They also want power ... It is concentrating all the time. The larger exporter groups now have more opportunity to find their own growers. They are actively looking for that, to avoid going through The Greenery ... [This] undermines the mission of The Greenery to concentrate Dutch horticultural supply, in order to be able to be a powerful party in the market. (van Haan, Interview)

Likewise, the supermarkets also have interests in either maintaining or extending their 'dedicated supply chain' model of organising supply:

> The relationships the multiples have developed with these small groups of growers in small units gives them a feeling they are being given a special service. That makes them feel comfortable. Every multiple wants to believe that the fresh produce he's being supplied with has been specially presented for him, and he's totally unique, and not the same produce is being served to Tesco's or Waitrose. (Barnet, Interview)[11]

As a growers' organisation, The Greenery is therefore trying to establish a unified and integrated grower base, on the one hand, and to mediate all external trade on the other. In their ideal scenario The Greenery would like to see their model (1) eliminate the other three.

If the growers' associations were a distinctively Dutch resolution of the demands for product differentiation on the part of the growers, The Greenery as an intermediary organisation or institution of a supply process is equally so. No other European tomato supply is organised like it. The concept of The Greenery is one of a centralised intermediary acting on behalf of the growers. It is still very much a growers' world-view of market organisation. Moreover, the four-stage structure of supply organisation is still largely retained: growers – marketing intermediary – distributors – retailers. Although the arm's-length trading typical of the daily spot market auction system has been completely transformed, it is replaced by an intervening marketing organisation undertaking the trading function for the growers. This is a peculiar response of a geographically concentrated industry open to a world of very diverse retail markets, and an attempt to bring coherence to an overwhelmingly export trade in which very small players (the growers) need to be able to trade effectively with very large ones (the retailers). Whether, and how far, it will succeed in simplifying the first pattern of conflicting and unstable trading organisations into the second pattern of Greenery hegemony is far from clear. But the stakes are high: the survival of the Dutch horticultural systems may depend on it.

In replacing the auctions, The Greenery necessarily assumes a wider role than merely acting as a centralised contract broker. It assumes the functions of a category manager to establish an integrated and coherent tomato product portfolio,[12] and of a distinctive Dutch tomato branding agency, with its own market identity.

The brokerage function is relatively straightforward, although it exemplifies the strategic limitations of operating as an exclusively intermediary function:

> The Greenery sells the product for the growers. We don't own the product. We are an intermediate ... It is more of a brokerage function. The growers deliver the product, and we sell it on. (van Haan, Interview)

To an extent, the brokerage function of The Greenery reflects its emergence from the auction: it is there only to sell produce on. This in turn creates tensions for the performance of its other two functions, if growers are too jealous of conserving their power. For, in terms of category management or establishing a sensible tomato portfolio of different varieties for the overall Dutch tomato supply, The Greenery strives to develop a clearly distinctive range, with quality produce adapted to the retail markets to which it is destined:

> We have to think of what is a sensible segmentation of tomatoes for consumers, and to implement a different segmentation ... (van Haan, Interview)

> Fifteen or twenty different tomato packs is no good. The multiples are looking to The Greenery for rationalisation in terms of category management. Gaining the confidence of the market, we can then go to them and say we can rationalise your product portfolio like this. That is the classic arrangement. If you are the category leader, you are asked to do that. (Barnet, Interview)

To perform its new function The Greenery must be able to go beyond acting merely as a broker and exert some degree of control over what the growers grow. In order to develop category management, they have engaged in major consumer research programmes for 'preference mapping' for all the dimensions of the tomato, taste, colour, shelf-life, shape, size, on the vine and off, and so on. They also involve the seed companies in constructing the necessary seed portfolio: the production of biological variety is thereby adjusted to the requirements of consumer segmentation in a process as far removed from natural selection as that which has produced the domestic dog. The difficulty of establishing a market-driven, rationalised portfolio, however, is that some varieties will be the 'moneymakers', whilst others will be the 'stars', and yet others the 'niche specialities'. Some growers' associations will have to accept a degree of cross-subsidisation in recognition of the differences in market segment to which their variety is targeted, a cross-subsidisation which challenges their proud financial independence and short-term price orientation. It is clear that The Greenery has yet to fully achieve this quite fundamental shift in production culture in their family business supplier base.

Downstream, however, a parallel problem presents itself. Exporting to Germany to Aldi or Lidl:

> They are not interested in added value. They are interested in one thing, and that is the lowest price. It's a big market, so we also have to deal with them. But it is not possible to establish category management, or that sort of thing, with them. (van Haan, Interview)

So The Greenery has to respond to quite contradictory market exigencies and could easily be undermined by growers thinking they might get a better deal in the German or UK market.[13] This 'facing many ways' aspect of the Dutch industry, in which a central intermediary organisation seeks to control the flows into different markets according to their specific characteristics, leads directly into the third main function of The Greenery. This is the establishment of The Greenery brand identity. For it is an identity that has to transcend the different markets it serves, a difficult balancing act. Like all the rest of us in this day and age, The Greenery has to struggle to overcome the perils of multiple fractured identities. In gaining market credibility, it therefore has to aim to add value and maintain standards for all products going under its name. But UK supermarkets require higher standards for category management, hygiene, and growing regime in terms of things like pesticide usage:

> We have translated all the requirements of the British supermarkets into a manual and directions for our growers. They are then certified by an outside auditing company ... You have other systems in Germany as well, but the UK standards are the highest. So the growers deliver to those standards, and are certified. (van Haan, Interview)

This upstream control over the growers to meet the exigent standards of the top UK multiples leads directly to tomato identity conflicts. As is well known, the multiples also assert their identities, and the whole ethos of direct supply chain management typical of the UK retailing sector is that the store's own label is prominent. The Greenery International's response to this has been to adopt what they call the 'Intel Inside' option: Tesco or Sainsbury have the dominant identity, but there is also a smaller Greenery brand label added to it. So tomato shoppers in UK superstores can now see 'The Greenery' label struggling to maximise its visibility. The 'Dutch girl' on the water bomb tomato is being replaced by 'The Greenery' logo for the new Dutch tomato portfolio – and other products, such as the Romero pepper introduced in 1998 as an innovation partly to enhance The Greenery's profile. It came with its own Greenery recipe.

Finally, in establishing itself as broker, category manager and tomato identity bearer, The Greenery is seeking to overcome the major obstacle presented by the albeit reduced seasonality of the North European glasshouse regime. As broker, it is at present constrained to renegotiate contracts seasonally, and also to re-emerge each year from a period of brand invisibility. The Greenery is therefore seeking to establish a continuous sourcing of Greenery products throughout the year. Dutch grower associations are setting up production facilities in Spain. Because of differences in climate and cultures of production, they have yet to produce tomatoes of adequate quality to be acceptable under the Greenery label. They are sold but anonymously, bereft of identity. The construction of a bio-socio-economic variety, 'A Greenery Tomato', requires new seeds and newly adapted growing techniques for different circumstances if it is to appear on the supermarket shelf in all its socio-economic clothing:

> The Greenery is wanting to develop a new sourcing system that will provide 52 week continuity of a Greenery quality product. It may come from pretty well any country in the world. But in the eyes of the ultimate customer, it will be understood as a Greenery product. (Barnet, Interview)

The culmination of this process of supply transformation, therefore, leads towards a market institution which, by distributing produce to its specification under its name, is Dutch only by virtue of where its marketing institution is located, rather than where the product is grown. 'Dutchness' would become Dutchness of the entrepôt nation. If – and it is quite a big if – this is where the present process of transformation leads, it will be an ironic destiny for a marketing organisation owned by Dutch family business tomato growers.

The two major transformations of supply organisation of the Dutch industry, namely the emergence of grower associations and the replacement of the clock auction by The Greenery, have entailed some quite fundamental institutional shifts. As yet unstabilised, they are still subject to conflicting and contradictory demands of different markets, different distribution systems, and resilience of family production units. It is far from certain that The Greenery will survive, at least in its present form. There are also many question marks over the future of the whole glasshouse regime in Northern Europe. But what is clear, in this complex mix of forces, is the very particular way they combine and impact on the Dutch horticultural industry. No other industry starts from where they do. And no other industry faces the same conflicts and contradictions as are presented to its emergent institutions. The pressures and conflicts experienced by the Dutch industry are transnational even global. But these pressures and conflicts are refracted by local institutional circumstances, and under these conditions local institutions themselves then generate further distinctively local institutional novelties.

Tomates españoles or Tesco-tomatoes[14]

Looking at Eurostat trade statistics where thousands of tonnes of tomatoes circulate around Europe, it is difficult to visualise how this happens. The trail of the Spanish fresh tomato leads to Paddock Wood Distribution Centre in Kent. The sheer size of the complex of warehousing and of individual warehouses is stunning. A single Trasfesa warehouse follows the railway line for half a mile. Already growing out of its space of 50 acres or more, Paddock

Wood is where fruit and vegetable produce comes into the UK for subsequent re-distribution from all over the world. Del Monte has a major complex of warehouses, recently constructed, and with their own in-house ethylene gas banana-ripening facility to complement another independent ripening company's operation.

Here too are signs of a struggle over the control and organisation of supply of Spanish tomatoes, paralleling that of the Dutch. Again, there are several different contesting models of organisation: the point of departure and the directions taken in Spain are quite different from those in the Netherlands. At Paddock Wood, a distribution company, Victoria Trading,[15] handles nearly all the Gran Canaria produce for the UK supermarkets. The company is owned by Bonny[16] whose label is also to be seen in UK supermarkets, 'Intel Inside'-style. But Bonny, a premier tomato-exporting company, occupies a quite different role from any equivalent in the Netherlands. About ten years ago, it bought out the co-operatives and independent growers, now owning the land and leasing it back to tenant farmers. Bonny supplies the farmers with seed, fertiliser and chemicals, and operates a tight system of control over production regimes:

> Everybody recognises that Bonny and Bonyssa are generally better than any of the other marques, because we've got more control than everybody else who's out there. We've got more technology. (Mellonie, Interview)

At the same time, though, they are locked in to the UK supermarkets and to their quality requirements. As in the Netherlands, these take the top of the market in terms of quality – and again, the German market just goes for the cheapest.[17] Bonny controls the packing stations at the Gran Canaria end, but the supermarkets 'call all the shots':

> I am provided with detailed specification from each of the supermarkets, the customer. They specify size, colour grading, this type of thing, in incredible detail. They say what pack, what plastic film, you're supposed to use, even what label and what supplier to get it from, what sugar levels there are supposed to be in the fruit. Every aspect. You cannot go wrong if you follow their documents, five or six pages, some of them. (Mellonie, Interview)

Exemplary of the dedicated supply chain model, there are machines for grading tomatoes in the packing-houses in Gran Canaria. One channel might go to Marks & Spencer, another to Tesco, and so on. They are packed in the supermarket livery at source. Tesco, for example, now have their own dedicated containers with Temtel temperature logging systems, replacing the old system where produce was transported ungraded or sorted in the general hold of the ship – temperature controlled, but without the traceability afforded by temperature logging for the length of the journey. In earlier days, the supermarkets would wield their absolute power ruthlessly in switching suppliers to obtain better deals:

> But now, supermarkets are building up relationships with suppliers. They've still got a tremendous amount of power. But they are realising that if they want a better product, they are going to have to make some sort of commitment. (Mellonie, Interview)

This paradigm case of the dedicated supply chain of supermarket-importer-packer/producer-grower, however, whilst typical of much of the Spanish export trade, is by no means an uncontested or singular model for the industry. Much of the Almeria industry has retained the co-operative structure described in the model above. The Murcia region, however, is more typically farmed by large export-oriented businesses, and both of these regions rely very extensively on migrant North African labour, much of it semi-legal. There are also distinctively Spanish–UK hybrids. Van Heiningen Brothers, by far the largest UK grower,[18] has not only set up high-tech production facilities in Portugal, but also a trading partnership with Duran, an exporting company, for fresh produce from Almeria. Sainsbury obtains its Spanish supply through this route, and relies on Van Heiningen Brothers for quality control and quality range.

But, just as Dutch growers did not wish to cede all power to the almighty retailers, the Spanish too have increasingly attempted to carve out some control and assert a distinctively Spanish identity to their tomatoes. At first, UK supermarkets, in conjunction with Novartis (an agrochemical and beneficial pest control company), had attempted to institute production regimes in Spain to match those of the Northern horticultural regime. Standards on Minimum Residue Levels for pesticides and Integrated Crop Management Schemes were introduced in Project Alicia in the early 1990s.[19] But it was quickly realised that any extension of this project to become a general model would not only yield control over supply and production to UK supermarkets, but also failed to recognise that much of the Spanish export business would be unnecessarily hampered by producing everything as if it were for Tesco or Sainsbury. The Spanish tomato, like the Dutch, was for export to diverse European markets and requirements. Consequently, together with grower co-operatives in Almeria and the larger growers in Murcia (including Bonny and Bonnyssa), the government body for setting trade standards, AENOR,[20] set out to create a distinctively Spanish quality and set of production, packing, and distribution protocols:

They are very well recognised, and they also set standards for nuclear power plants. It was the first time that they worked in agriculture. (Finlayson, Interview)

Tomatoes and nuclear power plants might not have much in common, but at least in Spain they now share the same 'stamp of authority' to indicate they are produced to the necessary standards of quality and safety. As yet only a small number of growers have attained the standards necessary to sport the AENOR label, but much as with The Greenery, the eventual aim is that the label will identify the 'Spanish Tomato' across all European markets.[21] AENOR too is operating in contested space, both against the dedicated supply chain models and against nationally distinctive operators with their separate channels of supply, whether from the Netherlands or the UK. At present it would not be an exaggeration to say that the 'Spanish tomato' is suffering from a multiple-fractured identity, with competing protocols defining the tomato and its production. Thus, Agrivera, a company engaged in the process of authentication and certification of these protocols, can stamp the same tomato either AENOR, or Nature's Choice (Tesco) or Migros (the Swiss retailer). Perhaps one of the significant differences to the Netherlands in this respect is that its own retailer base is weak and fragmented, and has never wielded the kind of supply control of some its Northern equivalents:

Spanish retailers are not even at the starting post. (Cox, Interview)

For both of these reasons, the rapidly expanding Spanish industry of the past decade has been far more exposed to the penetration of external models of supply control and organisation than ever was the case in the Northern horticultural regime.

BATTLE OF THE TOMATO REGIMES

A leading UK producer:

I go through periods of being regularly frightened by the thought that our [UK] industry might be overwhelmed by these massive investments in Spain, particularly Southern Spain ... (Lewis, Interview)

A top-flight UK grower:

The threat from abroad is becoming quite serious. They're getting wise to the fact that North European technology works well in Southern Europe ...

It's only a matter of time. So you have to make sure that you're one step ahead. (Pearson, Interview)

The Netherlands:

You can't stop the technology from being transferred to them. If we don't do it, the producers of the technology certainly will. The seed companies are very active in the South, and the biological insect control companies are also. The crux is in being ahead of them all the time. Make sure you always take the next step before they do. That's the only way to survive. (van Haan, Interview)

About the only thing that England could produce better out of doors is grass. (Barnet, Interview)

These views of leading players belonging to the Northern European tomato regime range from the determined, through the embattled, to the apocalyptic. There is a vision of technology racing to keep ahead in order to counteract natural climatic comparative advantage. There is also a view of expertise, rather than hard technology, as being a relative asset for the Northern production regimes but only temporarily so. Behind all this there also lurks an idea, common in much of the rhetoric of globalisation, that all national varieties will be flattened under a single competitive pressure of the world market. England will be left to grow grass. The Netherlands will be turned into a cycling nature park.

But, it should be noted, these remarks all emanate from Northern producers of Northern 'fresh' tomatoes. The 'battle of the regimes' is quite specific to this particular product market and the way that it has evolved and been shaped, largely by the dominance of the Northern conception of 'fresh'. This is where a competitive 'hot spot' is located. Flows of fresh and processed tomatoes in Europe have established patterns which sharply segment markets from each other, to a large extent isolating Italian and Spanish production of tomatoes from head-to-head competition: one exports processed, the other exports Northern 'fresh'. The Italians think that their Southern 'fresh' tomatoes are far too refined a product to be exported to palates acclimatised to the 'water bomb', and in general produce only for their own gastronomically sophisticated fresh tomato market.[22]

The 'battle of the regimes', therefore, is an interesting phenomenon that belies any generalised competitive melting pot, let alone a global one. Competition both occurs at different scales and is different at different scales. Thus, Dutch growers have sought to eliminate or at least reduce competition between themselves, and create a 'super-co-operative' which defends the integrity and effectiveness of their industry as a whole. Technological innovation is diffused as rapidly as possible amongst them through their learning circles and inspection of each others' growing regimes, rather than being used to obtain competitive advantage over rival national growers. As will be seen in the next chapter, there is a parallel if not identical case in the UK where the Tomato Growers Association has been recently established, and where regional Tomato Growers Groups also disseminate best practice amongst themselves:

> We have a tremendous level of co-operation. It's a Dunkirk spirit, this one. Together we float, divided we sink. (Agombar, Interview)

There is an awareness that each grower's own fate rests on the collective capacity of their respective North European horticultural regime to advance technologically.

The effectiveness of this horticultural regime in 'staying ahead of the game' over the past few decades is quite impressive, and is based on a whole series of technological innovations that will be described in the next chapter. Although the area under glass has dropped quite significantly in the North (especially in the UK) compared with a relatively stable hectarage in the South, this has been more than outweighed by the astonishing increase in yield per hectare. Figure 4.11 shows that in general terms yield per hectare of the capital-intensive Northern production systems grew from being roughly four times more productive than Southern regimes in 1965 to over *nine times* more productive in 1995-97. This is in spite of the fact that Southern regime productivity had itself doubled over the same period. So, in an expanding market for fresh tomatoes, the Northern regime has been able to hold its own, essentially by investing in more and more sophisticated and capital-intensive technologies. Perhaps more significant than yield, however, the glasshouse technology of the horticultural regime has the potential to create a distinctive 'bio-socio-economic' variety of tomato (Chapter 5).

Competition between regimes leads to ever-increasing divergence between them, in a competition to avoid competition. Distinctive bio-socio-economic varieties of tomato are developed in the closed environments of glasshouse production, and the comparative advantage of these systems is continuously reinforced to create a closed and sustainable ecosystem. Conversely, for the South, advantages of sunlight, cheaper labour and different seasonal peaks, whilst leading to intense competition at the margins of the respective regimes' optimal seasons, push towards yet more concentration in the standard 'commodity' tomato production. Pre-eminence in processed tomatoes is further buttressed by the proliferating speciality markets for sun-dried products.

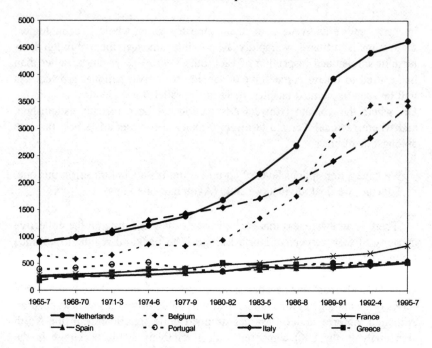

Figure 4.11 *The Northern outpacing the Southern tomato regimes. Yield per hectare in 100 kg. Eurostat.*

Each regime avoids competition with the other by creating an overall European market space and occupying different segments within it. In this scenario, Northern 'fresh' and Southern 'fresh' both flourish as bio-socio-economic species, with much Southern production continuing to supply an internal domestic market. Differences in cultures of production and consumption become accentuated rather than diminished by regime competition.

In an alternative doomsday scenario, the race of the Northern horticultural regime to stay ahead of the South by ever-increasing levels of capital intensity is a race to nowhere. North European glass could be on a trajectory similar to the cod-fishing schooners of New England that, in competition between each other and with the emergent steam and 'active' trawling technologies of Europe, became faster and faster, bigger and bigger, and riskier and riskier until finally the ultimate schooner, the *Teresa E. Connor*, was built never to sail.[23] As in Guernsey, the end result could be much broken glass. In this scenario, England would excel in growing grass, mainly for golf courses, leisure parks and, along with the Netherlands, would fashion its non-urban spaces into recreational 'nature theme park' Nature. An eighteenth-century aristocratic estate tableau for twenty-first-century mass consumption.

Whatever the outcome, there is likely to be a variety of bio-socio-economic spaces. The least probable scenario is that regime competition will drive towards an homogenisation or uniformity either of the tomato or of the socio-economic environment it inhabits. Competition is a source of variation.

NOTES

[1] The figures presented here are very approximate, based on the total tonnage of domestic usage of fresh tomatoes from Eurostat Bifrelega dataset (1998). Certain assumptions are made for presentational purposes, such as that there are eight tomatoes to a pound. More important, it is important to note that the category of fresh means only bought fresh, for reasons that will be explained later.

[2] The system involves mechanical harvesting of semi-ripe tomatoes, subsequently ripened artificially by exposure to ethylene gas. The process of developing mechanical harvesting and a distinct variety of tomato robust enough and yet easy to remove from the vine has been admirably described in the monograph by Friedland and Barton entitled 'Destalking the Wily Tomato'. This production regime was linked to a revision of immigration laws restricting the use of Mexican *braceros*, which was followed by relocation and concentration of tomato growing farms, arising from this process of industrialisation of agriculture (Friedland and Barton, 1975, 1976).

[3] Friedland has pointed out how what is meant by 'fresh' food has changed out of all recognition, both semantically and technically: food is advertised as fresh when it has been chilled, packaged in artificial atmospheres, ripened by ethylene gas, juiced, or subjected to all kinds of other treatments. The force of his argument is that there is no 'true' use of fresh. Thus also 'fresh' is a *'socially defined* description of foods that ostensibly have not been processed' (Friedland, 1994, 211). We are arguing here that different conceptions of 'fresh' are embedded in different production consumption configurations.

[4] Interviews at Heinz and Campbell, who both took as the prime sources of processed tomatoes ready for reprocessing into soups and sauces, Greece, Italy and Portugal, with increasing amounts from Turkey.

[5] We are grateful for the collaboration of Dr Marian Garcia of Wye College for interviewing 'the Spanish connection', and in Spain.

[6] Neil Culbey, Technical Director, Heinz, Interview, July 1998. In the USA, they have 300-gallon aseptic tankers for transporting tomato pulp. It was quite a surprise, when interviewing at New Covent Garden Soups, to see rows and rows of 50-gallon drums (like petrol drums) of tomato pulp from

Turkey and Greece, the raw material for their 'fresh' tomato soup. This contrasts with their advertisement showing a greenhouse shaped like a Tetrapack with tomatoes growing in it!

[7] It could be argued that innocent bystander nations, such as the English supermarkets, suffered collateral damage from stray Dutch water bombs and from competing with the dominant Dutch industry.

[8] 'These firm, shiny tomatoes are produced by the 45 members of the Evident growers' association. The association dates back to 1996 and has developed into a close-knit group, characterised by its motivation and shared vision.' Quotations here are from The Greenery International publicity material.

[9] The Dutch Market-Garden Food Co-operative.

[10] 'The Greenery bought two groups of exporters early last year, because it is important really to try to integrate the whole chain.' (van Haan, Interview).

[11] The same applies to Albert Hein in the Netherlands: 'Albert Hein, the biggest retailer, organised already over ten years ago their own growers, with whom they made contracts, taking their production at a price for a whole year. They told the growers to grow according to their guidelines, their regime, and so on. That was a movement which was undermining the whole auction system as it had existed.' (van Haan, Interview).

[12] Inevitably, tomatoes now also are enveloped in portfolios, and subject to portfolio management. *Sic transit gloria (lycopersicum) mundi.*

[13] 'What I think The Greenery would hope of is that as new products come on line, The Greenery will take ownership of the product, not the growers themselves, and allow us to market the product to the best advantage, without the restriction of the growers saying, Hang On!, I want to sell these in Germany … It is a little like trying to flog the product with one arm tied behind your back.' (Barnet, Interview).

[14] Dr Marian Garcia, Wye College, is to be warmly thanked for her invaluable contribution to the research covered in this section.

[15] Interview with Andy Mellonie, Technical Manager, Victoria Trading, February 1999.

[16] It has an equally important sister company on the mainland in Spain, Bonnysa, centred in Alicante.

[17] 'They buy on price and they will continue to buy on price.' Stephen Cox, General Director, Agrivera. Interview by Dr Marian Garcia, May 1999. Cox also states that foreign buyers seek out growers who have contracts with Tesco or Sainsbury if they need to be sure of the standards of the product and traceability.

[18] See Chapter 5.

[19] Interviews with Nazario Muños and Stephen Cox from AENOR and Agrivera respectively, by Marian Garcia, and with Ian Finlayson, Technical Director, Sainsbury.

[20] The Asociacion Española de Normalizaçion y Certifacaçion.

[21] A similar process of 'identity formation' is occurring for cherries. In Tesco, a pack of cherries appeared in July 1999 with the marque, 'Cereza del Jerte', with governmental standards equivalent to wine production under the Consejo Regulador de la Denomenación de Origen. See also Thévenot, (1995) Sylvander, (1995) and Letablier and Delfosse, (1995) for a discussion of the formation of 'conventions' for quality standards.

[22] See for example Minguzzi and Passaro (1993).

[23] See Mark Kurlansky (1999, 127–30).

5. The Fabrication of Nature

Sainsbury's farmers think that bugs can be good for you.

*Not all pests are pests. The little bug in our picture acts as a **natural** predator for the unwanted guests which prey on the tomato crop of Eric Wall.*

*Like all of Sainsbury's British tomato farmers, Eric is committed to using more **natural** farming methods.*
*So, if you're looking for a tomato that's **naturally** perfect, pick one up at Sainsbury's.*

Sainsbury Advertisement. July 1999

The contemporary (Northern fresh) tomato confounds categories. It is natural *and* artificial. Indeed, the more artificial, the more natural it becomes. This is not a paradox.

In the last chapter, the phenomenal growth in yield of the tomato grown under glass was demonstrated. Here, the evolving world of the glasshouse is explored. For the innocent who enters a commercial tomato glasshouse today for the first time, the experience is almost breathtaking. The plants are enormous beyond imagination, 5 metres high, with vines for any one plant reaching 12 metres.[1] They have to be tended and picked from specially constructed mobile ladders that run on rails that extend the full length of the rows of tomato plants, and these rows extend into the middle distance, usually over 100 metres. It is something like entering a tropical rainforest, but with important differences: there are only tomato plants, they run in straight lines, and there is no soil.

Yet, however enclosed the world of the glasshouse, it is a mistake to see the botanical vines as the only strands that sustain the life and growth of the tomato. The tomato, as ripened fruit, is suspended on one link of an 'innovation chain', where every link has been the focus of intense innovation:

seed manufacture, energy, atmosphere, pollination, nutrient provision, pest control, grading, packaging, distribution, information technology, consumption. Indeed, the interlocking and interdependent character of the innovations at *every* phase of the tomato trajectory is what really marks out the current phase of tomato innovation. There is nothing that has been 'left to nature'.

It is also a mistake, of course, to see this technology of the tomato as independent of the socio-economic relations between firms, organisations and markets, or of the new forms of labour (scientific, technical and manual), which create and operate within and between each link of the 'chain'.

This chapter takes its material from the development of the UK tomato glasshouse industry, tracing its connections to the 'innovation chain' and placing the technology in the fabric of its socio-economic relations.

TWO TOMATO 'LIFE STORIES'

Visibly, little remarkable has changed about the 'commercial' standard, round, red-orange tomato. But the invisible world behind it has changed. Some people may think of the tomatoes as they grow from their grow-bags,[2] or even in their own garden greenhouses. These are tomatoes on a human scale.

The space-age world of the North European tomato regime can be entered through two, now intertwined, tomato life stories, one that grew out of the earlier epoch of English tomato growing, the other acting as an external catalyst, new to all previous traditions.

Alan Parker, President of the UK Tomato Growers Association, and his partner Chris Hynes had met at a management course at Oaklands College, then part of Hatfield Polytechnic, and a specialist horticultural institution with a reputation for glasshouse technological expertise. Having with difficulty obtained some venture capital to set up as a business partnership, in 1975 they bought their first glass, 2.2 acres in the Lea Valley, a traditional market gardening area. They quickly concentrated on tomato growing, departing from the local pattern of multiple crops of lettuce, cucumber and pepper. But at first they slotted into the normal producer–market relations, taking over clients from the previous owner.

Before long, though, they made two decisive moves. On the technical front, they moved out of soil into hydroponic methods, using rockwool as the planting medium. Their irrigation and nutrient systems were computer controlled:

We were already high-tech growers, computer controlled, by 1983. One of the first in the country. (Parker, Interview)

And they switched from supplying wholesale markets to supplying direct to Tesco:

> When we were in the Lea Valley, we were supplying Tesco. We were the first mainland supplier to be supplying Tesco ... We've nailed our flag to Tescos over the years. They have been a very good customer to us ever since 1983 ...
> We had to do something different than just supplying wholesale markets. Even in those days their performance was appalling. It used to depress me thoroughly, seeing all the care and attention we paid into growing this crop and getting it into the market in good quality, and then a guy at a whim just got whatever he could for the product. There was no attempt to get top price.[3] (Parker, Interview)

On the back of a secure market, and to maximise the length of the growing year, they then moved to the Isle of Wight in 1986, soon after using their heating systems to re circulate CO_2 gases. This has the effect of further increasing yield by up to 15 per cent. When they had started growing in soil, they were producing 80 to 90 tonnes an acre. By the late 1980s they were producing 240 to 270 tonnes an acre, and had embraced space-age technology. With large, capital-intensive production units their 30-acre nursery, together with another and a joint marketing company, now handle the produce of 68 acres of glass, with a turnover reaching £15 million. To their long-term partnership agreement with Tesco, they have added Sainsbury as a second major client, as well as Waitrose. The combination of a technological revolution, capital growth and a completely different trading system, has resulted in tomato cultivation being established on a totally new basis.

In 1964, the Van Heiningen brothers emigrated from the Netherlands to Sussex to set up a new tomato business. They came from a horticultural industry where small family business dominated and where 2 acres was a large holding, especially at that time. In England, too, family businesses predominated and, although occasionally larger, 5 acres would have been about the limit. At the same time, both in the Netherlands and the UK, growers sold their tomatoes to wholesale markets or through the auction system. The Van Heiningens started their English business with *17 acres*. And they immediately started bypassing the intermediary markets or distributors and sold directly to the supermarkets.

In 1998, Arnold Lewis, the Company Chairman and previously a manager for Marks & Spencer, pointed through the tinted glass windows:

I think that the original thinking of the Van Heiningen Brothers was quite remarkable for their time in 1964. We had a guy here last week from Tesco, Sainsbury's as well. He told me that we must have been supplying Tesco since that nursery was built over there. He said he remembered that being built, and being invited by Leo [a Van Heiningen] to come and look at the new nursery. That was more than thirty years ago.
*(*Lewis, Interview)

Van Heiningen Brothers now produce tomatoes under 200 acres of glass, supplying 35 per cent of the total UK market. Two hundred acres amounts to a production capacity equivalent to three or four Dutch growers' associations put together, or around 100 growers. In the UK, VHB is in a league of its own, the next-largest grower being about one-tenth of its size. Alone amongst growing companies, they supply all five of the major supermarket multiples:

This year we will supply Tesco's with 1.3 million 6 kilo boxes of tomatoes. Well there aren't very many people who could produce that sort of volume. (Lewis, Interview)

From the time they arrived, therefore, the Van Heiningen's leapt out of the tradition whence they came, and helped to transform the setting in which they then found themselves. In contrast to the Dutch 'single tomato' growers, Van Heiningen alone produces 13 to 15 varieties of tomato, and trials and introduces many more. The hurricane in 1986 broke established customs as much as it broke glass, and a takeover in the same year combined to consolidate this break with the past. A major convenience-food manufacturer, Hazlewood Foods,[4] acquired VHB and put up the capital to buy several acres of devastated greenhouses. VHB rebuilt them and developed a highly automated, computerised system for growing cress and fresh herbs, adapting much of the technology from tomato horticulture but reducing labour to an absolute minimum. Automation has enabled the process to avoid the human touch of 'green fingers' from the moment seed enters the system, through germination, repotting, transferring into rockwool mats to individualised punnets, and leaving the facility already packaged and marked 'Tesco', or 'Sainsbury'. Carpets of cress on a slow-moving conveyor belt stretch for over 100 yards, giving the impression of a sea of green, ebbing and flowing, only monitored by the occasional white-coated and hygiene-conscious technician. 23,000 punnets of cress leave the glasshouses every week. If VHB have a dominant position in respect to UK tomato growing at 35 per cent of the market, for fresh herbs and cress they *are* the market. In 1998 they produced 95 per cent of the total supplies going through all supermarkets, according to

Retail Weekly. [5] Steve Chadwick, Technical Director of VHB, said of this labour-less world of 'natural' growth: 'This is the van Heiningen dream', nature – fully automated – doing its own work.

The other significant aspect of this second shift away from the patterns of the past was the even greater integration of the supply chain between producers and retailers. Hazlewood Foods is an 'own-label' company, one of the major players on the scene for producing directly to supermarkets:

> It is this that has made the UK lead the way ... *The trade is developing right from one end of the chain to the other*, tied in with the environmental credentials. These are quite powerful things to bolt on to our industry for the future. (Chadwick, Interview)

The contrast with The Greenery International, and with it, the whole relationship between growers, retailers and consumers, could scarcely be more marked. The UK tomato inhabits a different socio-economic space from the Dutch. Interestingly, despite the pre-eminence of Dutch horticulture in the North European Tomato Regime, Van Heiningen Brothers was recognised by the Dutch as being at the technological and marketing leading edge. It was VHB that pointed the way out of the vicious spiral of supply and demand that had led to the Great German Water Bomb Scandal:

> When the Greenery came into being, believe it or not, they actually came here and asked us what we were doing, and why we were doing it, and asked us why we thought the Van Heiningen model was better than the Dutch Auction model. And it wasn't long before they launched onto an unsuspecting world a whole range of products that were, yes, truly differentiated. (Lewis, Interview)

TOWARDS A TOTAL ECOLOGICAL SYSTEM

These two life trajectories of Ayreton Nurseries and the Van Heiningen Brothers supported the development of glasshouse cultivation as a total ecological system. The early utility and conception of the glasshouse was essentially to create counter-climatic conditions, allowing plants accustomed to grow in open Southern sun to flourish in Northern climes. But the glasshouse carried within it a much greater potential. Especially when considered for commercial purposes, rather than for private personal consumption or for aristocratic conspicuous and exotic consumption, the capital and labour investment of glasshouse production impels a logic of high success rate and high yield per plant. Nonetheless, only during the last 20 to

30 years has this logic been fully developed. An agricultural revolution under glass has entailed innovation at a new intensity to every single aspect of cultivation, and has engaged multiple sciences and technologies in a 'distributed innovation process' (Coombs and Metcalfe, 2000; Coombs, Harvey and Tether 2001). This chapter, moreover, only considers the cultivation phase, where seven interlocking dimensions have been subject to major innovation:

- the growing medium – the shift out of soil;
- the gaseous atmosphere in which plants grow, energy and light;
- seed (reliability, quality variation, disease and pest resistance);
- nutrient intake and irrigation;
- pollination;
- control of pests and diseases;
- information technology related and integrated across many of these aspects.

In short, the ecological system as a whole and each phase of the cultivation process becomes the object of multiple and interrelated transformations. This is the true novelty of enclosed systems of agriculture.

Diagram 5.1 summarises the successive 'fabrication of nature' involved in the creation of a new ecological system from the early 1970s onwards. Many of the innovations overlapped in their development and diffusion amongst the horticultural community: it is only from where we stand now that the total ecological transformation appears as such.

The Soil

Plants 'naturally' grow in soil and it is necessary to fully appreciate what it means agriculturally to stop working the earth. In outdoor regimes, from the invention of the plough, 'working the earth' has always been heavy labour, eventually leading to mechanisation. In glasshouse regimes, prior to hydroponics, the labour required was especially onerous. Each year, it was common to completely remove all the soil by manually digging to the necessary depth of growing roots, to place it in specially constructed containers, and to steam sterilise it, before replacing it. Looking back at inter-war horticultural equipment catalogues, there are weird and wonderful steam engine contraptions built for this purpose:

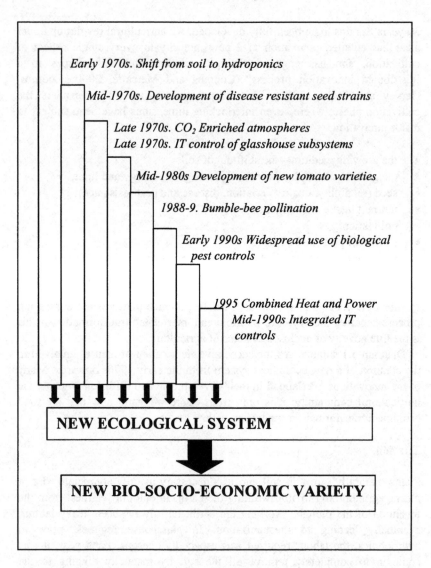

Diagram 5.1 The creation of new ecological system

I built three greenhouses to start. And then I gradually built until I had eight at the finish, 50 footers. In the winter I used to get the soil ready. I used to sterilise it. I'd make a big box up, about four five foot long. Then I used to have a bottom part on hinges, and then the top that I could open and shut down. I used to put in the steam pipes, and make me' own box of pipes, and put that in the middle, and put the soil all round the pipes. Get the fire going. And as soon as she was scalding hot, really scalding hot, see, then I'd undo the bottom and the soil would drop into the wheelbarrow. And then I was away. I never did use chemicals, no. Just the steaming.' (Parish, Interview)[6]

So, even before soil ceased to be utilised, glasshouse soil used to be 'reconstituted' by intensive labour, quite apart from manuring, in order to for it to be a suitable growing medium. It was far from a 'naturally occurring' substrate.

The significance of the shift out of soil, however, was that hydroponic methods allowed precise control of the flow of water and other nutrients over the plant roots, the mineral traces and all elements necessary for plant growth in scientifically determined proportions. Unlike soil, which might vary in composition by accident of history and/or location, hydroponic methods led to a completely controlled and 'fabricated' nutrient mix. Growers might have their different 'recipes' but they were all just that, dedicated mixtures, open to systematic experimentation.

Some growers shifted directly from soil into hydroponics. Chris Harvey did so in 1981 when it had become recognised that growing yields had reached a plateau in soil-based cultivation systems. He pioneered a particular hydroponic method, Nutrient Film Technique, where the roots are suspended into a continuous flow of nutrient liquids, across a gradient of the glasshouse floor, to be recycled via a catchment tank. More typically, the route to hydroponics was via a phase of growing in peat bags or blocks, and then to the most common hydroponic method of using rockwool, a spun mineral fibre similar to that often used in roof insulation, as the rooting medium:

We moved from soil to peat bags and through to hydroponics and ended up in rockwool. Rockwool offers the perfect medium for rooting and aeration. You can put on as much water and food as you like and you can't saturate the plant ... It is perfect. You have full control of all the feeding ... You have no diseases.

Each plant has a tube and there is a little peg on the end. There are two plants in each module, and each plant has own irrigation spike so that you can water exactly to the demands of the plant ... You are watering with water and fertiliser, perfectly balanced, computer mixed, computer controlled ... The plant is never wanting for water or feed ... There is no reason why you can't maximise growth. (Turner, Interview)

Almost from the beginning, the hydroponic technology was linked to computerised control, at first analogue and then digital, so as to ensure maximisation of yield and feedback control from each individual plant within the glasshouse. Information and cultivation technologies were developed in conjunction with each other. The shift out of soil was therefore a critical step in the development of an automated feedback closed ecology.

The Seed

The method of 'following our noses' led from Van Heiningen Brothers (as well as a number of other growers in the UK) to a seed company in the Netherlands, De Ruiters. Situated between Schiphol and Rotterdam airports, the trip there also led to the discovery of another remarkable world behind the supermarket shelf-life of the tomato. Passing through the typical Dutch horticultural landscape, a high-tech glasshouse adjoins each grower's well-appointed detached house or bungalow, accoutred with an immaculate front garden apron.

In the midst of these rows of family greenhouses stands the company headquarters, a modernist edifice to science. It is a recent, substantial and high-prestige investment, a multi-million pound molecular biology laboratory complex, dedicated to the development of new and better tomato seeds. A spacious and lofty 'glasshouse' atrium with tropical plants and displays of scientific achievement provides an architectural metonym for its economic function.

De Ruiters, along with a number of similar sized Dutch seed companies, exemplifies a firm that is equally 'global' and 'local'. Founded in 1945 as a private company, the current President is the second generation owner. It is global in several ways. The seeds it develops (tomato, capsicum, hot pepper, cucumber, melon, aubergine, and cyclamen flowers) are exported internationally and to all continents. For obtaining traits which it wishes to introduce into new cultivars, it uses a global 'gene bank'. In order to breed pathogen resistance in tomatoes, it acquires pathogen varieties from across the world. Once a new cultivar is developed, seed production (a labour-intensive process) is undertaken either by directly owned production facilities or by dedicated contractors, which are spread across the world, in South America, Thailand, North America, Northern and Southern Europe, all in order to ensure coverage of the global climatic zones where the seeds are destined to be used. A picture of Thai women in a glasshouse engaged in the painstaking activity of manual pollination adorns the company publicity brochure.

And yet the company is also distinctively 'local'. Arising from their horticultural expertise, and earlier, from their renowned tulip bulb production, the Netherlands is a centre of expertise in seed development. De Ruiter's seed portfolio is characteristically North European horticultural, unlike globally global companies such as the Seminis Group or Novartis: the portfolio specialisation is for seeds whose plants are all grown (although not exclusively) under glass. Finally, in a way exemplary of the 'polder model' of capitalism, De Ruiter is plugged in to the science infrastructure, where government, universities and commercial organisations work in consort. They own jointly with other similar seed companies a biotech company, KeyGene, which is closely associated with Wageningen Agricultural University. In these many ways, De Ruiter is 'embedded' in, and helps to form, the local politico-economic culture of the Low Countries. The headquarters and the research laboratory are thus both nestling among the greenhouses of the Westland *and* within half an hour of Rotterdam and Amsterdam/Schiphol international airports. Seeds, being light, travel by air. And the company seed portfolio is held within a metre-thick concrete vault, secured by steel doors that would grace any bank, as protection against possible plane crashes. As Erik Postma, the Technical and Research Director said:

A seed company would cease to exist if it lost its seed stock. (Postma, Interview)

The days of hybridisation through simple crossing by sexual reproduction à la Mendel of one chosen phenotypical tomato plant with another which has a desired trait (colour, pathogen resistance, taste, shape, and so on) have long gone. It was a lengthy and unreliable process of gradually establishing the desired trait into the chosen variety over several generations. Of course, this type of breeding itself was far from mutation followed by natural 'natural selection':

In a normal selection process, say in the environment, these plants would never be selected. This is a process of cultivation. A dog is an example that I always use. Look how many dog species there are! This would never have occurred if man had not interfered in the process of selection. Still, we consider all dogs to be normal. (Postma, Interview)

In terms of both fundamental science and technology, the process of developing new tomatoes (or other plants) by hybridisation has progressed from operating at the level of visible or manifest aspects of the plant (phenotypes) to the molecular biological level of the gene, and DNA sequences. As an intervening stage, hybridisation had already developed a biochemical technique using the presence of enzymes as 'markers' for the desired characteristic or trait, by means of enzyme assays. From this technique, enzymes were then used as 'scissors' to cut lengths of DNA sequences associated with these traits. These DNA sequences then themselves became the discrete gene 'markers', responsible for the expression of a given trait in the plant. The particular technique[7] developed for identifying the DNA sequences over the past ten years, and then using them as markers in the breeding process, established De Ruiter as a leading company in the world for hybridisation based on molecular biology:

> It is exactly identical to classical hybridisation. You don't change anything in the DNA. The only thing that you have is that whereas normally you would have a phenotypic marker or an enzyme marker, now you have a DNA marker. So you don't change anything, it's only a flag. (Postma, Interview)

The great advantage of operating at the level of DNA sequences is that it enables completely controlled cross-breeding, so that the DNA sequence and hence the desired trait is present in the cross-breed with certainty.[8] This both accelerates the normally laborious and long process of hybridisation, as well as ensuring much greater control. If, for example, the aim is to breed a resistance to a particular pathogen into a plant where a number of different resistances were required, it would be a lengthy and trial-and-error process before the necessary set of resistances were all established together. With DNA markers, it is possible to know that the required combination of DNA sequences is present in all plants involved in the breeding exercise, prior to expression in phenotypes. Given that earlier forms of hybridisation normally took ten years or more to establish some desired traits, the gains made by using DNA markers are very considerable:

> What we develop are markers that are associated with the trait of interest, and by just following whether if the marker is present within your germ plasm, it allows you, without any selection, without any visual selection, to keep the trait in your breeding process. (Postma, Interview)

There is another way of looking at this transformation of the tomato. The cultivation of the tomato has now recruited a whole new range of people. De Ruiter now employs molecular biologists, and has built its own in-house molecular biology laboratory. Through its joint ownership of KeyGene, it is involved in a network enrolling the work of university-based and fundamental molecular research. A new world has thus opened up behind the tomato.

High-tech hybridisation is developed within the context of a continuing demand for new varieties of tomato. Clearly, the greater control and speed of the hybridisation is a generic technology that provides both more rapid and more targeted development of new varieties. Three dimensions to new variety can be highlighted:

- pathogen resistance,
- fruit quality,
- production-regime or climate specificity.

Breeding resistance to the Tomato Mosaic Virus (TMV) was one of the significant breakthroughs that contributed to the massive growth in yield in tomato production over the past 20 years. But, as with the development of vaccines to eliminate viruses that attack humans, understanding both of the nature of the virus and of the organism attacked by the virus is equally necessary. Consequently, in the laboratory complex there are several laboratories producing the pathogens that might attack tomato plants, fungi, insects, viruses or whatever. It is a technological strategy of 'know thy enemy'. These facilities have to be highly sophisticated in order to ensure total isolation and are subject to the strictest governmental quarantine regulations. Moreover, like similar companies, De Ruiter has laboratories in every climatic area for the testing of pathogens specific to that area. Their laboratories in Zoetermeer specialise in producing pathogen specimens which attack North European glasshouse tomatoes, where it is easier to replicate the climatic and atmospheric conditions most favourable to the 'local enemy'.

But the new technology also promises some quite new possibilities for pathogen resistance. Using DNA markers, it becomes more possible to replace agrochemical treatment of pathogens with resistant seed varieties, given the much higher level of accuracy in targeting complex gene configurations. There is growing public resistance to the use of pesticides and, conversely, a growing market for alternative ecological solutions:

A completely ecological production, that is the ultimate goal. But I don't know if it is realistic. (Postma, Interview)

Moreover, because De Ruiter is a seed company independent of any interest in agrochemicals, it can pursue a market strategy of complete substitution, and is currently aiming to compete on a straightforward cost-for-cost basis with agrochemical alternatives:

The grower has to choose if he wants to use fungicide or pesticide, which costs him money, or buy seed with us with a premium price probably, and use that. If he adds up the costs of buying the resistant variety and finds it cheaper than the use of agrochemicals, of course, that will mean sales for us in that area (Postma, Interview)

The route to a pesticide-free regime, therefore, can be both ideologically driven, especially in terms of the shaping of consumer perceptions and also in terms of governmental controls of minimum pesticide residue levels, but also one of hard commercial calculation. If humans become 'pesticide-averse' plants may become 'pesticide-resistant'. Even companies like Novartis, with currently heavy investments in production of agrochemicals, are scouring the Andes for tomato varieties that are resistant to certain pathogens in order to breed back these traits into contemporary domesticated varieties.

Like breeds of dogs, new biological species are fabricated to tickle human aesthetics and, in the case of tomato plants, supermarket product ranges. The hybridisation process is pulled in two different directions for the creation of new varieties, one focusing on yield maximisation, the other on tomato aesthetics, taste, colour, scent and shape. The first is often, but superficially, described as producer-, or agribusiness-oriented; the second as consumer- or market-oriented. But the German water bomb scandal demonstrated that a yield-oriented producer system is intimately connected to a price-oriented consumer market; and conversely that an 'added-value' producer system is oriented to a highly stratified consumer market for a wide product range.

Van Heiningen Brothers have maintained a long-standing relationship with De Ruiter, as grower to seed-manufacturer, visiting them frequently, and claiming influence on the direction of their seed research development. It is clear that UK growers have been pushing for a different type of 'biological variety' in addition, of course, to pathogen resistance:

It is really very much as a result of the UK market place, pressure from people like ourselves and the big retailers, who went into the plant breeders and said, for goodness sake, you've got the ability in plant breeding terms, but you're not using it.
It's only in the last three or four years that really you have this amazing range of tomatoes, because they realised that the UK example was the one they were going to go for. (Chadwick, Interview)

When we go to the seed houses we stress flavour all the time ... flavour, flavour, flavour. (Hamilton, Interview)

From this type of interaction between growers operating in the UK market and Dutch plant breeders facing several different national markets, new biological species of tomatoes emerged. For the breeder, there is a concept of 'product plus', of some new added value deriving from the aesthetics of the plant construct. The 'tomato on the vine' is paradigmatic of the new aesthetics: the tomato looks more natural when attached to the vine, smells as tomatoes are supposed to smell. For the plant breeder and grower it is an opportunity to cash in on a 'product plus', and add a new 'fabricated natural' variety to the tomato gene pool. The potential of the new hi-tech hybridisation method is that, with much higher levels of control and targeting of desired traits, it is possible to breed in all the new shapes, sizes, colours, scents, vine-characteristics (abscission) whilst retaining and developing pathogen resistances. The Sainsbury or Tesco supermarket shelf is the natural habitat for the golden mini-plum tomato-on-the-vine.

The Atmosphere

Tomatoes in contemporary glasshouse do not breathe the same air we breathe. They grow in an artificial atmosphere, with enhanced levels of CO_2 to stimulate growth and yield by about 15 per cent.

> We've been leading in CO_2 enrichment for many years, pushing it to the limits. It has been one of the main influences on profitability over the last ten years. (Parker, Interview)

Of course, that CO_2 is beneficial to plant growth is a 'natural' fact, but CO_2 enrichment of the atmosphere fabricates a non-naturally occurring environment. The subsequent technological development of CO_2 over the past 20 years has been remarkable, going from the accidental by-product of heating glasshouses, to circuits of heat storage at night and gas emission during the day, culminating in the state-of-the-art Combined Heat and Power systems of the most advanced glasshouses today.

Woodhouse Nurseries, owned by Pearson and Sons just south of Manchester, recently installed Combined Heat and Power in 1998. Given the privatised electricity generating industry, Scottish Power put up the capital for the mini- gas-fired power generator, which provides enough electricity to supply the town of Alderley Edge in the near distance across the fields from the nursery. An Austrian Jambacker engine under computer control monitors gas and electricity outputs: the gas burned for electricity also produces the CO_2 emissions that then go into the greenhouses. On the assumption that the electricity is produced in any event, the plants absorb the resultant CO_2 'for free'. At the same time, heat is generated and stored as required during the day or used overnight. At the other end, as Philip Pearson put it:

It gives benefits to all parties, in that we've got people putting money into CHP, and they can tell their shareholders that they are generating power in an environmentally friendly way. Our customer [Tesco] likes it because we are being green. We like it because we are getting the economic benefits. (Pearson, Interview)

The ecologically 'virtuous circle' in terms of real economy flows of energy, heat, gas and tomatoes is presented in Diagram 5.2.

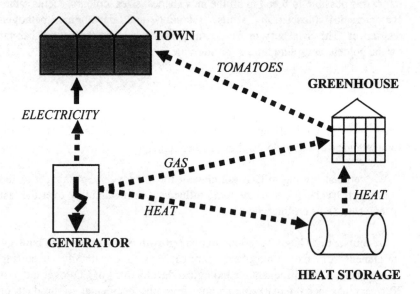

Diagram 5.2 The ecologically 'virtuous circle' of heat, electricity, gas and tomatoes

But there is of course also a money economy flow paralleling this real economy circuitry. Many of the growers installing these Combined Heat and Power systems have the generators financed by the power–generating companies, and their own investments underwritten by the supermarkets. The underlying trading relationships implied are therefore intimately connected to the scale of the tomato growing units, and the stability of their supply to one, or very occasionally several, supermarkets. CHP not only involves a new dimension that literally plugs the greenhouses into the national electricity and tomato grid, but also raises the capital intensity of this production system. As yet, the greenhouse is the only form of agriculture to divert 'greenhouse' gases from power generation, exploiting the advantages of its relatively closed ecology. In so doing, however, it demonstrates how horticulture can operate as an experimental laboratory for the cultivation ecologies.

Bees – and other insects

Following Mandeville,[9] this section could be entitled 'the fabrication of the bees'. Bumble-bees in vast numbers have been recruited to replace labour, or other mechanical and chemical aids to pollination. In every modern greenhouse, there will be brightly coloured cardboard boxes, labelled 'Brinkman's Bees', or 'Koppert's Bees'. Other insects are recruited for other purposes, but first, the bees.

Bumble-bees have now completely monopolised pollination in glasshouses for all kinds of crops. They just happen to be better at it than rival methods, as well as commanding lower wage rates. After all, they are doing something that 'comes naturally' to them. The fruit-set is improved, leading to more even fruiting on the truss and higher–quality fruit:

> It is to do with the way the bee visits every single flower – they never miss one. (Koppert, Interview)

Douglas Blair, now an organic tomato producer, experimented with honey bees in the early 1960s, but with no success, and had then used electrical bee simulators until the arrival of the commercial bumble-bee.

> The bees start at first light – they have a rest in the day and work in the evening – but the big advantage is that they work weekends and don't ask for overtime. (Blair, Interview)

The commercial bumble-bee package normally arrives at a nursery with one queen and about 40 workers, which then increase to several hundred. But, 'following our noses', the question posed itself as to how bumble-bees were mass produced. After all, 'in nature' a solitary queen normally nests in leaf-litter or a mouse hole in a manner that would seem singularly intractable to commercial exploitation. The technological breakthrough was achieved in Belgium and was developed in 1989–90 on a commercial scale. To produce bees on a mass scale, it was necessary to break with the normal annual generational life–cycle. Large warehouses with matchbox-sized 'nests' are programmed with different artificial light conditions to speed up the year:

> It is a giant clinical factory. Bumble-bees normally are one generation each year. So it's a matter of actually getting those generations going much

quicker than is the natural life-cycle. (Scopes, Interview)

The artificial light conditions, however, have to be attuned to the 'natural light' of the environment where the bees are being put to work. When bees were flown out to work in a glasshouse in Iceland, they folded their wings and downed tools, as they were maladjusted to the local light spectrum. There are also strict regulations on exporting bees, so that commercial breeding facilities are established in different locations, to prevent contamination or competition with wild bumble-bee populations. In the US, for example, different native species operate on either side of the Rocky Mountains, and Koppert commercially produce them accordingly. The same company has a partner producing in Asia for the Japanese and Korean market. In Europe, there is now intense competition between the bumble-bee producers Koppert, Novartis and Biopest for the lucrative and expanding Spanish tomato and horticultural industry, where it has been found that the bees work as well under plastic as under glass. In fact, there is an ongoing 'bumble-bee price war' between these companies,[10] with some offering to give bees away free with every package of some other commercially produced insect. Thus, as with tomatoes, bumble-bees can be seen as 'bio-socio-economic' varieties, mass produced but at the same time working naturally, fabricated and yet variable according to the ecologies they are bred to work in.

The same is also true for the other insects which now participate in the horticultural labour force, the 'natural predators that prey on unwanted guests' of the Sainsbury advertisement. Although the use of other insects predates the widespread use of bumble-bees, there is a clear connection in terms of insect-friendly ecological requirements:

We spend tens of thousands of pounds on bumble bees and the last thing we would want to do is to be throwing around a lot of pesticides ... *Anything that the bees don't like we don't use.* (Hamilton, Interview)

The development of biological pest controls has been a major innovation in horticultural production over the past two decades. Unusually, the Dutch pre-eminence was only reasserted through Koppert after the early development work had been achieved by the Glasshouse Crop Research Institute (GCRI) in Littlehampton, led by Joe Hussey, in the early 1970s. Van Heiningen Brothers, located very near to the GCRI, had already begun the adoption of biological pest control (BPC) by 1972.

It is important to recognise that beneficial insects had to establish themselves as much in an economic as an ecological environment. Like bumble-bees, the 'natural predators' also need to be mass produced on an industrial scale. Unlike bumble-bees whose main competitors were transparently inefficient and costly human pollinators, however, 'beneficials'[11] were, and still are, up against agrochemical alternatives to the control of pests and diseases. So both aspects need to be considered separately: how insects become economic agents in the first place, and how they establish themselves in the market place for pest control.

To survive, predators need prey:

> It was a massive decision to make to go biological. To leave a background level of pest in your crop rather than to try to eradicate it completely with use of chemicals was a big step certainly. If you have a policy of zero tolerance, you have to do that with chemical means, because a biological control needs a background level of food to exist. So we don't do that. We use biological control, rather than eradication. (Pearson, Interview)

The switch to the use of biological pest control thus means a change in the dominant mindset of glasshouse cultivation, where the closed ecology normally contains with it a high risk of the rapid infestation of the whole crop. The phrase 'zero-tolerance', borrowed from a moral panic about crime, is significant: before the new 'liberal' biological regime, any deviance was to be met with overwhelming chemical force.

But the mass production of the 'beneficials' also relies on the mass production of their prey. Creating an abundance of prey intensifies the 'natural' life cycle of the predator. One of the main beneficials, *Encarsia formosa*, is a microscopic wasp that preys on whitefly, a significant threat to tomato crops. The wasp itself is only 0.6 mm long, a small dot to the naked eye. Like the bumble-bee, this wasp had to change from being a naturally occurring insect in order to undertake its new role as a major economic actor within the glasshouse. The creation of a special biological cycle is needed in order to achieve a commercial production cycle for the insects. Some insects lend themselves well to being 'fabricated', whereas others are less adaptable.

At the Novartis Great Hawkesley production site, there are several large glasshouses full of tobacco plants, the ideal plant for whitefly infestation. When entering these glasshouses, swarms of whitefly soon cover the human body, and one of the new human tasks in the production process is the unpleasant one of disturbing the leaves regularly to ensure even distribution of the whitefly over the leaf surface. This is critical for maximising wasp-yield. The whitefly larvae-infested plants are then taken into *Encarsia* wasp breeding glasshouses, which then parasitise the larvae. The *Encarsia* develop, and are themselves harvested. A continuous wasp production process is established, with a turn round of plants and insects, all at different stages of development, between different glasshouses.

Early techniques of *Encarsia* pupae production involved cutting the leaves on which the wasps had originally bred into small pieces, each with about sixty pupae on them, sticking the leaf on a card, and selling them in that form. A lot of wastage occurred, and it was an extremely human labour-intensive process, involving an army of women, most of them part-time.

The contemporary method involves Emmet-like machinery, where the harvested pupae are first purified, then dosed by exact measure onto a sterilised adhesive strip. This strip is covered with an inert powder, to prevent the hatching wasps from sticking to the strip and stopping them from going out to work. The strip is then placed on a card, which in turn is inserted in a sachet, somewhat similar to size and design to a teabag. Once deployed, the sachets are hung on tomato plants at about 1.5 metres from the ground throughout the greenhouse. The labels on the sachets are in over 15 languages, including Japanese, indicating the wasps' global future employment prospects. And they are now branded Novartis wasps. If ever there was a need to go beyond any simple binary opposition between nature and culture, these wasps present the most compelling argument. The production process has been described in this detail to emphasise how 'fabricated nature' is both natural and extremely fabricated.

The point needs two further amplifications, illustrated by a pair of similar mites, *Amblyseus cucumeris* and *Amblyseus limonicus*. Both these minute insects attack thrip, also a common pest in tomatoes, but especially in cucumbers and peppers. The *lymonicus* variety has been demonstrated to be much more aggressive and efficient at destroying thrip. But unlike *cucumeris* they are difficult to produce. Specific natural characteristics distinguishing one related species from another can thus make all the difference between a minuscule mite having a big commercial future or not: in the language of actor-network theory, some insects are more easily enrolled than others (Callon, 1986).

The second amplification is that the use of 'beneficials' is not just a question of 'goodies' versus 'baddies'. In order for 'beneficials' to be effective they need the right fabricated ecology in order for them to go to work productively. This includes details of the sachets such as paper with a porosity to allow the right balance of gases and humidity to permeate them. The sachet's own micro-environment has to be adapted to the normal environmental conditions inside the glasshouse, which in turn presupposes the level of atmospheric control afforded by contemporary computerised systems. For that reason, and for many pests, the use of 'beneficials' is quite impractical in the open or semi-open plastic-covered production regimes of Southern Europe. Whitefly, which can transmit lethal viruses as well as directly damaging the crops themselves, easily invade the cultivated crop either from the countryside or from neighbouring, chemically controlled crops.

Insects need the right *human* environment too. At the instance of the supermarkets, many of the biological control companies are attempting to replace pesticide use in Southern Europe. Use of 'beneficials' presupposes a technical expertise in both the recognition of different prey-pests, and also in knowledge of their lifecycles and environmental conditions. Certainly, the physical infrastructures are being upgraded to nearly North European qualities for enclosed cultivation. But up to now, the obliterating use of chemicals in Southern Spain has made much detailed human understanding of pests redundant.

Novartis, together with Sainsbury, hence initiated Project Alicia in order to develop the technical human expertise required to complement the technical insect expertise in pest elimination:

> We realised very quickly that the growers knew absolutely nothing about pest control. Very often they didn't even recognise what was a pest. Northern Europe is unusual in the level of education there is amongst growers. [In Spain] training has proved the key ... If our training supports our product sales, the of course we are interested in training. If we don't do the training, we don't sell anything. There is a clear commercial incentive for us to do it. (Greatrex, Interview)

Insects need the right kind of humans, as much as humans need the right kind of insects.

For many UK growers, the supermarket multiples have been quite decisive in prescribing quality control and production regimes that require low-level usage of chemical pesticides. Alan Turner of Cantelo Nurseries is typical:

> We were basically just ignorant. I was spraying myself. I certainly wouldn't do it now. The main reason was our association with Tesco ten years ago ... They pushed us further. Initially, we thought it was going to be pretty tough to achieve, to grow with only limited chemicals. (Turner, Interview)

Tesco's 'Nature's Choice' brand for low-pesticide tomato regimes' and the Sainsbury advertisement at the head of this chapter, are evidence of a competition to be the most 'natural', to be on-side with Nature. For the expansion of 'beneficials' into Southern Europe, the supermarkets have been decisive:

You have the supermarkets, Sainsbury, Tesco, all the UK multiple retailers, companies in France, Germany, and Holland, all pursuing a very similar line. They dictate to the grower – Whoops! ... or advise the grower perhaps we should say, what pest controls they should use, what fertiliser regimes they may best use, all designed to satisfy the supermarkets, and the supermarkets' customers that the produce is grown in a safe environmentally friendly way and that there will not be residues there which will damage or potentially damage the public's health. So a lot of this, *is driven by the supermarkets' perception of public perceptions.* (Greatrex, Interview)

The supermarkets' perception of public perceptions is a nice phrase that encapsulates the opinion-forming role of the retailers, which in turn is translated into the production protocols which tomato suppliers are obliged to follow. It would be going too far to suggest that supermarkets are alone in defining what is natural about 'nature', but they certainly do lay down rules to follow, and so create an economic environment for 'beneficials' to become commercially viable insects.

But the economic environment for 'beneficials' is more contested than this suggests. It is significant that much of the initial inspiration for biological controls came from believers in a future without chemical pesticides. The Bunting family, closely linked to the Greenhouse Crops Research Centre, established a company dedicated to development of first *Encarsia formosa* and then a predatory mite, *Phytoseiulus persimilis*, that attacked spider mite, a major tomato pest. This company was then taken over by Novartis, and it is clear that there was a tension between pursuing biological controls alone and the new orientation of pursuing them within the context of Integrated Crop Management, or Integrated Pest Management. In these regimes, although dedicated to low use of pesticides, and the use of only those chemicals that are not harmful to the 'beneficials' and the bumble-bees, chemicals still have a significant role to play. Many companies, such as Zeneca and Novartis, thus argue that the use of 'beneficials' is unlikely in the foreseeable future to take over the whole market for pest control. They are rather seen as complementary weapons in the human armoury against 'bad insects'.

Moreover, the market space for 'beneficials' is further constrained by the global sourcing of produce by supermarkets from different production regimes, where beneficial pest control is not viable. Growers, such as Van Heiningen, might aim to achieve total elimination of the use of pesticides by the year 2000. But if they are to achieve this, they need attract the market premium to go with pesticide-free produce. For this to happen, supermarkets will have to create a new product market segmentation, which redefines 'nature' to exclude the use of all pesticides – a move they have as yet been unable or unwilling to make. There is thus at present an uneasy tension between ecologies and economies for this newly emerged economic actor, the beneficial insect.

Information Technology

> In the last ten years, we moved towards computer control. Priva [the IT system] now runs the nursery 24 hours a day. (Hamilton, Interview)

> Now we monitor by computer. We put suction pipes in at each of the testing points ...The temperature, humidity and CO_2 is measured at that point and back to the environmental computer in the middle – so analysing CO_2 constantly ... and it is turning on and off according to the demand. (Turner, Interview)

It might seem strange to include information technology as the final component of the new glasshouse ecologies along with soil, seed, atmosphere and insects. But it is striking how many of the different aspects of 'fabricated nature' were introduced together with computer control, and also, how the 'environmental computer' is central in bringing together diverse and disjointed processes of innovation into an integrated and unified 'total ecology'.

In re-writing the history of innovations surrounding glasshouse horticulture, it is important to recognise this was an 'emergent ecology' where the different aspects 'went together' but were not necessarily *pre*conceived together. Historically, the introduction of computer control into glasshouse was intimately linked to the introduction of CO_2 emission.[12] But computer controls also accompanied the introduction of hydroponics and NFT, monitoring and controlling the flow of nutrients to each plant. In other words, the emergence of computer controls was closely bound to particular technologies as they developed.

Moreover, apart from an 'integrated ecology' logic, there were other diverse or at least distinct logics to the introduction of computerisation. In the Pearson's hi-tech nursery, supermarket logic is central in binding IT to the traceability of tomatoes from the store shelf to the tomato vine:

> Traceability goes right back. Our system means that if there's a problem in a box in Tesco's, that goes right back to our packhouse records, to the grader. There's computerised grading. Each batch that goes through is

given a code by the computerised grader, which goes out through the boxes to Tesco. So we can trace it right back through to who picked it, and where it came from, and what day, and what time actually. (Pearson, Interview)

So, humans are also part of this computer-controlled environment, and yet another associated logic to IT is the monitoring of labour. The system PRIVA Assist is an on-line management tool, which enables a central terminal to monitor exactly what each worker is doing at any time and in what location, as s/he carries a portable handset on which activity information is entered:

We keep track of all their operations, so that we can work out unit costs and pay them for the hours they work ... We need to know how long they spend on each job, and how long their break time is, etc. (Turner, Interview)

Along with traceability, direct computerised monitoring of humans within the glasshouse enables simultaneous logging of both labour activity and responses to incidents of pest activity.

Nonetheless, in spite of this coexistence of different logics of control and information, there is clearly a way in which they are mutually implicated: economy and ecology are complementary, and the technology is therefore not simply a technical fix to a technical problem. Glasshouses are socio-economic ecologies. They are developing towards 'total environments', including human and non-human aspects, and integrating systems for traceability, labour, climate, nutrients and irrigation:

We look at the greenhouse as a total environment. We are looking towards a range of equipment, each piece integratable with the next piece, that is OK for the total environment.' (Addis, Interview)

SOCIO-ECONOMIC VARIETY: THE UK TOMATO

The extent of the transformation of the 'world behind the tomato' just outlined is quite astonishing, but levels of capital investment, intensity of innovation for every aspect of cultivation, takes place only within a developing economic environment. In the previous chapter, major characteristics of the North European production regime were outlined and the Dutch variant was analysed. Much of the glasshouse technology is shared, and it would therefore be erroneous to assume any simple causal links between economic and technological systems – in either direction. The dominant role of UK supermarkets has provided particularly favourable conditions for the emergence of greater tomato variety, of 'product plus', and of a competitive race to 'fabricate the natural'. These different conditions of emergence favour different orientations in technological development, but they also distinguish between the 'insiders' and 'outsiders' of supermarket supply chains.

The diagram representing the UK production-distribution regime (Diagaram 4.3) describes a hierarchy of supermarkets, a hierarchy of growers and, implicitly, a hierarchy of tomatoes. The relations between growers and supermarkets are clearly stratified, and those with the longest and most stable trading relationships were thereby enabled and encouraged to develop the new technologies. The diagram shows the top multiples (Tesco, Sainsbury) having a core of stable supply relations with the top-level growers. Middle-level supermarkets rely more extensively on a stable intermediary supplier (a distributor or marketing group), with middle-ranking growers. The lower, discounting end of supermarkets use the cheapest source whatever that might be, and consequently have highly contingent trading relations with any particular grower or group of growers. Off the bottom of this scale in the current retailing world are small greengrocers taking their supplies from residual wholesale markets, where trading relations remain locked in the previous epoch of arm's-length trading. This is, of course, a broad-brush picture of the UK paradigm of producer-retailer relations.

At the opening of the chapter, two of the top-rank UK growers were described, together with their distinctive relationship to supermarkets multiples:

> We see it that the multiples dragged the horticultural industry off the floor and turned them into one of the most efficient and effective groups of suppliers of anywhere in the world. The English horticultural industry can hold its head up anywhere. (Agombar, Interview [13])

With Tesco's, for example, Ayreton Nurseries developed the 'Tom and Jerry' packaging for cherry tomatoes and the infant market, realising the significance of 'getting them hooked young'.

For the ecological transformation described above, it is quite clear that being on the 'inside' of a secure and continuous preferred supply relationship with one or more supermarkets is of central significance. Long-term trading relationships, in some case five-year planning agreements, afford the possibility of capital growth and the risk of investment is often underwritten, formally or informally, by the retailers.

Almost in the form of a sociological 'experiment', three nurseries within 10 miles of each other south of Manchester demonstrate this interconnection between technological development and position in the hierarchy depicted in the dominant UK model. Again, starting at the top, there is the Pearson nursery, with a recently installed CHP system, now an exclusive and dominant supplier for Tesco in the North-West, and indeed, Number One in the Tesco National League table:

> They (Tesco) are prepared to underwrite investment to the bank as well. That's as far as their commitment goes ... We were determined we didn't want anybody else. We wanted Tesco. We wanted the best one. If you try hard enough, you get there. (Pearson, Interview)

The Pearson nursery, a wider family business, has broken the size barrier, cultivating just under 12 acres of glass, and employs a sizeable, full-time and permanent workforce.

Next in the hierarchy, there is the Frank Rudd nursery, only just under 2 acres, with the family workforce of mother and father and two ambitious sons determined to make it. At present, they have a medium secure outlet for their produce through English Village Salads (owned by Geest), which distribute to Sainsbury as well as the middle-ranking supermarkets. But consequently, they also both pay the middleman a percentage on their sales, and lack the long-term planning environment of a stable trading relationship. With one foot close to the door, they still both resent the power of the supermarkets and strive to enter the kind of relationship with them enjoyed by Pearson's. For them, the future lies with acquiring their own CO_2 boiler system, still one step down from full combined heat and power, and they are limited by scale to producing one, possibly two of the varieties to match the full supermarket tomato portfolio. They are in an 'East of Eden' scenario.

Finally, there is the Matthews nursery, a contingent supplier to supermarkets, forced also to trade through wholesale markets, and direct to small growers. Michael Mathews is struggling to install an initial CO_2 system on his small family holding. His view of supermarkets is quite different:

> Talk about the public demanding things! The public don't demand anything. The public only demand what the supermarkets tell them they should. That's basically the problem. The vested interest of the supermarkets is to make as much money for themselves as possible. And the way they do that is to leave as many options open as they can for themselves. They've got very little loyalty to the growers up here. (Matthews, Interview)

For Michael Matthews, too, there is no doubt that the wholesale markets are the dumping ground for the tomato remainders, having failed to secure sale to the supermarkets, and where prices for his produce are accordingly lower, with Bolton market being a slightly better class of wholesale market than Manchester:

Anything which doesn't come up to supermarket standard, they dump on Manchester Market, you know. So there's a lot of cheap tomatoes around, because it's usually 'grade-outs' from supermarkets, that the growers themselves have no other market for. (Matthews, Interview)

In contrast to the Dutch, with their unique style of grower association tomato identity, being at the upper end of the hierarchy of growers in the UK not only means being able to develop and invest in the most advanced technologies, but also to trial and produce the distinctive range of tomatoes now found on supermarket shelves. There is thus no wholesale market place where growers compete, head to head, on price. Rather there is inclusion or exclusion from supermarket supply chains, and attempts by outsiders to become insiders in a competition orchestrated by supermarkets.

At a different scale of competition between UK and Dutch national regimes and between Northern and Southern European regional tomato regimes, the predominant feature of the relations between UK growers is, like the Dutch, one of cooperation rather than competition, in face of a shared threat. Thus, the Tomato Growers' Association is the British variant of The Greenery International, very different in character and economic function. For over 20 years, Tomato Study Groups have operated at a regional level, much in the same way as Dutch growers' associations, learning from each other, visiting each other's nurseries, promoting the best techniques and growing systems:

Last year [1997] we reached a defining moment for tomatoes. We formed the Tomato Growers' Association, a coming together for branding. The industry is working exceptionally well together. No one company could do that. It has to be the industry. 85 per cent of tomatoes produced in this country are now produced through the TGA ... We do compete. But frankly that is a minor competition. We have a tremendous level of cooperation. It's a Dunkirk spirit, this one. Together we float, divided we sink. (Agombar, Interview)

Unlike The Greenery International, the TGA is not a marketing or brokering institution, standing between the growers and the retailers, but a branding and expertise-sharing organisation, to enhance the common profile of UK tomatoes in a direct producer-to-retailer supply system. Many of the growers stress what a close community they are.[14] There may be limits on just how much technology they share, but they see the strategic position of enhancing the competitivity of the North European production regime as a whole, and of UK producers within that regime. So, together with its very distinctive model of producer–market relationships, the 'British tomato' was launched in 1998, with its TGA logo now appearing on boxes of tomatoes alongside the supermarket brand and the nursery name – the 'Intel Inside' solution. The British tomato has achieved a new market identity of a distinct bio-socio-economic variety. A historically 'defining moment' indeed for the tomato!

NOTES

[1] One of the main reasons for the giant plants has been the breeding out of Tomato Mosaic Virus (TMV). 'Six trusses of tomatoes, up to here, and every single nursery would have tomato mosaic virus … People who'd been in the industry all their life, just could not believe it' when the new plants came along (Parker, Interview).

[2] 'People believe that tomatoes are a natural product, and grow like they do in a growbag outside the backdoor.' (Robin Barnet, Interview). The growbag is also no doubt as natural a phenomenon outside back doors as the tomatoes that grow in them.

[3] Alan Parker, Interview, March 1990

[4] See Chapter 8.

[5] We shall return later to consider the implications of this for the relation between innovation and competition: the most 'innovative' firm behaviour is in the area where they have a complete monopoly.

[6] Jim Parish, 84 years old at the time of the interview in 1998, is a retired tool-maker who had worked in many of the car and aircraft plants around Coventry until he ceased employment. Although working 48 hours or more a week, he worked his glasshouses in his 'spare time', but for commercial sales of the produce. His father and grandfather (a blacksmith) before him had also grown greenhouse tomatoes, a family tradition going back to the 1870s and 1880s when tomatoes were still considered by many to be poisonous red berries: 'my dad's dad was telling me that they used to reckon them as poisonous.' (Parish, Interview).

[7] The A/P technique.

[8] In view of the widespread confusions about what is involved in genetic modification, it is vital to be clear how this method of hybridisation, although relying on much of the same fundamental science of DNA sequence identification and DNA recombinant techniques, is not genetic

modification. So long as genetic material is passed from one plant to another by means of sexual reproduction, rather than by direct insertion into the germ cell, there is hybridisation and not 'engineering' or 'modification'. The difference lies in the means by which a DNA sequence finds its way into the plant.

9 Mandeville (1670?–1733) wrote an early precursor of political economy based on the division of labour and social organisation of bees, entitled *The Fable of the Bees* (1970). It has taken some four centuries to develop the reverse engineering.

10 'We know that in Almeria the price of bumble-bees has dropped by 80% in a very short period ... Bumble-bee wars, yes, the prices have been pushed down.' (Greatrex, Interview)

11 The word commonly used to describe the various insects engaged on the side of the humans.

12 Chris Addis, Interview, Managing Director of Priva UK, the leading player in horticultural IT. Priva currently has about a 50 per cent share of the world market in this field. The firm was established in Holland, and its UK counterpart was created some 35 years ago. Of the link between computer control and controlled CO_2, Addis said 'That is when the real Priva company started.'

13 Wight Salads is jointly owned by Ayreton Nurseries, and supplies supermarkets from 68 hectares of glass, substantial by UK (let alone Dutch) standards.

14 Alan Turner affirms that 'most of our innovations or technical improvements come by working together with other growers ... We are very open with each other'. And Chris Harvey suggests that: 'It has always been open ... It probably stems back to many years ago when market gardening was a kind of allotment culture. You could literally shout from your plot to the guy across the way.'

6. The Rise and Fall of the Genetically Modified Tomato

The fabricated total ecologies of the contemporary European greenhouses, and new tomato varieties 'classically' hybridised using recombinant DNA technology, represent an historical development of the tomato. Genetic modification has now created a further dimension of distance from first domestication. The tomato once more was to find itself a pioneer. It was the 'world's first genetically engineered whole food' (Martineau, 2000). Unlike RoundUp Ready soya or Bt corn and cotton, now established world commercial crops, tomatoes broke new territory for genetic modification by altering plants in order to change the quality of the food, rather than in order to enhance agricultural techniques, for example by linkage to use of specific proprietary pesticides. It was consumption- rather than production-oriented genetic modification. In the US, the genetically modified tomato appeared as a premium vine-ripened tomato in 1994, the Flavr Savr™. In the UK, a similarly modified tomato appeared as cans of purée in 1996. Both products were segregated and clearly labelled, with consumer information on the new technologies prominently displayed. People bought them in large quantities.

But in each case, if for very different reasons, the new products, one fresh, the other processed, disappeared after an economic life of little more than two years. Moreover, a second generation of differently genetically modified tomatoes was left stillborn. The significance of this episode in the history of the tomato is that, as a world first, the new biological entity *failed* to become economically instituted, to become stabilised in a new market. It secured a scientific life but only a very temporary and tenuous economic existence. The 'failure' needs to be put into perspective. The tomato and much else besides have become much better scientifically understood as a result of the process, and that gain is irreversible. Economically, much has been learnt and one of the leading players described the whole launching of the GM tomato as a 'proof of concept'.[1] The negative lessons on the conditions for creating an economic life for genetically modified foods are no doubt grounds for doing things differently in the future, in terms of market creation, clear *consumer* benefits, and regulatory processes including segregation, labelling and information. Just as scientific hybridisation has involved a fundamental shift in understanding of plant and animal biology, as well as a transformation of agricultural production and food, so too genetic modification can be seen to be in the early and turbulent stages of a fundamental revolution in the production and consumption of food:

> I think the general public, and certainly the newspapers, don't understand that this is a revolution in biology. Plants have between 30,000 and 50,000 genes. In 20 years time, half of them will be genetically engineered. I can't even dream of the consequences. But biology is a predictive and manipulable science in the same way that chemistry was in the 1890s ... It's going to be such a mega revolution, we would be astonished. I would be astonished. (Grierson, Interview)

This chapter will analyse the UK story of the emergence of the tomato as the vehicle chosen for developing that revolution in particular directions, using the US only as a point of critical contrast. The story of a process leading from first scientific engagements with the tomato for these purposes to the definition of an economic product and attempts to form a market is a complex one. The biological specificities of the tomato and of genetic modification are combined with social and economic specificities of the relations between firms and public science. Interactions between producers, retailers and consumers in different countries also all play a significant determining part. At the outset, it is important to emphasise that genetic modification is not a unitary phenomenon, there are many techniques, and there are many possible outcomes with different ecological, human biological, and socio-economic consequences. The story undermines a view of a single possible trajectory of science or technology rolling out in a universal or global way. Rather, whether for the GM tomato itself, the science, or the commercial product, the picture is one of institutional variety.   In attempting to explain this variety, the account could be summarised by a number of questions that might be asked of a can of genetically modified tomato purée (see Diagram 6.1).

1. Why tomato as the world's first GM food?

2. Why GM processed tomato (purée) in the UK?

3. Why did the purée come in supermarket own–label cans?

4. By whom and how was it decided to identify clearly that the product was made with GM tomatoes?

5. Why are the tomatoes Californian, exceptionally for the UK?

Diagram 6.1 Questions that might be asked of a can of genetically modified tomato purée

THE EMERGENCE OF A GENETICALLY MODIFIED PRODUCT: THE FIRST GENERATION

To give an overview of the chronology, Table 6.1 provides a summary of some of the chief events in the sequence that led to the appearance of a saleable GM product. In very broad terms, two main phases of genetic modification of food are posited.[2] Neither involve the introduction of traits foreign to the tomato. 'First generation' genetic modification, the focus of this main section, involves 'switching off' or inhibiting the expression of a natural characteristic of a plant. So, for example, fruit can be inhibited or prevented from ripening. 'Second generation' genetic modification, analysed in the next section, involves enhancing or amplifying an already natural characteristic of a plant. Enhancement, in principle, can apply to any plant characteristic: shape, flavour, proteins, vitamins, oils and so on. Gene expression enhancement is a means of increasing the nutrient or aesthetic values, including medicinal values already present in plants, and so has led to the emergence of the concept of 'Nutrient Dense Food' (NDF).

The history of the GM tomato is quite a long one, and is still very much open-ended. It took 22 years from the first scientific work to the appearance of a commercial product, a brief 'moment of glory' before it disappeared from the supermarket scene. GM tomato purée is unlikely to reappear again, at least in its original form. But, in the long run this is probably the first episode of a major revolution in the life of the human tomato. As can be seen from Table 6.1, the two generations overlap, the second beginning in the early 1990s, before the appearance of the first commercial product of the first generation genetic modification, the can of GM tomato purée in 1996.

Table 6.1 Schematic chronology of the emergence of GM tomato products	
1974	The preliminary scientific engagement with tomatoes
1978	Locking-in to researching the tomato system
1981-82	Grierson introduces Zeneca to the tomato
1987	First patent filed for GM tomato to 'switch off' a gene (polygalacturanase)
1988	The formation of the GM production network (aided by use of the Bostwick Trough to measure viscosity. The Zeneca GM tomato becomes purée.
1991	*Zeneca approaches Bramley for GM trait enhancement (lycopene)*
1992	Calgene creates Calgene Fresh Inc for developing and marketing the Flavr Savr tomato
1993	Zeneca goes to the supermarkets
1993	*Zeneca initiate the five year programme for development of Nutrient Dense Foods*
1994	The FDA gives approval to the Flavr Savr GM tomato, and the first tomatoes appear in US stores
1995	*Linkage with Guy's Hospital to study lycopene absorption*
1996	A can of GM tomato purée appears on the UK supermarket shelves.
1997	Monsanto buys up Calgene Fresh, and the Flavr Savr tomato disappears in the US
1999	GM tomato purée is removed from supermarkets

Note: 'First generation' normal script, 'second generation' italics.

First Engagements

At the beginning of the story of GM tomato purée, none of the eventual participants had the least idea that the product was going to be tomato, let alone tomato purée. In fact, what is striking about the historical accounts given by the main players is just how accidental was their engagement with the tomato, and yet, once engaged, just how inescapable the engagement became. This is as true for the leading scientists (Grierson, Bramley, Schuch) as it is for the companies (Zeneca, Petoseed, Hunt Weston, Safeway and Sainsbury).

At first glance, the tomato first became a scientific object for research in gene functionality, and then only later became an object with product potential. But that description misses something significant: the tomato addressed scientifically in the early 1970s for genetic modification was *already* a commercial agricultural product, and the outcome of hybridisation for horticultural purposes. As Kimmelman, and Mittman and Fausto-Sterling have shown, the choice of an agricultural crop as an object of scientific experimentation provides a determining context linking science with agriculture (Kimmelman, 1992; Mittman and Fausto-Sterling, 1992). *Post hoc*, Grierson had six rationalising reasons for his 'accidental engagement', mostly connected to the physiology and biochemistry of the tomato ripening process. Significantly one reason, however, was that an 'excellent genetic map' for the tomato had already been constructed by plant breeders, using classical Mendelian techniques. Two of the key genes subsequently involved in the story had already been identified and characterised by these methods (Rick, 1978). Indeed, subsequently the new molecular biology scientific paradigm absorbed and consolidated the Mendelian genetic linkage maps of the previous paradigm from which it emerged (Tanksley, 1993; Zabel et al., 1993). These *post hoc* reasons, no doubt already 'in the air', informed Grierson's appreciation and judgement of what was scientifically worthwhile. What finally tipped Grierson towards the tomato was that a Thai PhD student researching for a food science thesis on tomatoes brought the tomato to Grierson. Up to then, Grierson had been engaged in researching the physiology and senescence of the petunia, a plant that happens to be a close relative of the tomato (sharing the Solanaceae family). It was at this very early point, therefore, that the tomato, which had been the object of food science and commercial breeding, became the object for researching the genetic control of plant development. Don Grierson started working on the understanding of genetic mechanisms affecting tomato plant development in 1974. Four years later, his tomato engagement had become thoroughly path-dependent:

I thought, what are the questions? What questions do tomatoes pose which you've not thought about before? *What is the tomato really good for* [emphasis added]? The harder I thought about it, the more I realised that everybody else had missed an awful lot of things … I can remember actually saying to a scientific colleague of mine from Germany in about 1978, I think I'm going to concentrate on this tomato system, because it is really going to help us answer an awful lot of questions. (Grierson, Interview)

Silencing Genes, controlling the Ageing Process

In terms of gene modification technology, tomato purée relies on techniques for switching off gene expression. It is important, especially given a tendency to treat all genetic modification as one and the same, to distinguish between different forms of genetic modification, if only because the product potential derived from enhancing gene expression is radically different from that which can be generated by gene suppression or silencing.[3] Thus even a House of Lords Select Committee Report (1998) opens with a common, and much-voiced, conception that genetic modification as such 'involves the insertion of genes from one organism into another so as to produce a modified organism with different characteristics' (op.cit. para.1).[4] In fact, what is here termed first generation genetic modification of the tomato is distinguished from the second generation partly by virtue of 'gene silencing' being an effect of inserting genes cloned from the *same* organism, which induces silencing precisely because of an homology with the target organism's genetic constitution. By contrast, enhancement of gene expression is primarily achieved by use of non-homologous genes,[5] hence gene material cloned from *other* organisms, transferred to the target organism.

In terms of the science, it should be emphasised that both first and second generation genetic modification are concerned with the fundamental understanding of processes of plant development and fruit ripening. The scientific understanding of plant physiology and biochemistry was unified and integrated with molecular biology to a new degree. Moreover, given that plants contain some 50,000 genes or more, this unification depends on the identification of gene sequences in terms of gene functionality. A cDNA (cloned DNA) library was developed, and through this gene identification, understanding of gene expression was advanced. As part of the progress from first and second generation genetic modification, in terms of the science the first generation had concentrated on discrete gene identification linked to discrete gene functionality in a tradition of Mendelian gene particularity, whilst the second generation began to explore multi-gene complexes and gene interactions.

Don Grierson started a collaboration on first generation genetic modification with Zeneca (then ICI) in 1982–83 which has lasted to this day. He said of the start of that collaboration:

In the general scientific sense, we knew where it was going. And in the commercial sense, absolutely no idea .... They had no tomato business whatsoever. They didn't come to us saying we need to know about tomatoes. They said we need to know about plant genes. The tomato system is as good as any for finding out about plant genes. They had seen the future. Because they had the corporate laboratory and the biotechnology group, and they knew that plant biotechnology was coming, they knew they had to be in there. (Grierson, Interview)

For Zeneca, striking up a relationship with the tomato was more of a blind date than an 'accidental engagement'. Zeneca had in fact been committing itself by making substantial investments in a very different area of biotechnology, one much more oriented towards their core business. In the previous period they had been buying up seed companies in the main commodity crops of maize, wheat and soya. The ICI-Zeneca orientation was therefore then similar to Monsanto, directed towards farmers and agrochemicals. The shift to the tomato represented a fundamental break with that orientation.

The early basis of the collaboration was a complementarity of different capabilities rather than fundamental science residing in universities and applied technology in an agrichemical company. Grierson had expertise in plant physiology and developmental processes that Zeneca lacked, and Zeneca had capability in molecular biology and the techniques of DNA cloning that Grierson lacked. Together they were able to identify a DNA sequence of the gene that controlled the pectin chain, or the process of senescence of the cell walls of the tomato fruit. The PG or polygalacturanase gene (named pTOM6) was identified, cloned, cut by molecular scissors, reversed in its sequence to form anti-sense DNA, and transferred into the cell nucleus using *Agrobacterium tumefaciens* Ti plasmids. The result was the almost total inhibition of the production of the PG enzyme, and hence fruit was produced in which long-chain pectin in the cell walls did not suffer the normal processes of senescence (first publication, 1988).[6] In this one respect, after a given developmental stage the cells never rotted. This enabled fruit to remain longer on the stalk, so improving fruit quality, but also meant that once picked, the fruit had much higher viscosity. It was discovered quite shortly after this (first publication in 1990) that a very similar effect of gene suppression was surprisingly achieved by cloning the same gene, not reversing its sequence, but adding a second copy back into the nucleus. This was called sense-gene suppression or co-suppression. Thus the same cloned gene being transferred in the same sequence back into the same organism could produce the same effect. That both anti-sense gene suppression and sense-gene suppression resulted in the elimination of PG gene material in the cell has led to the use of the generic term of 'gene silencing'. For the PG gene the aim was more or less total inhibition.

This research programme and technique was also developed with pTOM13, the gene that controlled the production of ethylene, also critical to the process of fruit ripening. Zeneca initially decided to assist the University of Nottingham in patenting the ethylene gene and gene suppression technique, but not to develop the technology into a commercial product. Grierson, appreciating the scientific reasons for understanding the role of pTOM13 in ethylene synthesis, pursued an independent, intellectually driven research programme over seven years, making significant advances. But, this is *the product that never happened* – at least not yet. At the time, this was partly because of an intention to focus on getting one product to market. But also if ethylene gene expression is totally suppressed a fruit is produced that never ripens:

> The question in the ethylene story is that if you make no ethylene, you end up with a green tomato which you can keep on your desk until you die, and it's still alive, sitting there, not doing anything. So it wouldn't be particularly useful to the consumer. (Schuch, Interview)

The assessment of the utility of ethylene suppression was also related to the already existing industrial usage of ethylene gas as an artificial ripener for harvested unripe fruit, prior to its consumption as a fresh fruit. For the US fresh tomato market, the tomato is mechanically harvested green, and then ethylene gas is subsequently applied at the appropriate time to induce ripening to deliver a 'fresh' ripe tomato on the store shelf.[7]

> This is the standard practice for non-GM tomatoes grown in the field for table tomatoes. (Grierson, Interview)

In Europe, however, the whole system of fresh tomato produce and market is quite different, as tomatoes generally are picked non-mechanically and relatively ripe. Zeneca therefore assessed that the market for the fresh tomato business using ethylene-controlled gene expression was too small and fragmented to be of interest. But:

> If you can do all this wondrous stuff with bananas, then you would have something quite sizeable there. (Bright, Interview)

Bananas, melons and other fresh fruit produce have distinct problems of controlled and chilled storage during transportation, are often picked unripe, and can be artificially ripened by application of ethylene gas. There is no doubt a substantial potential product market for GM technology involved in genetic modification to induce controlled and delayed ethylene synthesis in fruit. For this reason, Zeneca later bought back in to the Grierson research programme into ethylene synthesis. But not for tomatoes, not in Europe.

Until 1989 there was still a real possibility that Zeneca would disengage from the tomato and concentrate in the area of their core expertise in broad-acre crops. A new commercial manager analysed the tomato market and, convinced that Zeneca had a leading genetic modification technology, supported continued research and pushed this towards defining a product. The decision was made to concentrate on the polygalacturanase gene identified by Grierson and Schuch[8] in the mid-1980s. But the final product or utility of this science was yet to be fixed.

Closing in on Purée

Two further developments then combined to steer the process of product emergence and definition towards its culmination in purée. The first critical point was that Calgene, the US biotechnology firm, had acquired the patent for the use of the same DNA sequence (pTOM6) for fresh tomatoes (Redenbaugh et al., 1992). Calgene had only narrowly come second in the race to patent the gene, and had been working with financial support under license to the Campbell Soup Company. One of the terms of the agreement was that Calgene was excluded from entering into the tomato business (Martineau, 2001, 11), and it was only in 1991 that Campbell relaxed these conditions to allow Calgene Fresh to enter the fresh tomato market in the US for which Campbell's had less competitive interest (ibid., 126). As a consequence of negotiation, Calgene and Zeneca agreed to split the market with Calgene producing the Flavr Savr™ as a 'fresh' tomato, and Zeneca looking for a product in the area of processed tomato. The US tomato industry had long been oriented towards the mechanical harvesting of semi-ripe tomatoes, with ripening occurring post-harvest because of the more robust harvesting method (Busch et al., 1991; Friedland and Barton, 1976; Friedland and Barton, 1975). The genetic modification resulting in delayed ripening, allowed the fruit to remain longer on the stem whilst maintaining its robustness. It was thus considered to be well suited to the American style of fresh tomato production. By contrast, Zeneca had judged that the same modification was more suited to processed tomatoes, because of the greater flavour, decreased wastage and increased viscosity that might be derived from the same genetic modification.

After this deal, there was no turning back. Calgene was locked in to the genetically modified fresh tomato; and Zeneca was equally bound to the development of a genetically modified processed tomato, with brief, but much more positive outcomes. The potential market institutions had taken decisive further definition.

The second decisive development involved the almost chance purchase of the Bostwick trough. It is not a piece of high-technology laboratory equipment, but a plastic container measuring some 18 inches long, with a little gate at one end. Juiced tomato is poured into it, the gate is released, a 30–second interval is timed, and a measure is taken of how far the juice runs. It cost Zeneca the significant sum of $50. Zeneca applied this equipment to their GM tomato juice, and the tomato industry was convinced by their own standards of proof that GM tomatoes were commercially promising by virtue of being physically less runny. Zeneca were no longer 'bozos from Europe', as the American industry had once described them (Poole, Interview):

> So somewhere or another, we suddenly came across this trough, which only cost about $50 to buy. It was the cheapest business investment we have ever made. It gave us a clear steer about where the work really needed to go. (Schuch, Interview)

The product took a major step forward in definition. Zeneca then approached seed companies and tomato processors in the US, in order to construct a value chain capable of taking a product through to market. Pre-existing contacts with the seed company Petoseeds, and the prohibitive costs of buying into fruit and vegetable seed companies, channelled Zeneca towards the US as the place where the product would be developed. Hunt Weston, the established US tomato processor, was then recruited as the partner responsible for this phase of production.

Equally if not more important was that a clear and defined regulatory environment had already been established in the US. Approval for commercial development was thus procedurally much easier to obtain from the USDA and the Food and Drug Administration (FDA) than from the patchwork of regulatory systems in Europe (House of Lords, 1998, paragraphs 44–50; Lindemann, 1993; Schuch and Poole, 1993). In this respect, moreover, Calgene had led the way in developing the regulatory science necessary to obtain regulatory approval from the FDA, achieving this in May 1994 (Martineau, 2001). They had undertaken new and significant experimental work to prove these genetically modified tomatoes were safe for consumption and cultivation.

So, the first genetically modified tomatoes for Zeneca's processing were destined to be of Californian origin, making them the only Californian tomatoes to enter UK markets on a significant scale. For reasons related to the food retailing of supermarkets in the US, price is at a premium over quality, and this has led to the use of the hot-break technology in the processing of tomatoes, where volatiles are burnt off during sterilisation, collected and re-amalgamated (Gould, 1992). This contrasts with the more costly cold-break methods used in processing in Europe. Moreover, hot-break, because of its relatively destructive nature, is much more technologically attuned towards paste, as the Americans call it, than to diced tomatoes or sauces. Thus partly because of inter-firm linkages, and partly through the difference in regulatory regimes, Zeneca was steered towards a definition of a final product: genetically modified processed tomato sold in the UK was to be purée.

> We then hired somebody from out of the food industry, who'd worked with Campbell's Soups … He said, Why don't we do it? … Let's put a product on the shelf. That was when the retailers came in on this. In order to do that, you have to get the retailers on side. (Bright, Interview)

In 1992, four years before its final launch, Zeneca opened up discussions about the marketing of the tomato purée with UK supermarkets. Zeneca approached all the major retailers with their proposed genetically modified tomato purée. Eventually Sainsbury and Safeway took up the challenge to create a new product. It was clear to Zeneca that, in view of possible consumer rejection and campaigns against genetically modified 'Frankenfoods', it was important to get at least two major retailers involved. The Institute of Grocery Distribution was also concerned to promote a national and industry-wide policy on the introduction and labelling of genetically modified foods.[9]

> We needed to get a consensus built, such that retailers and the food industry wanted to do this. It was a good introduction for the food industry. (Bright, Interview)

Out of this process came a quite unique series of meetings between Zeneca, Safeway and Sainsbury during which they jointly developed a programme over a period of more than two years for a product launch. Trust in commercial confidentiality between them and in Zeneca's ability to deliver the product had to be secured. Crucial decisions were taken by Sainsbury and Safeway to assume a significant share of risk by launching the product under their own label, rather than an early proposal for Zeneca to establish a brand.

Finally, agreement was reached between the three parties on packaging, labelling, pricing and market share. The two retailers unusually agreed a common price in order to avoid competition over what was in effect a jointly launched product. A 40 per cent reduction in production wastage allowed the product to sell 15 per cent cheaper than the existing non-GM equivalent. As quality was also deemed superior, the consumer was seen to benefit on both counts:

> It was probably the first co-operation between two major competitors in the UK market. (Coombs, Interview)

By the end of 1997, Sainsbury had sold over 1 million cans, and Safeway 600,000, all clearly labelled. Where both products were in store, GM products outsold conventional cans of purée by two to one (Coombs, 1997). Although this final stage of the process of bringing GM tomato purée to market was clearly a tripartite one, and involving a long period of mutual testing and cooperation, it is equally clear and also unusual that Zeneca was the orchestrator of the triangular relationship:

> Q. *It was Zeneca that took the lead through all of that process?*
> Absolutely, yes. Obviously we worked with them, but it is a classic example of working with a supplier, a textbook example, quoted throughout the industry on how retailers and suppliers should work together. That was a major contributory factor to the tremendous success that this product has had. (Coombs Interview)

In concluding the story of the economic institutionalisation of first generation genetically modified tomatoes in the UK, it can be seen that a complex set of processes were involved. The contextualised first engagement with the tomato; interactions between a firm and a university science department; differences between European and US tomato production and marketing; differences in regulatory environments; transatlantic deals involving a key player in the tomato world, the Campbell Soup Company; firm-to-firm collaborations, most significantly engaging supermarkets as strategic players in the UK; all contributed to the specifics of the final appearance of the can of tomato purée with which this story started:

> We can write the history to say we wanted da-dee-da. But it wasn't like that. There was a product concept there. But it moved around quite a lot ...
> I think one thing is absolutely clear. This is not a linear model of innovation [where] a brilliant academic has an idea and then industry reduces it to practice. (Bright, Interview)

SECOND GENERATION GM AND NUTRIENT DENSE FOODS

'Plants are clever things', said Professor Peter Bramley on being presented with a yellow tomato by Zeneca. A further 'accidental engagement' with the tomato now occurred for the second generation of genetic modification. In this instance, Zeneca, already thoroughly tied to the tomato, introduced it to a scientist researching the biochemistry of carotenoids in other plants.[10] Creating an 'open laboratory' between Royal Holloway and Zeneca, a second generation scientific collaboration undertook their research using Ailsa Craig, a pre-eminent horticultural variety of salad tomato, in association with Van Heiningen Brothers.[11] Although they knew by that time that the eventual commercial product was likely to be in processed tomatoes, Ailsa Craig was the 'right tool for the job' of researching genetic expression of carotenoids. Its genetic map was well known through horticultural science and it possessed distinctive ripening characteristics:

> One nice thing about Ailsa Craig is that you see a nice developmental ripening on one truss, whereas in processed tomatoes, they all ripen together. The genetic background is very clear. So it is also good in that respect. (Bramley, Interview)

The science was developed by engagement with an already commercialised, already technologically and scientifically developed object.

The yellow tomato's carotenoid gene had been suppressed using first generation anti-sense 'silencing' techniques. Bramley's original assumption was that the yellowness was an effect of beta-carotene, but it was discovered that the yellow was in fact an effect of a flavonoid that produces skin colour and Vitamin E. It was excessively produced by the plant to compensate for a loss of the antioxidants necessary for physiological survival, consequent on the suppression of the carotenoid gene pTOM5. So began the next generation of genetic modification research, which opened up an entirely new range of tomato transformations. Instead of gene suppression, the search was for enhancement of genetic expression with the objective of raising the levels of key nutrient characteristics of plants. These include proteins, vitamins, antioxidants, and in the particular case in point, lycopene which is related to the red colour of the tomato, and is important both as an antioxidant beneficial to cardiovascular disease and as a possible anti-carcinogen for prostate cancer. It also produces beneficial effects for macular degeneration for those countries whose Vitamin A consumption is low in the normal diet. At the time, Boots, the chemist retailer, were marketing capsules of lycopene concentrate from non-genetically modified tomatoes as a means of conveying the health benefits of a Mediterranean diet.

The second generation GM thus involved two things: an important extension of GM technologies on the one hand, and a completely new field of possible food production on the other, with the potential to revolutionise what has historically been understood by 'food'. Rather than treating foods as constituents of diets, so requiring a balanced intake of foods, GM can take the nutrient content one step further back, by modifying the nutrient quality of all food components, across the whole range of plant life, both for animal and human nutrition. This is the true scope and scale of the Nutrient Dense Food concept, and the tomato emerged as the primary pioneer with lycopene enhancement. Zeneca was quite explicitly using the tomato as its tool for learning about this new generation of food products, about shaping of demand and the market, and about negotiating and influencing its regulatory environment.

The techniques of modification were also necessarily different. Enhancement is produced by adding additional copies of genes for particular gene expressions. But as was already demonstrated with gene silencing, copies which are from homologous, or identical, organisms have the effect of gene suppression. So, for the development of lycopene enhancement, non-homologous genes with analogous functions were taken from yeast, on license from a Japanese brewing company Kirin; together with a gene promoter from the CNRS laboratory at Strasbourg, cloned from a capsicum gene. Enhancement by use of additional copies can produce a totally red plant, so absorbing carbon unnecessarily, instead of maximising its effect for the economic object of the modification, the fruit. Thus, use of a promoter gene triggering the lycopene enhancement only as the fruit ripens, concentrated the effects at the fruit ripening stage. This control over the timing of lycopene enhancement in the carotenoid pathway leads to some quite fundamental developments in understanding of plant biochemistry and physiology, insofar as it requires working with the physiology of plants, without killing them, in such a way as to target precisely the required gene expression enhancement:

> We really want to know whether and how we can control over-expression genetically ourselves by transformations, or whether there are in-built safeguards in the plant, such that, if you overcome them, you kill the plant ... I think we are in a position now where, with this new generation of plants, we are pushing from the top and pulling from the bottom. We really will start to see if we can guide the carbon exclusively, or more or less exclusively, where we want it to go. (Bramley, Interview)

In contrast to the first generation GM tomato, therefore, even if final product definition was far from being defined, the fundamental science was oriented to the production of a health-yielding product. It is not so much that fundamental science was shaped by commodity markets and production. The development of the science was itself a part of initial product development. The nature of research funding also changed,[12] with the European Union becoming a major source of finance but on condition that there were clear and demonstrable potential health benefits:

> The reason for this significant funding over the last six years or more for EU purposes has been this potential health benefit, the antioxidant levels in the diet. So there is some very nice fundamental science to do, which we like to do ... So the fundamental work goes on, and continues to go on. But the practicalities are that without the health benefit, and potential commercialisation, that money would not have come through. The economic argument is vital. (Bramley, Interview)

As a consequence of this change in orientation of GM research and its funding, other scientific disciplines have been brought into the process of developing the product. Thus, Guys Hospital undertook collaborative research to explore how human physiology interacts with plant physiology. It is one thing to produce enhanced levels of lycopene in the tomato, and quite another to ensure that these enhanced levels are absorbed, or are 'bio-available' to humans. Both plant and human physiology played a role in determining the possible product characteristics. Fresh tomatoes with enhanced lycopene are minimally absorbed however much consumption is increased. Volunteers were fed whole cans of lycopene-enhanced purée in a single sitting, and apart from being an unpleasurable experience, this too was discovered to be less satisfactory than GM lycopene-enhanced tomato paste cooked with oil, such as found on pizzas or pasta sauces. The irony of this 'scientific discovery' of the virtues of pizza tomato concasse was not lost on the researchers. Thus psychology and food design, along with dietary science and human physiology, have become integral to the process of developing the new GM science. Peter Bramley put it very nicely:

> I was a carotenoid person. That's pretty narrow, isn't it? In recent years, I've started learning about antioxidants, dietary components, and bio-availability, and all these things. It is rather like you saying you chose the tomato [for research], and look where it has taken you. There was I on carotenoids, and now they are expanding quite nicely into all sorts of areas. It's very interesting. I think it is in for big growth. I am sure Nutrient Dense Foods are going to be a big thing over this next few years. I really do. (Bramley, Interview)

The 22-year trajectory of the genetically modified tomato culminated in a potential for developing the first Nutrient Dense Food tomato product. But as a UK company entering the UK food industry with a genetically modified food product, Zeneca was faced with the tension created by having started the production process in the US and now selling the product in the UK. A GM food originating from an 'easier' regulatory regime in the US had far greater potential for undermining the consumer market in the UK than genetically modified soya and soya oil, as products directed towards agribusiness. It was certainly an issue of labelling and segregation, but also much more than that. The idea of importing a food product produced under a regulatory regime that did not even impose segregation and labelling into a market that did, was clearly not viable in the long term:

> Zeneca is a British company, and we are fighting in this country. We have to defend ourselves to the London stock market. You can call it ethical, but it was also common sense. If you can't sell in your own country, you have really got problems ... We saw a lot of problems. We always saw that Europe would be a lot harder than the US for selling GM foods. It was hard to see why, but it was to do with consumer instincts ... We had to prove that we could do it. It was a real test for ourselves. Could it actually work, and could we actually work with these people in the food industry? (Poole, Interview)

Thus from 1997, Nigel Poole of Zeneca clearly saw the need to develop a European production base for GM tomatoes, and was actively negotiating for EU regulatory approval for over a year to achieve that (*Wall Street Journal*, 1998, and Poole, Interview). This transitional phase had already exhibited the peculiar anomaly of supply shortages due to a hesitation to expand the acreage under GM production in California beyond 17 acres. They could not even supply enough GM tomatoes for the tomato purée for all Safeway and Sainsbury stores. In establishing the next phase of production of GM tomatoes and for the next generation of NDF GM products, Zeneca set about constructing a supply system with European growers, processors and retailers.:

> We just want to get the chain running. Just make sure the chain is running, and then we'll get out of it. (Poole, Interview)

To conclude the last two sections, Diagrams 6.2 and 6.3 schematically represent networks of distributed innovation for the two phases of bringing the GM tomato product to the supermarket shelf. For the second phase, much

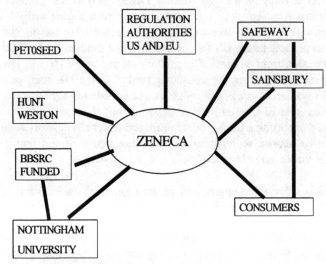

Diagram 6.2 First generation GM network

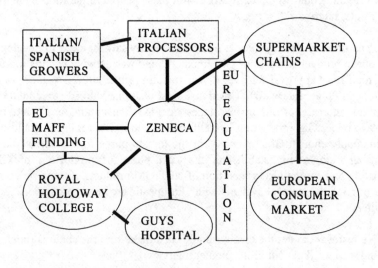

Diagram 6.3. Second generation GM network

was left uncertain before operations were suspended. But it is nonetheless clear that a quite new platform and configuration was being developed both for the continuation of first generation products and for the emergence of second generation products than the one established for the original product launch.

Comparing the two diagrams, it is clear that the appearance of a Sainsbury or Safeway can of genetically modified tomato purée on a supermarket shelf, at a given price, and in a given format, is intelligible only within this market configuration, distinctive to certain geographical regions and scales. Equally, the second generation demonstrated a shift in configuration, in terms of regulatory frameworks, funding authorities, geographical location of growers and processors, and probable scale of the market, covering a wider range of supermarket chains, in all likelihood European-wide rather than in the UK alone. It is not the result of a technology push process, and indeed the 'pre-history' of the emergence of a specific processed GM product demonstrated that many and complex shaping processes were at work. Zeneca may have been orchestrating relationships between certain players and constructing a web of complementary capabilities, but within contexts and under conditions that were developing quite independently of Zeneca. The entry of a GM object into the supermarket atmosphere is subject to a wide range of forces, not least of which is the as yet unpredictable resistance and counter-reaction of those opposed to genetic modification. The regulatory framework itself, in ways that need further examination, is subject to continual change, and this change takes place within a wider context, one aspect of which is doubtless public opinion and political environmentalism.

A TWIST IN THE TALE: NOW YOU SEE IT, NOW YOU DON'T

Two and a half years after the first can of GM tomato purée appeared on the supermarket shelves, it was withdrawn, along with all other identifiable GM products. The lycopene-enhanced tomato was held in abeyance, with no immediate future prospects. The disappearance of GM tomato purée was a result of a general policy on GM foods undertaken by first one and then all major supermarket food retailers in the UK. It is quite likely that this particular GM product has disappeared never to reappear. But it is much less likely that this will be the last GM product to appear on UK supermarket shelves, or that the technologies behind especially second generation GM foods will not eventually produce a radical transformation in future foods (Harvey, 1999b). Genetic modification, unlike for example food irradiation technology, is a much more radical and widely transformative technology. The disappearance was the result of a resurgence of public hostility in the UK to GM foods, following some high-profile demonstrations against the scientific trialling of new GM crops prior to commercialisation.

The disappearance two years earlier of the Flavr Savr™ tomato stands in marked contrast to the events in the UK and Europe. There, a convincing argument has been made that Calgene as a biotechnology company made a major strategic error in attempting to vertically integrate and become a tomato producer, distributor and retailer 'Calgene had no business to be in that business' (Martineau, 2001, 223–4). Zeneca never made the mistake of departing so radically from its core competence. But secondly, and equally important as a lesson for the creation of GM food markets, there was no clear evidence that the particular GM technology produced tangible and demonstrable benefits to consumers for the fresh tomato version. 'The Flavr Savr™ was, at best, of marginal value to a fresh-market tomato business' (ibid., 224). There is a lot to learn in the development of precise benefits from particular GM techniques.

The UK and much of the European food market has been hit by a number of significant health shocks, starting with salmonella poisoning, followed by E-coli, and culminating in BSE (bovine spongiform encephalopathy). In Europe, this has been followed by contamination of Coca-Cola supplies from France and Belgium, and dioxin contamination of much of the Belgium food chain, from milk, eggs and meat to chocolate. Of these, BSE was probably by far the most significant because it combined the most extreme examples of industrialisation of agriculture (by turning unwitting cattle into cannibals through recycling of bovine animal matter into fodder) with a discomfiture of official science. Scientific panels constantly shifted their position on the safety of eating contaminated beef, resulting in political switches in regulatory measures. Predictions of the scale of mortalities from Creutzfelt-Jakob Disease still range from minor incidence to a pandemic. The result has clearly been a substantial undermining of consumer confidence in both food and science.

Yet it would be quite wrong to suggest that UK and European consumer confidence – or final demand – in GM foods was simply an effect of the impact of these food disasters. Apart from a widespread and political campaign waged by many newspapers against GM, there have also been deep divisions within the UK government. Supermarkets saw short-term competitive advantage in being the first to eliminate GM products from their food chains, and once Iceland took the high moral panic ground, others stampeded behind them. In addition the UK has witnessed a distinctive alliance of oppositional organisations bringing together a number of quite different political and commercial interests around the defence of 'Nature'. This alliance has made the opposition effective, at least for the present. Ecological movement organisations such as Greenpeace and Friends of the

Earth have thus joined forces with the organic farming movement, and especially the Soil Association which owns a commercial monopoly on certificating organically 'natural' produce.[13] This Association is moreover symbolically headed by Prince Charles, to give it the added weight of 'tradition', and it invokes a return to 'traditional' farming, uncontaminated by industrialised science.

This peculiar combination of radical ecologists and agricultural traditionalists has been reinforced by other major public nature conservancy organisations (the National Trust, the Royal Society for the Protection of Birds) and the medical profession (the British Medical Association), defending the biologically 'natural' body against possible commercialised-science-borne disease. Indeed, the focal theme which has enabled these disparate organisations to unite has been the self-styled 'defence of Nature'. This defence has been buttressed by a demonisation of science as that which manipulates nature to Nature's detriment. These champions of Nature can thus be characterised as developing a form of 'nature fundamentalism' (Harvey, 1999b), insofar as they counterpose a vision of pristine Nature to nature as contaminated, cultivated and manipulated by humans. Ignoring hybridisation, the Greenpeace International internet biotechnology homepage had as its banner: 'NO GENETIC MANIPULATION OF NATURE'.[14] Many photographs of protests against scientific trialling of GM oilseed rape prior to commercialisation, portrayed science as an alien invasion of Nature.

To a consumer 'moral panic' and a peculiar political, commercial and establishment oppositional configuration, there must be added the clash between the two very different GM production regimes and cultures across the Atlantic. There is little doubt that Monsanto, with its focus exclusively on the market for agribusiness, developed a GM technology with little end-market concerns or sensitivities. The absence of segregation and labelling of GM products exemplifies the difference in both context and orientation in the US. The impact of introducing non-segregated products into the food chain, especially through soya and rapeseed-based oils, created the worst possible circumstances for eventual consumer acceptance of GM products, simply because consumers were given no choice and were treated with disdain. The European imposition of segregation and labelling by governments in order to negatively counter the US regulatory regime, rather than initially establishing a positive regime, only further stigmatised GM products. The current turbulence being experienced in Europe, resonating through the World Trade Organisation, reflects a clash between two very different regimes. In part it results directly from a lack of recognition by Monsanto that end-markets, and in particular end-markets in Europe, might be very different from those in the US. This attitude was encapsulated by Monsanto's Chief Executive, Robert

Shapiro, when he affirmed to a shareholder meeting that GM crops had been the:

> most successful launch of any technology ever, including the plough. *Guardian*, October 1999, 15

Subsequently, after resistance to unsegregated crops and field trials in Europe had developed, export markets were increasingly threatened, and Monsanto share values dropped in value by 35 per cent. Deutsche Bank recommended investors to sell Monsanto shares. In these circumstances, eventually Monsanto arranged a secret meeting in the UK with Greenpeace, the Soil Association and Friends of the Earth, in recognition that these organisations were significantly shaping its world markets, and that consumer and retailer markets could no longer be disregarded (*Financial Times*, 27 September 1999). Monsanto was brought to a realisation that it inhabited a quite different configuration to the ones inhabited by Zeneca, illustrated in the two charts above. In an interactive video-link conference with Monsanto, Shapiro then declared:

> We have irritated and antagonised more people than we have persuaded ... Our confidence in biotechnology has been widely seen as arrogance and condescension. *Guardian,* October 1999, 15.

Furthermore, Monsanto took the significant decision to cease development of its Terminator gene modification technology. Again, strategically this decision had a particular focus. Whilst Terminator technology would limit if not eliminate risks of genetic pollution as seeds are restricted to a single generation, one of its perceived socio-economic effects is to prevent the re-use of seed, so increasing farmer dependence on seed manufacturers. It is thought that less–developed economies would be especially severely affected, and yet these are amongst the principal global markets for GM technologies of the future. Thus, by this decision Monsanto once more primarily addressed its agribusiness constituency, rather than accommodating consumer or ecological concerns.

The growth of consumer moral panic, the particular organisational and political alliance opposed to genetic modification, and the clash between two different production-market regimes, *in combination* have significantly altered the course of development of GM products in Europe, and possibly the future trajectories of GM technology and fundamental science as well. If the charts of the Zeneca networks describe instituted linkages which eventually combined diverse elements in order to make the can of GM tomato purée appear 'economically', it is quite difficult to place these three disruptive causal elements which made it disappear on the same plane. Partly this is a result of the absence of instituted linkages. Partly, too, it is a result of the lack of stability, the unresolved outcomes. But it is more because oppositional relationships are difficult to subsume under 'consumer demand' or 'selection environments'. The concept of political opposition is made anodyne if characterised as a 'hostile environment', which, as it were, just happens to be there. The opposition may be hostile but it is not an 'environment'.

CONCLUSION

To analyse the rise and fall of genetically modified tomato has involved demonstrating the effects of interactions between different socio-economic domains. The different biological species of tomato inhabiting US and European cultivation, and their modes of production and processing, fundamentally affected the trajectories of genetic modification technology, leading in one direction in the US, another in Europe. Moreover, much of the analysis has brought together quite different causal domains (biology, regulatory authorities, politics), involving other significant and strong interactions.

Three important consequences can be drawn. The first is that an analytical opposition between production-driven innovation and consumption-driven innovation is unsustainable. What is significant are the different societal configurations of the relationships between them, and the ways these change over time.

Secondly, the analysis is lifted from a level which looks at a firm on the one side and its market environment on the other, to one which looks at differently instituted *relationships* between firms, markets, consumers, public institutions and regulatory systems.

Thirdly, an 'instituted economic process' analysis is well placed to take account of interactions between different causal domains, particularly in cases where processes do not culminate in the institution of the specifically 'economic', as when GM tomatoes fail to become stable market commodities. Tracing the appearance and disappearance of genetically modified tomato purée thus embraced phases of economic institutionalisation, de-institutionalisation and non-institutionalisation. Processes of co-formation of radically new technical products and their markets can be long–drawn–out and deviously tortuous.

NOTES

[1] Nigel Poole, Interview.

[2] This schematic representation refers to a range of GM technologies, but does not cover all areas of GM, such as animal GM, or indeed the development of plants producing biodegradable plastics where traits not present in an organism are introduced. It is not intended as a comprehensive 'staging' of GM technology.

[3] The terms 'gene suppression' and 'gene silencing' used for the switching off of gene expression are currently used, whereas controversy still surrounds the understanding of the dynamics of elimination of DNA material in the cell resulting from the transfer of cloned DNA (Grierson and Schuch, Interviews).

[4] The EC Directive 90/220/EEC is more circumspect by defining a genetically modified organism in terms of genetic material altered 'in a way that does not occur naturally by mating' (Article 2).

[5] There are other techniques, but these are the ones currently being developed by Zeneca.

[6] The fundamental science of creating a DNA library, and of identifying gene functionality for different genes, as well as undertaking the biochemistry of transgenic plants, was pathbreaking in its own right.

[7] As Martineau (2001) puts it, this is the 'gassed green' tomato: 'The reason why they tasted like cardboard was that they weren't allowed to undergo the normal ripening process on the vine' (Martineau, 2001, 8).

[8] Wolfgang Schuch, the chief biotechnology scientist in Zeneca in this story, was a central figure in the development of both the science and the technology, as we shall see below.

[9] By contrast, Calgene Fresh Inc. in the US struggled to develop a brand of their own or to gain wide access to supermarkets, given the much more fragmented character of retail markets there.

[10] 'Tomatoes were new to me experimentally when this connection occurred.' (Bramley, Interview)

[11] See Chapter 5.

[12] Grierson's research at Nottingham University had been funded primarily by British government sources, under the SERC Biotechnology Directive, now part of the BBSRC (Biology and Biotechnology Science Research Council). Although Zeneca contributed some finance, and material resources, these were minor elements in the research programme. See also Diagram 6.2

[13] The monopoly in certification for defining what counts as 'organic' is an interesting market-institutional phenomenon. The supermarkets need one universally accepted standard to ensure clear product definition in order to attract higher prices for a distinct market segment. Multiple alternative definitions would undermine this market segmentation. Agreements between the Soil Association and supermarkets have therefore resulted in the Soil Association being able both to acquire monopoly rents from

certification and at the same time impose a monopoly definition of what is 'organic'.

[14] This headline banner must either be bizarrely ignorant, which is unlikely in view of their normal scientific advice, or deliberately and opportunistically misleading. The expansion of cultivated areas, and normal classical hybridisation techniques, have resulted over many centuries in a substantial 'genetic manipulation' of nature, one that has affected the naturally occurring gene pool in significant ways. Their argument cannot surely be to abandon agriculture and stop using hybrid cultivation.

PART II

Twentieth–Century Tomato Configurations

7. Tomato: A Pioneer of Mass Production

TOWARDS A NEW IDENTITY

A can of Cambell's Cream of Tomato Condensed Soup and Andy Warhol. This combination might have been sufficiently inspiring on its own, without the can from the previous chapter. For, the tomato achieved its true prominence in the social world of objects labelled 'Campbell's' and 'Heinz', canned soup and ketchup, whereas before, at least to the turn of the twentieth century, it lurked on the fringes of mass popular acceptance. The August 1978 *Scientific American* celebrated the meteoric rise of the tomato on its front cover, and testified to the tomato becoming

> at the top in total vitamins and minerals provided in the US diet. (Rick, 1978, 68)

Annual consumption of tomatoes in the US had risen from 8.2 kilos per capita in 1920 to 25.5 kilos in 1978, overwhelmingly as a result of the growth of processed tomato consumption (Rick,1978,76), to which bottles of ketchup and cans of soup were the outstanding contributors. But the inspiration of the can of tomato soup may soon run out of breath, at least in the UK. Its rise to fame at the turn of the century and through the inter-war period has been followed by a major tomato identity crisis. The serried ranks of branded goods are at risk of tumbling down, to be increasingly replaced by a more varied display of supermarkets' own-label products from the 1980s onwards (Corstjens and Corstjens, 1996; Doel, 1996).

Warhol's *100 Cans*[1] was selected for a recent exhibition called 'Objects of Desire'[2] in order to project into the public mind the idea of a dance between the representing and the represented. It is not only that in their still life Pop Artists represented the world differently than a Cézanne, but the world of objects to represent had also been totally transformed. As Eco put it:

> The tin of Campbell's soup, whether painted or rebuilt is still, obsessively, a tin of Campbell's soup ... The [artist's] way is to react to an obsession by plunging into it up to the neck, and to admit industrial objects as part of

157

the natural landscape. Pop art created an omni-ecological society in which there were no differences between nature and industry, between unspoilt landscape and desecrated landscape. (Eco, 1989, 227).[3]

Unlike a still life of 'natural objects' (fruit, flowers) appearing in 'natural light' and (often) domestic space, stacks of cans on supermarket shelves squeeze out all but manufactured objects, space, light. The retailing mode of 'pile 'em high and sell 'em cheap' *is* an object of the still life. Moreover, standardised[4] 'objects of desire' first appeared dressed in the uniform of brand images. Artistic representation became a reprise of a manufactured mode of presentation, the already aestheticised commercial design (Livingstone, 1990).[5] Thus, *100 Cans* is almost a plagiarism of one of the earliest-ever branded food advertisements (1898), by a Campbell's commercial designer, in which the Stars and Stripes motif was substituted by an equally national flag with repetitive bands of the red and white cans of tomato soup, going for a dime a can.[6] As Eco (1989) suggests, moreover, the circle between represented and representing can be turned around, with commercial designers mimicking Pop Art. Or even closed: in 1999, Campbell unveiled their latest makeover design for soup labels. Where? The Warhol museum in Pittsburgh (*Guardian*, 28 August 1999*)*.

Evidently, a book of 'The Tomato in Art' has yet to be written, and this one does not attempt to fill the yawning gap.[7] Nonetheless, and without wishing to overstate it, the tomato's appearance in art, and in Pop Art form, is an expression of its new societal salience. For America, tomato soup and ketchup joined apple pie to become important elements of national cuisine, and national symbols. When a writer of the history of ketchup (with recipes) appropriates it as 'America's national condiment' (Smith, 1996), he is also implicitly exhibiting how cuisines are constitutive of national cultural identity.[8] But it is also a cultural symbol inextricably linked to another feature of this national identity: America as the land of mass production.

PIONEERING MASS PRODUCTION

The emergence of branded foods, of which Campbell's soups and Heinz ketchup are prime examples, was part of a revolution in food. It is difficult to see something so ordinary as a bottle of Heinz tomato ketchup or a can of Campbell's tomato soup as the outcome of revolutionary change. In a classic work, Jefferys (1954) argues that:

The period 1875–1914 witnessed a transformation of the distributive trades comparable in many ways to the revolutionary changes that had taken place in the industrial structure of the country in the previous century. (ibid.,6)

There were linked changes in each of four poles of production, distribution, retailing and consumption, enshrined in the new products. This chapter explores what brought about this revolutionary new configuration,[9] in order to understand how this new tomato phenomenon emerged to effectively dominate the central decades of the twentieth century. By first understanding how this configuration became normal, it will then be possible in the next chapter to comprehend the dynamics which are beginning to threaten and replace that configuration with a new one.

THE RESTRUCTURING OF DEMAND AND RETAILING

Starting with consumption, urbanisation in the late nineteenth and early twentieth centuries created spatially concentrated masses of people who were newly dependent on purchasing food on an unprecedented scale and continuously over time. This was a macro-social shift in the nature of demand for food products, especially a mass market of an industrialised working class with low income and emerging clerical, professional and managerial salary-earning classes, with quite dispersed income bands. Thus, one of the earliest-ever market research exercises in 1911, conducted for Campbell's Soups by the Curtis Publishing Company, discovered that consumption was 'not bound to any one income class: a great majority of the people eats 1 or more of the 21 varieties' (Collins, 1994, 90).[10]

At the retailing pole, multiple chain stores emerged. In the US, large retailing chains such as the A&P Company (Strasser, 1989; Tedlow, 1990; Ortega, 1999a), broke the traditional divide between retailing and wholesaling by purchasing direct from manufacturers or primary produce suppliers. As Campbell's business historian put it in terms reminiscent of more recent times:

> The buying power of these chains and their concomitant ability to sell food at a discount were so enormous that they threatened to put the smaller mom-and-pop corner stores completely out of business. (Collins, 1994, 86).

In the UK, where this development was particularly pronounced, firms like Home & Colonial, the International Tea Company and Liptons established themselves with over 500 branches by 1920. The Co-operative Society, a leader in this respect, had piloted the development of low-cost, standardised and branded goods to sell throughout its chain, which had over 1000 associated Societies by 1890. The multiple chain retail outlet was the vehicle for standardised goods, with central or coordinated buyer power, rather than the independent local outlets or individual producer-traders which declined as the chains grew.

The emergence of the multiple retail chain in turn entailed new systems of distribution, increasingly replacing the weekly or monthly fairs and markets as well as itinerant traders, to create a new division between retailers and wholesalers for fresh produce, on the one hand; and retailers and manufacturers for processed food on the other. Rail, steamship and increasingly the combustion engine provided the necessary logistical counterpart for the mass flow of goods to more widely dispersed but affiliated retail branch outlets. One of the early photographs of the Campbell's Soup Company is of a fleet of horse-drawn trucks in the Campbell livery standing outside its Camden plant in 1912, followed by its motorised equivalent in 1921. The plant was sited on the Delaware River, a main trading route and linked to a railhead, so giving access to rapid national distribution. A lithograph of the Heinz factory complex at the turn of the century similarly has in its foreground a freight railhead and an international steamship port (Smith, 1996) on the Allegheny River in Pittsburgh. But speed of transport was only one of the necessary components of this system of retailing. It also required conservation and preservation of foods, and hence canning and processing to achieve sterile conditions.

MASS PRODUCTION

With forgivable hyperbole, 1869 can be said to be a climacteric year for the human tomato. It was the year of the coincidental appearance of the first Heinz company, the first Campbell company,[11] and of the *American Grocer*, a journal which was to play a shaping role in the rise to fame of tomato ketchup. It was the point of origin for an entirely new phenomenon: the mass-produced, globally distributed, standardised and industrially processed tomato. Whether in soup or in ketchup, new bio-socio-economic varieties of tomato were to be bred, cultivated, processed, branded, advertised, distributed, retailed, purchased and consumed in a manner undreamed of until this historical epoch. From next to nothing, with few capital resources, both Heinz and Campbell's were to become very big tomato business, front runners of mass production and of this first wave of convenience foods. By 1906, Heinz was producing 5 million bottles of tomato ketchup annually, and by 1905 Campbell's were producing 40,000 cans of condensed soup a week (Collins, 1994). By his death in 1930, John Dorrance, the innovator of condensed tomato (and other) soup and by then owner of the Campbell's company, was valued at $115 million, and rated the third-richest person in the US. By the 1990s, Heinz alone was producing 400 million 14-ounce bottles of ketchup out of a world total of 840 million. Also in 1990, David Johnson, President of Campbell's Soup, declared: 'If you're in the soup business, you have to be in China' (Collins, 1994, 182), if only because it is the market where there is the highest per capital consumption of soup.

The emergent 'mass-produced' tomato was also an emergent biologically designed tomato. In the earliest days of this new industry, biological 'adaptation' to a new socio-economic environment took some quite bizarre forms. An example of American 'gigantism', the Anderson & Campbell Preserve Company were developing the biggest beefsteak tomatoes imaginable, both for canning and for ketchup, claiming that a single tomato was sufficient to fill a can. Amongst the earliest advertisements, the fruit reached phantasmagoric proportions, one beefsteak tomato being slung under a pole carried by two swarthy men.

As the two companies developed towards large-scale industrialised production, there was also a gradual move towards 'science in command'. Each began to develop scientific breeding to develop dedicated ketchup tomatoes, dedicated condensed soup tomatoes. For Campbell's, John Dorrance, an organic chemist educated at MIT and Göttingen, and the firm's General Manager from 1910, had at first experimentally bred tomatoes on his own home farm. Harry Hall in 1912, a plant breeder, professionalised the process as Superintendant on Campbell's Soup Farms, where contract farmers grew on crops on an exclusive supply basis. At the time, before most tomato production moved to California, New Jersey was described by Hall as 'the land of the good red tomato' (cit. Collins, 1994, 110). Hall hybridised different varieties working in conjunction with the New Jersey Agricultural Station[12] to eventually develop the perfect tomato for tomato soup production (the Rutger variety). By 1918, this process of hybridisation was extended to adapt to different climates in order to extend the seasonality of the tomato by growing crops in Georgia. In 1918, Campbell's distributed 40 to 50 million of these dedicated soup tomato seedlings to their contract farmers in both regions.

H.J. Heinz, the founder of the company, had from the outset supported the establishment of experimental scientific agriculture, and had promoted the experimental research stations developed by the US Department of Agriculture even in the early 1860s (Alberts, 1973, 47). Like Campbell's, Heinz exercised tight control over their supplying farmers, providing them with the seed and laying down cultivation procedures. H.J. guaranteed to buy their entire harvest at a price agreed on at the time of planting. Thus he secured his source of supply, the quality of the yield, and reduced the risks both to himself and the farmer, a startling precursor of supply chain management. In what today would be considered as a 'mission statement', Heinz had 'Important Ideas', number three of which was:

> To improve the finished product that comes out of the bottle, you must improve it in the ground, where and when it is grown. (Alberts, 1973, 47).

In the 1920s, further advances were made in breeding a dedicated ketchup tomato, the beefsteak being definitively abandoned for a smaller, high-pulp, fig-shaped tomato. In 1926, Heinz developed their own variety (Smith, 1996, 122), with high viscosity and pectin, now especially modified to ripen on the truss all at the same time to suit mechanical harvesting. Thus, the new bio-socio-economic variety was adapted to the farm and the bottle, to processing and consumption. This process of 'socio-biological evolution' has continued and developed with hybridisation techniques. By the 1990s, Heinz's seeds were produced globally in India, Chile, Thailand and Taiwan. In 1994 they patented the use of DNA markers[13] for selection of the desired ketchup traits, and a new ketchup tomato variety, H9382. In that year, 56,000 pounds of seed, with each ounce containing 10,000 seeds (Smith, 1996, 123) were produced. This co-evolution of commercial ketchup or soup and dedicated biological tomato varieties from Giant Beefsteak to H9382, was triggered rather than prefigured in 1869, and yet that was its critical starting point.

As a production process the early stages scarcely hinted at the significance of this food innovation. Indeed, there is something almost quaint about the way in which both Heinz and Campbell's launched their enterprises. Before constructing their astonishing factory complexes at Pittsburgh and Camden, H.J. Heinz employed his own handwritten notebooks with traditional recipes for pickling and cooking, arranged alphabetically, and taken from his own family traditions. Likewise, Campbell's, with their wider range of ready-made canned foods, adopted the recipes directly from homecooking. In the early factories:

> Manufacturers prepared foods and still set up their plants like large-scale kitchens. Ingredients were washed, cut, cooked and stirred much as they would have been by a homemaker. (Collins, 1994, 27)

The labour process was simply transferred from the home to the factory and scaled up, early photographs showing rows of women undertaking these formerly domestic tasks. Anderson & Campbell products had labels emphasising the continuity between home cooking and factory processes, using handwriting 'scripts commonly used by housewives to identify home preserves' (Collins, 1994, 25), much in the same way as, a century later, New Covent Garden Soups distinctively ornamented their tetrapacks with a font that suggested affinity with the domestic recipe book. Behind this apparent similarity, however, can be seen diametrically opposed logics, the former emphasising continuity with home cooking, the latter discontinuity with mass standardisation.

Nonetheless, intensive manual labour was progressively replaced by machinery, although certainly never eliminated as Margaret Bourke-White's photographs of onion-peeling and chicken-skinning in *Fortune Magazine* in 1935 demonstrate.[14] Apart from the mechanisation of canning, which had vastly increased production,[15] the invention of pressure cooking in 1874 speeded up sterilisation and cooking processes for the filled cans. By the end of the nineteenth century, Heinz could produce 40,000 sealed and airtight cans from one machine in a single day. Various new machines for cleaning and cutting vegetables were adopted in the 1880s; a machine for shelling peas in 1892, one for cutting corn from the cob in 1899, technologies for canning asparagus (1891), sardines (1900), olives (1901) and pineapple (1903) (Alberts, 1973).

John Dorrance's invention of condensed soup in 1897, and its first production in 1898, can however be seen as a decisive break from the scaled-up kitchen, both as a technology and as a product. Condensing soup as a means of reducing volume to make it lighter and more transportable, cheaper to can, and yet convenient to cook, was a new development of a specifically commercial commodity food. Mass manufacturing was then extended in Campbell's construction of Plant No.2 in the early 1920s, erected solely for the processing of tomato pulp for the famous Campbell's Condensed Tomato Soup. Following Chandler, Best has described the emergence of the American Big Business corporation, of which Campbell's and Heinz were premier examples, thus:

Mass production is the American System[16] plus the principle of flow. (Best, 1990, 52)

The flow-line of the factory organisation, replacing production by batches, was combined with decentralised departmental functions for business organisation. Campbell's Plant No.2 was set up very much along those lines.

Tomatoes arrived at the plant at 5.45 am, when they were graded by Campbell's inspectors, the farmers being paid according to grade. Conveyor belts took baskets of tomatoes through three washing processes, which were then passed down assembly lines of women further selecting for quality. The fruit then met a hammer mill, a large machine with two sets of interlocking fingers, which crushed the fruit to pulp. A vast flow of tomatoes poured into 14,600-gallon copper breaker kettles for steaming:

> Each kettle was manned by a single worker who stirred it with a huge wooden paddle. (Collins, 1994, 114)

The cooked pulp then passed through three centrifuges, 'Cyclones', each with a specified fineness of mesh, removing skin and seeds. The resultant liquid was transported in stainless steel trucks to the soup-making building, where butter, herbs, spices and other ingredients were blended in 110-gallon kettles. There were detailed procedures for industrial cooking, times, sequence and quality of ingredients all laid down to a master recipe. Once cooked, the soup was submitted to further centrifugal forces and sieving, before being canned and placed in pressure cookers for sterilisation. By the late 1920s, 10 million cans of soup rolled off the assembly line in a single day:

> Beginning in late summer and continuing through the end of October, a line of trucks and farm wagons, sometimes nine miles long, began forming before daybreak along Second Street in Camden. It was the tomato season, the time when this relatively fragile vegetable was ripe and ready to be made into Tomato Soup .... The streets of Camden literally turned red. (Collins, 1994, 106)

FACETS OF STANDARDISATION

Imagining this vast flow of fresh tomatoes coming in at one end, and millions of identical cans of condensed tomato soup coming out the other, it would be wrong to give too much emphasis to the 'hard technology' industrial aspect of standardisation. Standardisation is a much broader principle which, whilst embracing the mechanisation of production processes, involves something much more profound. This is partially obscured now that we take standardisation for granted. Standardisation has even acquired a certain negative aura of unending, uninteresting, unsatisfying uniformity. So it is necessary to imagine the time before standardisation.

Food as an organic, variable, raw material, which is fundamentally unstable over time, was a major challenge to standardisation. The process of mass production had to overcome this 'lumpiness' and instability in a uniform way in order to establish a tradable product. Put crudely, to produce food as a tradable mass commodity, the initial problem to be resolved was to make the contents of every bottle identical to that of every other, every can identical to every other, and to make sure the contents did not variably or inappropriately deteriorate. Both these pioneering mass food-producing companies had early put 'science in command'. John Dorrance, the Managing Director of Campbell's from 1910, trained as an organic chemist, as did Sebastian Müller who conducted experiments on food preservation at Heinz as early as 1904. In 1902, Howard Heinz, who majored in chemistry at Yale, became a Company Manager, and as General Manger in 1918, recalls that with Müller,

> we began to apply new scientific controls to quality, and actually referred to the section doing that work as the quality control department. We think we may have been the *first in American industry* to use that phrase. (cit. Alberts, 1973, 216)

Overcoming variability and instability by scientific development of a uniformity and reliability of product was a precondition for the creation of a mass market for food products.

But a further dimension of standardisation, that of the labour process, was also central to preventing contamination and ensuring hygienic processes on an assembly-line scale. Great play was made to journalists during factory visits of the link between purity of the process and cleanliness of the labour force. Both firms were conspicuous for their uniformed, 'respectable' workforce, and Heinz proudly displayed their 'Heinz girls' in early advertising of their products. Lillian Weizmann, typically a central European migrant, started work at Heinz in 1888, working from 7 am to 5.40 pm on weekdays, and to 4.40 pm on Saturdays. She was held up as the paragon employee:

> Lillie's day began in the dressing room below the five-storey bottling building, where she changed her street clothes and where she had the luxury of a private locker with her own key ... Her caps, ready-made from fine Irish dimity, cost her twelve and a half cents. She was required to begin each day in a freshly laundered uniform and white apron. Since she handled food, she received a weekly manicure. (Alberts, 1973, 136)

Campbell's and Heinz shared a paternalistic view that betterment of the quality of the workforce would result in betterment of the quality of ketchups and soups. Howard Heinz, in 1902, described this aspect of educational and recreational facilities, coupled with discipline and cleanliness, as 'The Sociological Work Connected to the Factory'.

Standardisation is also about the creation of standards of food purity. Throughout the nineteenth century there had been a problem of adulteration of food (Burnett, 1985, 99–120), which could range from contaminants or additional ingredients finding their way accidentally into food, to systematic and deliberate substitution of ingredients and addition of dyes or chemicals to disguise the results. In the early days of tomato ketchup, many small-scale manufacturers[17] used fermented tomato waste as a basic ingredient, but often substituted pumpkin or squash pulp for tomato. Aniline dye derived from coal tar, although toxic, was commonly used to keep and enhance the red colour. Boric and salicylic acid were used as preservatives, especially after the latter was produced synthetically from phenol and carbon dioxide.

So it is highly significant that the promotion of 'pure food', and the eventual establishment of a regulatory regime through Pure Food legislation, developed together with the emergence of mass-produced, nationwide, standard food products. Indeed Heinz and tomato ketchup can be said to have played a leading role, and for the first time created a demand for purity by engineering a food scare through a negative advertising campaign. This proved to be both a technical and propaganda victory.

The Heinz chemist Muller successfully managed to produce a preservative-free tomato ketchup industrially[18] and this gave Heinz the opportunity to combine forces with the leading advocate and proselytiser of food safety, Harvey Washington Wiley.[19] Heinz's view on food safety was that:

Regulation would make the industry respectable and trusted – an achievement *beyond any price* [emphasis added].' (Alberts, 1973, 171).

One of the key preservatives used ubiquitously within the canning industry had been benzoic acid, derived from the benzoin tree, and which was white, tasteless, odourless, antiseptic – and toxic. From the early twentieth century Wiley and Heinz waged war against benzoates (Smith, 1996),[20] but despite some success with the passing of the 1906 Pure Food and Drugs Bill, failed to get it banned. Wiley joined forces with the Consumers' League, and the General Federation of Women's Clubs. He and later Heinz vigorously publicised their campaigns through the *American Grocer* and the *Ladies Home Journal*. The *American Grocer* became an important vehicle for the pure food campaign. Opposing them, the National Canners' Association and the Association of Manufacturers and Distributors of Food Products (which in the early days included Joseph Campbell) equally vigorously defended the continued use of benzoic acid. After securing the partially successful 1906 legislation, Heinz undertook a major advertising campaign and together with Wiley founded the American Association for the Promotion of Purity in Food

Products. But the canners and the food manufacturing industry challenged various State bans, winning significant court cases culminating in a case held in the United States Supreme Court in 1914. Despite defeat in the courts, Heinz continued the advertising campaign with the slogan:

'Good Ketchup Needs No Drugs'

Although benzoic acid remains to this day a legal preservative, Heinz created such a moral high ground as to ensure that all competitors were forced to follow suit in producing preservative-free products. The extent of Heinz's success in creating a demand for pure food can be measured by the fact that, although their ketchup cost 25–30 cents a bottle compared with the rivals' 10–12 cents:

> Heinz's more expensive product dominated the ketchup field, often controlling more than half of the total market share. (Smith, 1996, 110)

In the absence of chemical preservatives, sugar and vinegar became much more dominant in tomato ketchup, and the sterilisation process and cooking, as well as the tomato varieties used, led to a much denser paste. As the historian of ketchup has proclaimed:

> Ketchup sales skyrocketed. Thick ketchup was more appropriate for hot dogs and french fries, which were increasingly becoming part of America's diet. (Smith, 1996, 111).

The establishment of food purity standards, partly by legislation, partly by aggressive marketing strategy, thus contributed to the emergence of a particular tomato product, with distinctive qualities, making it ideally suited for the new fast food industry that was developing. Tomatoes were metamorphosed, assuming new consistencies and tastes in a changing culinary environment, and for the first time inhabited the now instantly recognisable glass bottle. Interestingly, the American hamburger also established its key position in American diet in the early 1920s as a mass-produced product by distinguishing itself from the suspect variability of boarding house and mobile stall food, and by distancing itself from manufacturing processes associated with adulteration and low-quality ingredients. White Castle, the true pioneer of American mass-produced fast food (Hogan, 1997), built its reputation and business on the promotion of standards, uniformity and purity.[21] The hamburger had to be the same, the white uniforms had to be the same, the prefabricated restaurants had to be the same,[22] wherever their increasingly mobile customers were, *as a demonstration of standards.*

Looking backwards, there is such an apparent logic to the mutual reinforcement between these different strands of standardisation that the contingency and overdetermination of their coming together becomes obscured. From 1869, it was probably 40 to 50 years before all the different aspects of standardisation developed higgledy-piggledy into what now appears a coherent bloc. Business organisation, mass-production technologies, discovery of preservative-free means of creating a stable food product, messy regulatory and legal environments, new techniques of hybridisation, a market demand for 'pure food', did not run to the same timetables or even necessarily share common destinations.

CREATING TOMATO IDENTITY

With standardisation came identity. Heinz and Campbell's were pioneers in branding, and with it, advertising of food. Tomatoes not only acquired new shapes and forms, they also acquired the names by which they would be known by the public at large. New York's first-ever large neon sign, appearing in 1900 and six storeys high, was for Heinz Tomato Ketchup. Only in the late nineteenth century did mass production, nationwide distribution and selling by advertised branding of foods come together. Both Campbell's and Heinz led the way in the use of fleets of delivery vans dressed in distinctive advertising livery, and to enhance visibility of the Heinz brand, the company-owned 400 freight wagons for railway distribution circled the nation. Both companies also had their merchandising gimmicks, the Heinz 'pickle brooch', and in 1910 Campbell's promotional giveaway dolls, taken from earlier advertisements of 'the Campbell Kids':

> with their puffed cheeks and plump bodies, they were pictures of health, vitality and good nature. (Collins, 1994, 50).

Heinz's innovative 'pure food' advertising campaign has already been discussed,[23] but Campbell's were also inventive in multimedia and broad-spectrum advertising. There is an all-American origin myth for the famous Cambell's can: a company executive went to a football match between Cornell and Penn in 1898, and decided he wanted Cornell's colours on his soup cans. The company web-page, touchingly called Campbell's Community Centre, describes the red and white design as:

> the single most successful promotional decision Campbell has ever made.

The Campbell's advertising budget went from $20,000 in 1899 to $400,000 in 1911 and $1 million in 1920, when it amounted to 5 per cent of total sales turnover, Heinz following a very similar pattern of advertising growth. This way of developing a market for products identified by brand was quite revolutionary at the time. Dorrance himself was well aware, as the advertising strategy grew from its tentative beginnings, that it reflected a radical break in the trading relations between manufacturers, distributors and retailers, through its fabrication of consumer demand:

> When you have the consumer sold, you have finished the worst part of the campaign. If the consumer makes the demand, the dealer will stock, and if the dealer stocks, the jobber is bound to get the business, and if he lists it for the dealer, we have to make the soup. It is perfectly simple and eliminates a complexity of selling methods. (cit. Collins, 1994, 97-8)

Soups, however, had a double obstacle to overcome: they were not a customary or regular course or food in many of the diverse ethnic cuisines of America at the time, and people were not used to buying it ready-made, let alone in condensed form. Campbell's therefore piggybacked on the trend of the time by producing its own cookery and household books as a promotional tactic, a menu book, and *Helps for the Hostess*. Brand reputation was enhanced by the fact that Dorrance himself had studied the art of soup-making with Escoffier, and had been to study with chefs in the Café de Paris, Paillards and the Waldorf, much in the same way that contemporary convenience-food manufacturers play off and work with celebrity TV cooks. To create demand for manufactured soup, the soups were presented as the best that the best chefs could concoct.

REVOLUTIONARY FOODS

The tomato metamorphosis manifest in ketchup and condensed soups resulted in revolutionary types of food, the first as the essential accompaniment to the burgeoning fast-food market, the second as what might be described as a first wave of convenience foods. Ketchup, from being the traditional condiment and preserve of the nineteenth century, piggybacked on other significant changes in eating out, as well as home cooking in the twentieth century. The condensed tomato soup was sold, in advertising copy, as embodying both savings in time and labour, as well as being economical:

> Their use means true economy, for each can contains a condensation. They can be made ready instantly in any emergency. They do for you, at the cost

of a dime, what you would find it difficult to accomplish at an outlay of four or five times the money at home. They save the ordeal of toil, boil, pare, blend, fret and heat. (Campbell's advertisement, 1905)

The emphasis on instantaneity and release from the ordeals of preparing and cooking, ('Just add water and heat') certainly suggests a particular and emergent form of convenience (Warde, 1999), where the instantaneity rests on new infrastructures of gas or electricity rather than solid fuel stoves (Glucksmann, 1990). Campbell's Condensed Soups, with Tomato as the flagship, were accompanied by a range of canned ready-made meals, a range which was extended when Campbell's acquired its main rival in 1915, Franco-American, which sold to the more refined end of the market, appreciative of French cuisine.[24]

In tracing the emergence of a new form of human tomato, an upward spiral has been climbed. Starting with the development of new forms of retailing and distribution, the metamorphosis was traced through new biological varieties. The tomato was then pursued into the factory, where it became subject to a new feature in food manufacture of 'science in command' in flow-line production. From next to nothing, these new forms of mass-produced tomato products spread across the nation, and indeed, before long, the globe. In order to do so, they became standardised in multiple and interlocking ways, purified and replicated, made uniform whilst passing through many hands of newly uniformed and quality-controlled employees. Once successfully identical, they acquired a new identity, were branded and as such were advertised, designed and represented. In these various ways, they also acquired the identity of 'American food'. And they became path-breaking exemplars of entirely new types of fast and convenience food. They were engaged in the construction of a new culture later recognised by an ironically celebratory art.

Of course, the tomato was not responsible for all this, and all this cannot be entirely encapsulated in the metamorphosis of the tomato. Nonetheless, without exaggeration, the tomato was a leading player in a revolutionary process of complex, multidimensional and overdetermined change. The metamorphosis resulted in major new interlocking institutions of firms and markets, a stable pattern of human tomato enshrined in the branded standard product, that became dominant in many parts of the developed world over a number of decades. *It eventually became normalised.* Going backwards in history to pre-normality, extraordinary and often chaotic processes were seen to underlie what now appears obvious.

But that which has been ravelled can also be unravelled.

NOTES

[1] Warhol produced a large range of works representing Campbell's Soup cans.

[2] Hayward Gallery, London, South Bank, October 1997 to January 1998.

[3] See also Barthes (1989) in the same volume, where he argues that in pop art: 'the fact ... is not longer an element of the natural world: what appears as fact is the stereotype: what everyone sees and consumes' 236.

[4] Just as Warhol commented that he painted what he ate for lunch (same soup, same can) for 20 years, so Thiebaut also commented of his paintings *Five Hot Dogs* and *Salads, Sandwiches and Desserts* in America 'the food is the same wherever you go, even down to the napkins and salt and pepper shakers on the restaurant tables' (cit., Livingstone, 1990, 71).

[5] This has led some to critique much of Pop Art as a celebration of commercial design (for example, Kuspit, 1989; Kozloff, 1997/1962)

[6] The current fad over consumption of signs, which even cites Warhol's cans and pop art, appears thus to be fundamentally historically mistaken, and forgets both that Warhol consumed soup but painted labels, and that the labels and soup are historically indissociable (Lash and Urry 1994; Featherstone, 1991).

[7] In Western high art, the tomato makes its first appearance in a painting attributed to Caravaggio in 1607, and in another still life by Bartolomé Murillo of 1646 (Grewe, 1987).

[8] Hogan (1997) likewise makes the argument that the White Castle hamburger (with ketchup) became *the* American ethnic food in the inter-war period, in the construction of a new ethnicity: 'White Castle and its imitative progeny were instrumental in helping create a uniquely American ethnicity ... the hamburger is to America what fish and chips is to Britain or the tamale is to Mexico. Each of these foods helps define the country's ethnic identity yet is usually disdained or at least downplayed by the elites in their societies' (Hogan, 1997, 3).

[9] This is not to suggest that the configuration appeared uniformly across advanced capitalist economies. The growth of branded goods, for example, occurred in the UK and US to different extents, and yet the UK witnessed the earliest and most pronounced development of change in retail outlets even at the turn of the twentieth century, partly through urbanisation accelerating demand for wage-purchased commodities, partly through spatial integration across the national economy facilitated by the railway network.

[10] It was called the 'Ash and Trash Survey' because sampling was of household rubbish by socio-economic status.

[11] There is an even more intimate link between the origins of Heinz and Campbell's, with Campbell's first partner, a skilled tinsmith who turned from roofing to canning, Abraham Anderson, providing the debt-troubled Henry Heinz with a loan to assist start-up (Collins, 1994, 13, 26).

[12] Experimental agricultural research stations, promoted by the US Department of Agriculture, played an important role as a science infrastructure for the generalisation of scientific hybridisation (Kimmelman, 1992).

[13] See Chapter 5.

[14] Indeed, as we shall see later, the most contemporary of convenience ready-made meals still combine the use of high-technology equipment with basic domestic cooking labour processes according to their own peculiar economic logic.

[15] See Chapter 2. Already in 1870, 30 million cans were being produced in the US per year, or 1.3 cans per inhabitant. Heinz started using cans in 1877.

[16] The 'American System' is one that emerged in manufacturing in the 1860s where parts were machined to an accuracy that allowed mass production of interchangeable parts in batches, for subsequent assembly, thus reducing substantially the role of handicraft finishing and master craftsmen (Best 1990).

[17] Including H.J. Heinz and Anderson, and Campbell's in the early days.

[18] Wiley engaged the husband and wife team of microbiologists, the Bittings, to first demonstrate scientifically that it was possible to stabilise ketchup over the long term without use of chemical preservatives (Smith, 1996)

[19] Harvey Washington Wiley was Chief Chemist for the United States Department of Agriculture, and established the Association of Official Agricultural Chemists in 1884.

[20] The account of the 'benzoate wars' is largely taken from Smith (1996), who gives an excellent and thoroughly researched narrative of the various battles and phases of these campaigns.

[21] In this history, an unremarked but nonetheless significant aspect of the 'whiteness' of White Castle was that, in spite of many periods of labour shortage, the company only ever employed one black person, a cleaner, during the Second World War (Hogan, 1997, 115). It was company policy not to employ black Americans. White Castle clearly meant white American ethnic identity.

[22] One interesting aspect of this creation of standards was that White Castle developed a very high level of vertical integration: for meat supply, for paper caps and uniforms, and even for the prefabricated restaurants that were its hallmark. Ownership of these separate businesses translated into

control over standards across all the different inputs to the whole new package of the hamburger restaurant service. This contrasts markedly with the McDonald's phase of fast food outlets, characterised by franchising.

[23] The parallels with the creation of an organic food market in the UK, also at much higher price, in combination with negative food scare (BSE, GM), are striking.

[24] Franco-American was established by a French émigré, Biardot, in 1887.

8. The Battle of Tomato Identities: The Rise of Supermarket Own-Label

A CLASH OF CONFIGURATIONS

The context is the United Kingdom in the late twentieth century. Supermarkets have risen to power. The extent to which they orchestrate supply chains for fresh tomatoes has already been shown. The branded manufacturers Heinz and Campbell's are beleaguered. As nowhere else, supermarket shelves are filled by the supermarkets' own-label products, Tesco or Sainsbury tomato soups, ketchups, sauces, pizzas – whatever. It is war that appears on the surface as a conflict of identity. It might be asked, what is in a name? Heinz or Tesco, Campbell or Sainsbury? The answer, everything. Just as the rise of the mass production was intimately bound up with the manufacturer's brand identity, as a mark of a distinct configuration of how food is produced, distributed, retailed and consumed, so a change in identity is a sign of a change in configuration, and of the emergence of new foods, new forms of tomato.

Campbell's factory near King's Lynn was first established in 1933, as part of a creation of a global product, and the site is now the European headquarters. The real surprise for a global company, certainly the largest soup manufacturer in the world, is that in the UK, *half of its total production* is dedicated to producing retailer own-label soups:

> Retailers have started to develop their own store personalities, they want to develop their own unique products, and products developed specifically for their business. So you find there is the conflict between the products you are developing for brands, Campbell's brands or whatever brands you want to talk about, and the innovation that you would direct towards an own-label brand. (Woods, Interview)

Many dimensions are involved in a change in configuration as it challenges the beleaguered brand manufacturers. As a conflict between different configurations, it is very much affected by relative balances of power between the players involved. In the UK, Campbell's are constrained to produce under retailer labels. Heinz, as the dominant branded soup manufacturer in this country, resolutely resists, and only produces their brand label. The position is exactly the reverse in the USA, where Campbell's as the dominant soup manufacturer exclusively keep their Campbell's brand flying, whilst Heinz only produce under retailer own-label.[1] At first glance, putting a name to a product is proclaiming a certain proprietorial relation to it: this is a Campbell's soup, and remains so even after the consumer buys it. From an entrenched branded manufacturers' point of view, the old configuration was quite clear-cut. They owned the product. Retailers owned access to market. They were two neatly defined classes of economic actor, one performing one economic function, with production sufficient to secure ownership of products, the other performing another, a service function of distributing products to consumers. Manufacturers and retailers could not – and still cannot – be seen as competing with each other, as neither is attempting to perform or take over the function of the other, or encroach on each others' market.

But then along came 'own-label'. The heretofore exclusive rights to ownership of product identity was challenged. This led branded manufacturers to accuse own-label manufacturers of copying: the contents were the same, only the name and packaging were different. Retailers were, from the brander's viewpoint, abusing their ownership of access to market by using it as leverage to gain ownership of products. The dominant and 'normal' trading relation between manufacturers and retailers was destabilised.

Robert Bailey, European Market Manager for Heinz, used a battery of resentful phrases to characterise their own-label enemies: they were 'parasites' 'ripping off' brand manufacturers by 'copy-catting', making 'look-alikes'. In the absence of patenting,[2] for a branded manufacturer everything rests on the reputation of the brand. It is their name on the product that counts. The recipes, even the processes of cooking and manufacture, cannot be protected from copying. The brand and its reputation are what gains market share.[3] It is worth returning to John Dorrance's formula for success, at the inception of brand manufacturing. Before branding, companies like Heinz and Campbell's employed armies of salesmen to visit thousands of separate retail outlets, to sell the product *to the retailer*. If by branding and advertising consumers *demand* products, he argued, the rest is easy. The manufacturer no longer bothered to 'sell' the product to the distributor or retailer, for the retailer to 'sell' to the consumer. Retailers were forced to stock the brand, because consumer demand had been created. Brand reputation, supported by advertising, short-circuits the loop.

The emergence of own-label products scrambles that short-circuit. A quite different set of relations between consumer, retailer, distributor and manufacturer is involved. The brand and loyalty is *to the supermarket*, to the whole range of its products, shopping facilities and services, not to the product as such. For the branded manufacturer, locked into their loop, market share is created by loyalty and reputation essentially to their range of products, and amongst them the 'classics' on which their reputation was built. Tomato ketchup and baked beans for Heinz, tomato soup for Campbell's. Thus, the conception of copy-catting (sinful copying) only makes sense as copying of a brand product, and this only makes sense within the mindset of the old configuration. Represented very schematically, this aspect of the old and new configurations is contrasted in Diagram 8.1.

Old configuration

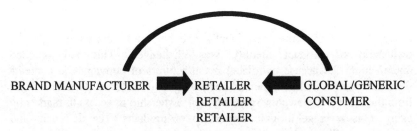

BRAND MANUFACTURER → RETAILER ← GLOBAL/GENERIC
RETAILER CONSUMER
RETAILER

New configuration

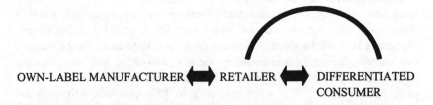

OWN-LABEL MANUFACTURER ↔ RETAILER ↔ DIFFERENTIATED
CONSUMER

Diagram 8.1 Old and new configurations of supply and demand

In both cases, the retailer is the locus where arrows travelling in opposite directions meet, where, as it were, supply meets demand. But in the old configuration, the retailer stands, much as in classical economics, as the black box (shelf space), the place were products merely pass through on their way to the consumer, with the product, as promoted through advertising, being the central object of demand. In the new configuration, by contrast, the supermarkets play a critical role in shaping demand (Chapter 10). They no longer stand as the passive space, the 'black box' and hiatus point between supply and demand. Supermarkets, partly through the vehicle of own-label manufacturing, actively orchestrate product and price differentiation. Moreover, with relatively secure access to shelf-space, own-label manufacturers have no need to appeal direct to consumers through advertising, and demand is channelled in quite different ways back to manufacturers via supermarket retailers (Chapter 9).

This difference in relations between manufacturers, retailers and consumers has profound implications for the ways firms operate and innovate, and ultimately, in shaping the food we eat, including, of course, the tomato. For, the structures of branded and own-label manufacturing firms are quite different. The former have marketing divisions, including advertising and consumer research. These are costly operations, and lead to very different overall management structures than in own-label manufacturers who have no need for advertising and promotion.[4] The risk for a branded manufacturer, given the 'hiatus' or 'black box' in this configuration of supply and demand, is much greater when launching a new product and the costs of sustaining established products through brand promotion are substantial. The branded manufacturer has to launch a product into the great consumer world 'out there'. The tendency, stated with pride, is to produce products which maximise demand, universal products like tomato ketchup or condensed tomato soup (or Kellogg's Cornflakes, Coca-Cola and so on), and products that endure. The own-label manufacturer supplies a product into an available space on a supermarket shelf with the consumer already in there – assuming the supermarket has successfully secured its consumer base.

The effects of this different set of relations is dramatic. Given their risks and costs, even the largest branded manufacturers produce only four or five new products per year. Own-label manufacturers typically produce one to two *thousand*. The products of the former are 'built to last', because investment in research, development and marketing require a longer period of return. Many products of the latter are designed for novelty and obsolescence. The innovation style of the branded manufacturers can thus be described as 'conservative radical', that of own-label as more 'variable geometry'. Heinz tomato ketchup and Campbell's Condensed tomato soup have both been subject to continuous and significant innovation. The switch to a plastic bottle for Heinz was a significant break, the plastic acting as a multi-layer oxygen barrier, requiring all aspects of tomato consistency, filling and sterilisation to be changed for the ketchup to successfully inhabit this new plastic environment. Campbell has continuously been engaged in developing new hybrids of tomato, but also fundamental technologies of heat transfer to accelerate cooking processes. Both of these are considered fundamental research and development. But both are sustaining a product that has the appeal and appearance of a 'classic'. The packaging, processing, contents, cooking and variety of tomato have all undergone a total transformation from the time the product was originally launched. It is not the same tomato ketchup, not the same tomato soup as that of the 1920s. But all this innovation is directed at achieving the classic status, something that endures and remains the same through time.[5] Indeed, many of the advertising makeovers, for both companies, now even play up the nostalgic appeal of the classic design. But, the status of a classic is accompanied by a loss of territory: what was standard, universal and dominant type of product, is now shifted sideways on the shelves to become a 'classic', making way for new types of food product.

In a clash of configurations, the result is necessarily uneven, much depending on the balance of power in different countries, but also in different product areas. It is not as if the old configuration has disappeared or been eliminated. Consolidations and mergers between branded manufacturers have responded to the enhanced power of supermarket chains. Moreover, the UK supermarket model (Chapter 10), is itself insecure: discount retailing, American- or German-style, engages much less in the new configuration type of own-label retailing, initially pioneered in the UK by Marks & Spencer at the top end of the market (Rees, 1969).[6] Discounters, driven by competition focusing on price, use their power to obtain lower-cost supplies, helping to sustain manufacturers with standard branded products gaining economies of scale from long production runs. So the conflict is many-sided.

Nonetheless there has been clearly a displacement and realignment, exemplified by the leading players in the UK, Tesco and Sainsbury, where for many product ranges own-label predominates. So, in talking of the 'battle of tomato identities', it can be seen that the whole configuration that saw the emergence of standard, branded products is becoming destabilised. It is for this reason that relations between primary producers, manufacturers, distributors, retailers and consumers are analysed here in terms of 'instituted economic process'. Patterns become established and normalised, products of a particular kind become typical and enduring. Trading and purchasing relations become settled and routine. And then, power relations change, and what had been institutionalised is destabilised. Those who operate in the old configuration appear to find it incredibly hard to view the world in any other way, and meet the resultant conflict with the new configuration with interpretations appropriate for the old, accusing upstarts of cheating according to their rules. Their capacity to innovate, according to their pattern of innovation, becomes restricted. No longer as dominant and increasingly squeezed out of shelf space, losing their prime eye-grabbing easy-reach position, returns on investment become less secure, and research and development investment is reduced.[7] They are forced to become increasingly 'conservative conservatives'.

NEW TOMATO FORMS AND IDENTITIES

Meanwhile, own-label manufacture has opened up new areas of food, convenience ready-made chilled meals, and chill-fresh foods, many of which are novelty or fashion driven. They are characterised by a short product life that would be terminal to the brand manufacturer. It is more than coincidence that branded manufacturers have been frozen out of the chill-chain, squeezed out of the sandwich business, and are peripheral to pizzas: it is an alien environment for their type of food. They were never seriously there. It is to these new forms of food, and a further metamorphosis of the human tomato that focus now shifts.

In an earlier chapter, it was shown how a new range and variety of fresh tomatoes became established in the new socio-economic environment of the UK supermarket. Here, the extraordinary versatility of the tomato is demonstrated by a new range of diverse cuisines assembled on the supermarket shelf and exemplified by the explosion of innovation in chill foods from the early 1980s. There are Mediterranean tartes tatins, basil and tomato fresh soups, a dozen or more fresh pasta sauces, marinated tomato-mozzarella-herb-olive tapas, quiches with sliced and diced tomatoes, Goan curries, a proliferation of pizzas each with their characteristically tailored tomato concasse, and, in perhaps the fastest-growing business area, sandwiches with all types of breads trapping all sorts of tomatoes, not least the robust and enduring BLT. The list is endless and everchanging. To take the two major own-label food manufacturers, Hazlewoods and Northern Foods, each uses over 6000 *tonnes* of processed tomato a year in these new tomato food forms, and a further 3000 tonnes of fresh tomato as garnish or main ingredient.

The emergence of these new food forms has required a reconfiguration of all the relations between consumption, end-market, distribution, and production. New forms of food co-evolved with this new configuration:

> The two of us, Hazlewoods and Asda – or Sainsbury, or M&S – we own the most important bit. We own and have total access to the shelf space. Shelf space is everything. If you are a brand [Campbell's, Heinz, etc.], you have to go and get shelf space. You own the product. (Craig, Interview)

This stark statement of property rights, contrasting who owns what, encapsulates the configurational revolution. In the old configuration, the world was neatly divided between manufacturer and retailer. In the new configuration, the key object of ownership is market access. The name on the product is now the name of the market outlet. Identity has shifted from the producer of the product to the owner of market access.

But to the consumer, that is the visible aspect of the change: the shelves are now widely filled with own-label goods, displacing branded goods. That change, however, is but one aspect of a many-sided and interlocking series of changes which we shall now explore. There is the emergence of a quite peculiar power asymmetry and complementarity between own-label manufacturers and retailers which affects the whole supply chain for the different foods. There are new styles of innovation linked with new types of production process, and the development of 'fashion' and 'novelty' foods. This is linked to where new ideas for these foods come from, TV chefs, restaurants, fast food, and takeaways from across the world. These changes in turn are linked to new forms of competition, where both the units of competition and what is being competed about change. The 'sin' of copying, so mortal to the branded manufacturer, no longer ranks even Number Seven. There is a new social stratification of food and social patterning of consumption, with foods targeted at both vertical hierarchies of wealth and disposable income, as well as horizontal groupings of families, kids, singles, lifestyles and so on. There are new temporalities running through every stage from production to consumption, shelf-life, product life, distribution schedules, production schedules with flexible working time, which all sustain the different consumption temporalities of ready-made recipe dish meals, fast-food convenience, and snacking. So it is to each of these articulated aspects of change that we now, in turn, afford closer examination.

'MULTIPLE MONOPSONY'

Probably not many people stop to think what the implications are for the manufacture of the own-label goods they buy in the supermarkets, or ask by whom and how they are made. The relationship between own-label manufacturers and retailers is one of 'multiple monopsony'. This ungainly term has been chosen to describe own-label manufacturing because it defies accepted categories of thought (including common sense), and therefore needs at the outset not to be falsely slotted into them. To make things easier, some concrete examples.

First, Hazlewoods: it is an important own-label manufacturer, with an annual turnover of £800 million in 1998, with production sites across Europe, and employing 10,000 people. They have already been encountered as the owners of the Van Heiningen Brothers. They grew, largely through successive acquisitions, from a small company to their current scale during the 1980s. Currently, sandwiches are their fastest-growing business, producing 1.5 million a week, with an annual rate of growth a phenomenal 40 per cent. But:

> Our product portfolio is quite diverse. I guess the big product ranges are in ready meals, sandwiches, pizzas, cooking sauces, and cakes. (Craig, Interview)

How does a large manufacturer, exclusively producing own-label products, supply the retail multiples?

> We have factories which are totally dedicated to certain retailers. For example, we pack all of Safeway's beef and lamb for their Scottish and Northern stores. That factory does nothing else but Safeways. We have a fish plant in Wrexham that does nothing else but Sainsbury. That's an own-label. We have a big ready-meal plant in Warrington, which is divided in two, one half of which is totally dedicated to Tesco, and the other half (there are two factories on the same site) is probably 90 per cent Tesco. As far as Tesco is concerned, that site is theirs [sic]. They are by far the dominant customer. (Craig, Interview)

This gets a certain distance in understanding 'multiple monopsony': the own-label manufacturer divides itself up into different units each producing exclusively for one retailer. But the exclusivity works the other way round too: Albert Hein, the Dutch supermarket, gets all its 50,000 own-label pizzas a year, and Sainsbury all its 50 million, from Hazlewoods. Moreover, an own-label manufacturer can have a virtual monopoly supply across nearly *all the major multiples*,[8] as with chilled lasagne:

> We currently make chilled lasagne for every retailer bar M&S. We do it in a mixture of factories, and *we are the primary suppliers of chilled lasagne for almost everybody* [emphasis added]. We do it from a combination of different factories or different development teams. You just have to learn how to do it. You have to learn to recognise that if Sainsbury is going to go for yellow round boxes, it's not a very good idea to let Asda do orange round boxes. They will get excited about that. (Craig, Interview)

There are thus *multiple mutual and criss-crossing exclusivities* with retailers, with plants dedicated to supplying exclusively one retailer, and a retailer exclusively getting a particular product or product category from one particular own-label manufacturer.

Turning to Northern Foods, there is a similar pattern. One of their flagship subsidiaries, Pennine Foods, grew from very humble beginnings in 1984 and now has an annual turnover of £85 million, making chilled recipe dishes exclusively for Marks & Spencer:

> We were the first people involved with recipe dishes, certainly with M&S. It was a real toe in the water job for everybody. We didn't know whether the concept was going to work, or whether the customer was going to buy into it. So we started off about sixteen years ago in a converted factory. It was a huge success from day one … We filled it to capacity within two years. (Stanley, Interview)

They then built a further factory, also dedicated to Marks & Spencer, Fenland Foods in Grantham, to be followed in 1990 by a purpose-built, steel and glass, supermodern facility, at Pennine Foods.

In the entrance, advertisements acclaim 'Proud to be exclusively providing the best in food to Marks & Spencer', and in turn, Pennine Foods are by far the most substantial, in most product categories the exclusive, supplier to Marks & Spencer. The factory itself is a testimony to the creation of the new food appearing in the supermarket chill cabinet. It is situated in Mosborough, a greenfield village satellite of Sheffield, adjoining the equally sparkling retail park Crystal Peaks[9] built in the mid-1990s, both, though, an incalculable distance, near and far, from the Sheffield of *The Full Monty*. But, like Hazlewood Foods, Northern Foods is also a multiple combination of such mutual exclusivities. Their subsidiary in Nottingham, The Pizza Factory, exclusively produces pizzas for Tesco, 14 million a year. But, and such is the peculiarity of these trading relationships, this exclusivity applies only to the seven pizza varieties of Tesco's Thin and Crispy range and, shortly, their big 12-inch family value range. Geest, another major own-label producer, complements this category exclusivity, by being sole supplier of the Tesco Classico pizzas. When Tesco decides to upgrade all its pizza range, it brings together all its separate own-label partners to the party to orchestrate and coordinate the re-launch. Riverside Bakery, also a Northern Food subsidiary, manifests another typical peculiarity. It has a split personality on the same site, half producing casseroles, steak and kidney pies, stews, and tartes tatins for M&S, the other half producing Sainsbury's total range of quiches and flans. This split personality[10] of exclusivities is only now being given fully material form, with a factory extension being built to keep the two personas physically apart.

So, this pattern of overlapping and interlocking mutual exclusivities is what lies behind the term 'multiple monopsony'. It is a business landscape utterly strange to that of the branded manufacturers described in the last chapter. But it also does not fit with notions of vertical integration, where a firm acquires ownership over upstream companies providing its inputs. To be sure, one of Hazlewood's factories was described as 'Tesco's factory'. David Stanley of Pennine Foods talks similarly as an M&S factory, while acknowledging that 'it is a very alien situation'.[11] 'Ownership' is described in these terms:

> The thing that M&S feel very strongly about is that we don't produce recipe dishes for anybody else ... M&S feel comfortable about the direction we are going, because we don't produce recipe dishes for anybody else. So there is no competition. There is no chance of anyone in Northern [Foods] talking to one of their colleagues who is producing something for Tesco's, because it won't happen. (Stanley, Interview)

It might therefore be thought possible to squeeze this bizarre relation between retailers and manufacturers into a concept of 'quasi-vertical integration'. But, there are many aspects of this 'multiple monopsony' that are *not like* vertical integration. Firstly, many of these own-label manufacturers (Hillsdown, Geest, Sun Valley, Northern Foods, Hazlewood Foods) are large players in their own right, with turnovers around or above the £ billion mark. Secondly, as they produce own-label products for all or most of the major multiple retailers, they can scarcely be said to be owned by one, more than one, most, or all of them. And thirdly, there are some product categories where the own-label manufacturer has a monopoly or near monopoly supply to all the major retailers. This is not even 'quasi' vertical integration.

'LOCK-IN' AND 'CHINESE WALLS'

So 'multiple monopsony' describes this strange set of relationships between manufacturers and retailers which support the growth of these 'new foods', and the new forms of tomato that appear within them. Three further characteristics define these relationships: asymmetries of power and dependency; 'lock-in'; and 'Chinese walls'.

The fundamental difference in economic function between retailer and manufacturer is by no means abolished by the emergence of the own-label configuration. Retailers retain the power to de-list and to deny access to market and, indeed, in none of the cases so far discussed are there written contracts of agreement about the longevity of the relationship. Conversely, retailers are dependent – utterly dependent – on manufacturers to produce the goods. Between retailers and manufacturers of any configuration there is power asymmetry *and* mutual dependency. What is new about own-label is the way that the asymmetric power relationship is configured. Vince Craig describes the emergence of this relationship over a period of more than a decade, as a process taking years:

> You are either a category champion, a mainstream supplier, or a 'we have you, but don't really want you'. Our role is to make sure we're in the number one category, and, if not, the second category. Certainly not the third. So there are closer relationships. The word 'partnership' is bandied about a lot, and everybody likes to talk about it. But partnership implies equality. In a buyer–seller relationship that is quite difficult to genuinely maintain. But you become much more important to the retailers as things get more and more complex, when you are doing more and more across the range. (Craig, Interview)

Over time, there is an increasing 'locking-in' to this asymmetric relationship, in terms of providing packaging design, logistics, promotional activities. Apart from producing products across a range, the manufacturer is delivering a manufacturing *service*. An almost decisive aspect to this service relationship is the *capacity to innovate*, to constantly produce new products and relaunch old ones. Jan McLoughlin, the Managing Director of the Pizza Factory and David Stanley of Pennine Foods describe a very similar process of lock-in with Tesco's and Marks & Spencer respectively. As Tesco grew its pizza range, so the Pizza Factory gained in experience and capabilities to provide a dedicated service to them and, as they approached their goal of becoming 'category champions', became more and more indispensable. When the relationship is one of providing a complex service, an innovation capability, across a range of products within a category, and in many cases, across categories, it becomes increasingly difficult for any 'new entrants' to break in. A putative competitor has to do more than produce a cheaper product, or even a few cheaper products, and be capable of providing a competing *relationship*, a manufacturing service across a range of products. As a relationship 'locks-in', there is a kind of asymmetric balance between seller and producer power. The two 'grow into' each other and intermingle functions. They each have development teams with 'man-to-man' marking (McLoughlin, Interview).

. The best 'Chinese walls' are not visible but highly impervious. Given the mutually dependent exclusivity described above, and given also that own-label manufacturers have multiple exclusive relationships, a business organisation is developed to keep these exclusive relationship exclusive, retailer-dedicated. That requires Chinese walls. The most obvious way, one used by Northern Foods, is for different subsidiaries to be exclusively dedicated to one retailer. Hazlewoods, likewise achieve a similar result with distinct factory units:

> Sites tend to work independently for a start. In large sites, you tend increasingly to have business teams that work with specific retailers. That business team will normally consist of national account people, development people, and technical people, who are involved in the process. (Craig, Interview)

In other cases, insulated exclusivity is achieved by a factory producing one category of product for one retailer, and another for another, so minimising potential cross-over (Riverside Bakery). Chinese walls are most visible, not unsurprisingly, in hybrid manufacturers like Campbell's, where they intrude into the model of a brand manufacturer. Walls (of communication, information sharing, accounting) between different teams producing for different retailers appear most artificial (Woods, Interview). But, in the nature of things, Chinese walls become most conspicuous when they break down. When this happens the own-label relationship is immediately threatened. An example of this happened in Northern Foods apparently by accident. The story goes that Marks & Spencer discovered an identical product, down to details of packaging design, being produced for another retailer by Northern in another factory unit. The claim within Northern Foods was that neither unit knew what the other was doing. Marks & Spencer threatened to break off the relationship with its unit on grounds of a breach of trust and exclusivity, depriving Northern of several £ million of business. Legal proceedings were imminent, until harmony was restored, difference in product created, and walls re-erected. Nonetheless, the very existence of such walls, visible or invisible, is absolutely central to the complex web of relationships of mutual dependence and exclusivity between major multiples and major own-label producers. There is a checkerboard of criss-crossing interrelationships, with retailers avoiding the total dependence on one manufacturer for its whole range, and own-label manufacturers diversifying their clients amongst the big five. Given the relatively low number of players of each kind, the overall result is a complex matrix of retailers, manufacturers and products. As an instituted structure, this relationship between major players on both sides of the fundamental divide is quite unique. Significantly, a similar matrix is to be found in the relations between retailers and logistics companies (Chapter 9), suggesting that these are indeed 'configurational' properties.

In an earlier chapter, it was shown how there was a hierarchy of suppliers of fresh tomatoes matching a hierarchy of supermarket outlets, the most durable trading relationships being the top-to-top ones. Vince Craig described a similar hierarchy for own-label manufacturers between category champions, mainstream suppliers and contingent suppliers. Nowhere is this aspect of lock-in at the top better illustrated than in the relationship between Marks & Spencer and Pennine Foods. This leads directly into why these relationships facilitate the development of such powerful and distinctive innovative capacities for the new foods we see on the supermarket shelves.

When the chilled food revolution began, Marks & Spencer were the unchallenged market leaders for the recipe dish formula, with Pennine (and its sister Northern Foods company, Fenland Foods), growing with it. As the market became established, the novelty of the lasagnes, cannellonis and other core products wore off. There was a diffusion of skills outwards from Northern Foods, so that Tesco and Sainsbury began to match M&S. In the current phase, therefore, Pennine's relationship to M&S is to continue to enhance their exclusivity by remaining market leaders through both continual improvement and relaunching of their core range *and* the creation of new food concepts, with a leading edge marked by novelty and fashion. The exclusivity is then linked to sustaining, jointly, the position of market leaders by being unique at the leading edge:

> We are the biggest recipe dish supplier to them. For them to get what we deliver, in terms of capacity and innovation, would take them a long time to take us out of the picture. We don't want to come out of the picture. We want them to grow and become more successful. (Stanley, Interview)

In this process of jointly aiming to secure leading market position, a top-to-top relationship where the bonds are strongest, innovation drives right through the chain of supply. Because the tomato in one or other guise is an almost ubiquitous ingredient across the range of products, it became the particular focus of attention in terms of quality and variety, processing and logistics.

Picking up on the trail (Chapter 3) of where processed tomato comes from and goes to, the processing and canning industry in Italy was ill-adapted to the new kind of market for high quality and value opened up by UK supermarkets in processed tomato, as was the Dutch or Spanish fresh tomato industry, with their similar focus on price and yield alone. Pennine Foods sent teams of auditors and technicians to establish the new standards, first merely in terms of purity and consistency of the product. They met with considerable resistance from a price-driven industry but progressively established relationships with particular processors:

> We quickly realised that it was about mentality. We wanted to find people who wanted to be with us for the long term, and who were prepared to give us the quality standards of product in the factory if we have the volume year after year. (Stanley, Interview)

So the same kind of relationship as between M&S and Pennine Foods percolated down the chain:

> Within M&S we were the only people who were putting resource into approving a processed tomato supply ... We've very much dictated what the M&S code of practice was on tomatoes. Everybody else followed. (Stanley, Interview)

Once new standards had been established, the next phase was to introduce entirely new tomatoes into the canning process with the aim of enhancing flavour. To do that, they went to the tomato breeders, and with Camden and Chorleywood Food Research station, they experimentally tested out new tomatoes for canning. Eventually, they adopted none other than the Marks & Spencer patented tomato variety, the Melrow. The M&S own fresh variety entered into Pennine Food own-label food chain, yielding a new bio-socio-economic processed variety of tomato.

A similar process of quality enhancement drove innovation in tomato processing. Once more the Pennine Food team scoured the Mediterranean for new processes. The journey itself was revelatory about contemporary tomato landscapes:

> The first time I went to Turkey, it staggered me, because it's a pretty backward country. We got to Istanbul, went across the Bosphorus, got into this car, and drove into the middle of nowhere. Literally, the middle of nowhere, where you were lucky if you saw a car. Then in the middle of nowhere, there are all these incredibly high-tech tomato factories, with fantastic equipment and all the processing controls you could dream of. The guys running it had a very, very good mentality. It is a really weird scenario, quite surreal.'[12] (Stanley, Interview)

These factories were, moreover, Japanese owned, producing tomato juice for the Japanese market, and using a revolutionary new technique of reverse osmosis to produce a thick juice without heat treatment and evaporation:

Basically it delivered a passata, which is obviously a completely smooth, relatively thin sauce, with no skins or seeds, just like a thick tomato juice. It used no heat at all. The flavour coming out the other end was absolutely staggering. We thought, God, this stuff is incredible. *This is the Holy Grail!* This is what I've been looking for all these years. (Stanley, Interview)

When touring Italian processing plants, Pennine discovered the same technology, but used to replace one of the evaporation stages in an otherwise normal heat treatment process. The firm, ARP in Piacenza, one of the largest processing plants in Italy, was then persuaded to engage in a joint investment in pipework so as to divert the tomato juice out of the evaporation loop and create a juice by reverse osmosis alone:

Now what we have is a world first. Nobody else is using it for this, in terms of an ingredient for soups and recipe dishes. We have got exclusivity on it. (Stanley, Interview)

The top-to-top relationship between M&S and Pennine Food percolated down the chain across to the quality and flavour of raw material and processing methods appropriate to the new chilled food range. This distinctive own-label, monopsonic relationship provided the essential context in which this type of innovation can occur.

NEW STYLES OF INNOVATION

A distinctive style of innovation is made possible in the own-label context, from which the new tomato forms emerge.[13] It has already been argued that a key aspect to this multiple monopsony is that it gives the own-label manufacturer access to shelf-space.[14] The contrast between the handful of new products launched by branded manufacturers has already been noted. Hazlewood Foods, a relatively modest company, develops 1200. Pennine Foods, one company out of a dozen subsidiaries of Northern Foods, produces several hundred a year; and the even smaller Riverside Bakery launches about 40 out of several hundred pilot products put up for review to M&S and Sainsbury.

As suggested above, after the market matured[15] the pattern of innovation altered. Pennine describes in terms of how once 'treatie' food has now become the core business, bedded into people's main consumption habits. This core is then surrounded by a periphery of novelty, of fashion-driven food, with relatively short product-life. Similar patterns occur in other own-label manufacturers, and the sandwich business is typical:

We launch 20 maybe 10 new sandwiches most weeks of the year. They are fashion products. I mean if you go into Boots to buy a sandwich, I guarantee you will always find a BLT. You will find an egg mayonnaise. You will always find a prawn salad. And there are two or three other products that fit into that category. But I really don't want to eat the BLT everyday. I'll want to try some weird and wonderful mixture of chicken tandoori and some special leaves and mozarella cheese, that may be fashionable. It may be well-liked for a while, but probably won't survive in the long term. But it doesn't actually matter. (Craig, Interview)

So this kind of innovation creates two categories of food, the ordinary and routine and the 'treatie' and fashionable. However, even for mainstream producers of the core business, there is constant revival and renewal, with relaunches to new recipes and new packaging occurring as much as twice a year. Branded manufacturers, under their configuration, take two years or more to launch a new product. Own-label manufacturers take four to six months, but also have the ability to 'fast track':

We put it in the kitchen, and four weeks later, it's on the shelf. (Stanley, Interview)

This speed to market, from concept to supermarket shelf, permits these foods both to create and follow fashion, in contrast to the branded classic lasting for a hundred years. There are many examples of this. The recent sudden rise to prominence of Thai food is typical. Likewise, sun-dried tomatoes suddenly appeared whole, chopped-up, marinated, herb-coated, across a range of product categories. *Where do new ideas come from?* The whole character of fashion-driven, reactive, innovation of this kind is that it can be responsive to trends, and shifts in trends. The speed to market creates the possibility of a feedback loop into the process, most notable perhaps in the way that own-label play off and work with TV chefs.[16] Apart from occasionally branding their goods 'Rick Stein' or 'Ainsley Harriot', a celebrity TV chef with a series on Mediterranean food highlights ingredients and styles of cooking, which are picked up by the convenience food and recipe dish makers. Versions then appear in supermarkets, including ingredients, and this fabricated familiarity can then feed back into subsequent more pedagogic cookery programmes. Ideas, rather than having a fixed locus of origin, are in a process of circulation. As a style of innovation it is far from a supply-side or linearly driven one. Another main component of the circuit is restaurants:

> Have a look at some of the products that we've got now in our Café Range, which is quite trendy. We've got things like Crispy Peking Duck. In terms of price point, it's a new challenge because it's that much higher than a customer is used to pay for a recipe dish. But that is very much what you would get in a trendy café or wine bar in middle of London. They're the sort of products we are trying to be innovative in. (Stanley, Interview)

All the own-label manufacturers interviewed had chefs dedicated to a particular category of food who then regularly trawl round restaurants, picking up on what is currently happening out there, and feeding it back into the factory. Pennine have chefs for their Italian, Indian, Chinese and American ranges, and they travel the world to sample restaurant practices of their particular category, or work for a while in their respective leading London restaurants, like Café Spice, in order to learn the skills.[17] Jan McLoughlin of the Pizza Factory described a trip to the United States, deemed the trend-setter a couple of years ahead of the game for their particular category of pizza. The team rented an apartment in Chicago, went round dozens of restaurants, brought back hundreds of pizzas for test 'at home' cooking and tasting, as the prelude to their launch of Tesco's Chicago Pizza Pie.

Within this context of ready-made, recipe dish convenience food, therefore, it is not just that ideas come from restaurants, but own-label becomes a vehicle for bringing restaurant-type food into the home, a form of 'eating in eating out':

> We spend a lot of time focusing on what the restaurants are doing, to be able to create that image in the home. (McLoughlin, The Pizza Factory, Interview)

At the top of the range, Marks & Spencer, with Pennine Foods, aim at 'restaurant-presentable' foods, where the visual effect of food in a trendy restaurant can be reproduced in the home. Thus their Café Range provides a series of dishes which leave the finishing touches to the consumer to complete, thus conferring to the home 'cook' a certain ownership at the same time as making possible a less pre-cooked flavour and appearance. The trick, and not an easy one, is to make the food appear as if it has just been cooked in the home, rather than manufactured in a factory six days before:

> We are trying to be more and more innovative in giving the customer something to do, so that they feel they actually own it, without making it too complicated, when they'd think it's no longer convenience food. (Stanley, Interview)

Own-label chill fresh foods thus challenge branded manufacturing canned or frozen products partly because they have come full cycle in producing fresh-made food for the home. One aspect of the 'globalisation of cuisine' that has so transformed UK own-label ready-made food is that, in addition to convenience, a range of food at a level of quality beyond most domestic competencies has become possible within the home. Most people cannot make and cook fresh pasta with a variety of fresh sauces, at the same time as being equally competent in Thai, Chinese, Indian, Mediterranean, Italian-American, Mexican, Cajun, etc. foods, now available. These foods are thus largely not replacing foods once cooked in the home, but expanding the market for manufactured foods.

All of these facets of the distinctive innovation process for own-label presume a context of coordination between retailer and manufacturer that could not occur, and does not exist, with branded manufacturers. Rather than the 'arm's length' trading of the branded manufacturer, there are processes of product development where own-label manufacturers produce ideas that are then subject to a review process by retailers. Before product launch, and indeed before a product goes into full production, retailers decide on and influence the shape of the final product, selecting which ones are to go forward. Suppliers of raw materials are audited by the retailers before they can be used by manufacturers, for all new as well as existing products. Since the design and packaging has to conform with the overall style of the retailer in question, there is necessarily much co-development of a product before it reaches the shelves. If a retailer wants to renovate a whole range of food, it will often orchestrate a number of own-label manufacturers who will then be required to produce a portfolio covering at least the particular fraction of the range for which they are the privileged producer.

Consequently, the 'lock-in' between the large retailers and the large own-label manufacturers is one that hinges on the innovation capability of the own-label manufacturer, the capacity to renovate existing ranges and innovate new ones. Insofar as there is competition *within* this strange matrix, the competition is thus not between manufacturers' products as such, as it is with branded goods, but between their services and capabilities.

Nowhere is this more clear than in the issue of plagiarism. Branded manufacturers make it clear that they look at all product copying as a form of underhand cheating engaged in by own-label producers. There may be a case for making that argument in food ranges where branded and own-label manufacturers overlap. But it is difficult to sustain in markets, such as chilled foods, where branded manufacturers have scarcely entered. The style of innovation of own-label producers, one of constant change and fashion-led innovation, with short product-life and novelty, is one where to *be copied* is the prime market position to hold. To be copied is a sign of success, to copy is a sign of failure. The drive for innovation is to be always ahead of the game:

> There's plagiarism all the time. They have even plagiarised it down to the packaging, even the background colours on the packaging. It's nice to know there are probably more things that have been plagiarised over the years from this factory, and in its own funny way that's got to be nice for the guys who are developing this stuff. (Grainger, interview)

STRATIFIED PRODUCTION FOR STRATIFIED CONSUMPTION

The changing tomato identity embodied in the new range of foods also involves the tomato being socially stratified in new ways. Supermarkets aim to create a comprehensive and differentiated range for any product category. There is a nice image of strata of pizzas (with tomato concasse to suit) matching stratification of consumption. Supermarkets rank and group consumers by their disposable incomes, as well as by their consumption characteristics. Thus for Tesco, at the top of the pizza social hierarchy are the hand-crafted, low-volume pizzadellas, piccadellas and strombolas; then comes the mainstream layer of pizzas (Thin and Crispy, Deep Pan), within which there is some further subtle social differentiation between the Classico Italian and the American-Italian; and at the bottom the economy range:

> There are these three or four tiers within the pizza range. They have grown at different rates within different retailers, because they offer differing purchasing opportunities for the shopper really. You have got to satisfy all the different social groups that go into the supermarkets. That's what the supermarkets are focused on. (McLoughlin, Interview)

So, when The Pizza Factory aims for the mainstream and middle of the second tier, its exclusive relation to Tesco is predicated on it also being dedicated to producing for middle- and lower-income groups within the pizza social hierarchy. Analysing the social market for pizzas, it discovered that Tesco lacked a pizza social group compared with Asda and Morrison, supermarkets tilted towards middle and lower purchasing power groups, the large family-size pizza. Taking information from loyalty cards, they could detect a group of shoppers going from Tesco to Asda or Morrisons for their family value pizzas. It was a social gap in Tesco's otherwise comprehensive social range, and one that The Pizza Factory, with its middle market social characteristics, was well placed to plug.

A similar social hierarchy can be seen to exist between Pennine Foods and Riverside Bakery, different subsidiaries within Northern Foods. The former is dedicated to the top-of-the-market range for Marks & Spencer (the restaurant-presentable recipe dishes and the top-of-the-market ready-made meals), the latter for the more mainstream products, at the same time as producing the mainstream middle-tier products for Sainsbury. To be sure, the matching between factory unit and social group via supermarket shelf is far from being one of rigid social division. There are many crossovers. But the characteristic of supermarkets differentiating products vertically by price and quality and horizontally into different consumer categories (families, singles, kids, and so on) and aiming for comprehensiveness of range is the one to which own-label manufacturers are tailored.[18] It is into this social code, in whatever product range, that the newly versatile tomato feeds, changing shape, quality, variety and consistency to do so. The manufacturers have a 'library' or 'portfolio' of tomato ingredients from which to construct this code: processed from Turkey, quick-frozen (IQF) from Hungary, reverse osmosis from Italy, diced and crushed from various European and even Australian sources, and then the range of fresh already discussed for garnish or main ingredient.

The contrast with the global brand foods discussed in the last chapter could not be sharper. The social logic of Campbell's, Heinz, Kellogg's, Nestlé, and others has been to maximise the market rather than differentiate it. The boast, from the very first social survey, was about the classlessness of the brand. The standardisation aimed to achieve a quality, uniformity and affordability that produced social standardisation. Certainly, there have also always been luxury branded goods and there still continue to be. But now these are set at the top of a social hierarchical pyramid in which most tiers, including top and bottom, are increasingly occupied by own-label products. Own-label has been the primary vehicle for establishing a finely tuned graded hierarchy of food, replacing dichotomies of standard and luxury.[19]

NEW TEMPORALITIES OF PRODUCTION AND CONSUMPTION

The social differentiation of supermarket own-label food is also articulated with new temporalities[20] of production, distribution, retailing and consumption. In passing, it has already been observed that 'fresh' in the context of the chill chain means a six-day shelf-life, and that many of these products, unlike their branded predecessors, have short 'lives'. A distinct temporal nexus is related to these new foods.

One of the immediate temporal implications of the mass-manufacture of fresh food is that each and every product is made fresh every day to maximise sales within the six-day limit:

If you take anyone round the factory, the thing that absolutely gobsmacks them every time is the fact that we do every product fresh every day. And each product is not a single process. You've got maybe eight or nine different processes that all funnel into together to make an end product. So you have got 140 of those funnels every day, day in day out. That is the biggest challenge for us. (Stanley, Interview)

Manufactured freshness, sustained by the chill-chain, is thus more than a form of 'just-in-time', because it is constrained by the bio-temporality and perishability of food on the one hand, and the socio-economic manufacture of the 'fresh' in ready-made soups, ready-meals on the other. Moreover, especially in the top-of-the-market products, where fresh herbs or a garnish of fresh cherry tomatoes may be used, the time scale is driven always by the most perishable ingredient.

But, in addition to this temporal logic of freshness, the innovation style of own-label and the need to reflect the latest TV show impose time constraints on introducing new products, and reorganising supply chains and production processes accordingly. Furthermore, given the dedicated linkage between own-label manufacturing units and retailers, there is an expectation of instant reactivity to changes in demand for particular products at the supermarket. Once The Pizza Factory has been fully reorganised to supply only pizzas, the daily orders it receives at 7.00 am will be out of the factory by the end of the second shift. In the case of Pennine Foods:

The M&S orders are so reactive to what's on the shelf and their current demand, that on some things we have zero lead time with them. They just ring up and chase us for this, that and the other, for today's pack. (Stanley, Interview)

If these foods were not fresh, but frozen, canned or dried, stocks could be held and drawn from to meet fluctuating demand. The instant reactivity involved in fresh and chill-fresh thus more closely fits with the own-label model of locked-in trading between manufacturer and retailer. Thus, in the event of a promotion for a particular product (a 'bogoff' or buy-one-get-one-free), this presents distinct time constraints and considerable fluctuations of production: at Riverside Bakery, on a normal week they might produce 9000 bacon, tomato and mushroom quiches; in a promotional week, ten times that number.

To support such product temporalities, there have to be in place appropriate working-time temporalities, and a distribution temporal organisation capable of providing rapid daily deliveries from factories to the nationwide chain of supermarkets. A logistical system, working on a 24-hour basis, is capable of ensuring daily delivery from all the own-label manufacturing units to all the retailing units. The articulation between dedicated own-label manufacturers and dedicated retail distribution networks is one of the key aspects of 'multiple monopsony'.

The temporal logic of sandwich and pizza production requires flexible working regimes to varying extents. Clearly, this in turn is related to the flexible working-time regimes in place in supermarkets, enhanced by the development of widespread 24-hour opening (Lehndorff, 1999; Ward et al., 1998; Beynon et al., 2002, Chapter 7). As might be expected, the most variable working-time regimes operate in those factories which are most subject to the kind of product variability and reactivity described above, and least where mainstream core products are primary.[21] Pennine Foods, with high levels of product innovation and novelty as well as instant reactivity to superstore shelf demand, operates flexi-hours, between five and ten daily (Trail et al., 1997; and Stanley, Interview):

> We guarantee the workforce a certain number of hours, but in return they have to guarantee that they will be available to work whatever hours we need to get the job done – bank holidays and things like that as well. We have very flexible work patterns to allow us to supply what M&S want. And the workforce is all local. (Stanley, Interview)

Other factories work a double shift, 6 am til 2 pm, and 2 pm til 10 pm, to make sure that total daily production meets total daily orders. Yet others, those especially producing only core mainstream items, deal with the fluctuations mainly coming from promotions by a combination of standard working weeks with large amounts of overtime.

Lastly, in terms of consumption, the products of this system of production are a new wave of convenience food which approaches a formula of integrated convenience meals, the supermarkets promoting the combined purchase of several courses and, within each course, of several dishes often in integrated packaging. As suggested above, some of this 'convenience' is as much about purchasing cooking for the home that falls outside the competence or orbit of most home cooking. Some is also about the 'convenience' of eating food in the home of equal quality but lower price than restaurant food. But there is also, in this commodification, the temporal aspect of time spent cooking in the home being substituted for purchased time spent on other people doing the cooking in factories. Ready-made meals, pizzas, quiches, soups and sandwiches can be all prepared and eaten more or less instantly, and are packaged in quantities for single consumers, couples and families, allowing the full range from individual eating times to domestic commensality. They are produced for variable temporal household organisations just as they are produced for variable disposable income.

It would be too neat a picture, however, to suggest that product and production temporalities, the flexible working hours of the workforces in own-label manufacturing and supermarket retailing, the logistical network sustaining 24-hour delivery, and the consumption temporalities of food in the household, all fit tightly together as an integrated system. Many of the people producing, distributing and retailing the Café Range, for instance, are certainly not those who normally eat them. Conversely, many of those who do eat the new wave of convenience foods, may not lead as flexible working time regimes as the people who produce them. Nonetheless, it is clear that even if such a temporal nexus of production, distribution, retail and consumption merely pioneers and prefigures a more full-blown and articulated temporal order, the different temporal phases of this nexus do 'hang together' and mutually imply each other.

CONCLUSION

In this chapter, it has been demonstrated that much lies behind tomato identity. Own-label is more than just a change in name. It entails a peculiar relationship between retailers and manufacturers that has many dimensions. The way it articulates asymmetries of power with mutual dependence form that distinctive phenomenon of 'multiple monopsony'. This in turn enables new ranges of products, new styles of innovation, new modalities of competition, to emerge and become institutionalised. Allied to these distinctive forms are new patterns of social stratification, market segmentation and, along with that, new temporal orders interlinked across each dimension of the emergent configuration.

In this chapter and the last, two very different configurations have been analysed. The emergence of the standardisation, advertising and retailing systems associated with the development of the first industrial mass production of branded food commodities contrasts on all fronts with the system of 'multiple monopsony' characteristic of a regime where supermarkets put their names on products. The difference in the processed tomato that enters into the new range of foods can be seen to parallel the difference between the domination of the old standard fresh tomato and the proliferation of varieties now present in UK supermarkets. In both cases, different systems of production, distribution and retailing sustain different patterns of consumption.

The clash between one configuration and another is at present far from resolved: Campbell's and Heinz, the chosen tomato examples of super-brands, are global players in a way that Sainsbury or Tesco are not. It is far from clear what the next round of supermarket or manufacturer consolidation might lead to in terms of new asymmetries of power and mutual dependence between them. Moreover, although in one week in early 2000 the *Financial Times* reported that Kellogg's had capitulated in its long-standing opposition to producing own-label breakfast cereals by reaching an agreement to produce own-label for Aldi, and that Unilever had decided to scrap 400 brand items to concentrate on its narrow core of universal brands, it would be premature to write brand manufacturers off as dinosaurs belonging to an earlier epoch.

It is of course quite possible that brands and own-labels will settle down to some new harmonious accommodation, with perhaps different levels of territorial occupation in supermarket shelves of different countries, or indeed, different global chains. Instabilities may occur at the boundaries, and recur with major power realignments provoked by acquisitions and mergers. But a division into relatively stable and unstable zones need not imply extinction of one by the other, just continuing dislocations and relocations. In this long historical process, it can be seen that the tomato gained an identity, and was indeed at the leading edge of forging this type of identity, only to meet a crisis out of which multicultural, biological and socio-economic varieties have proliferated to further exploit its material versatility.

NOTES

[1] Culbey, Woods, Interviews.

[2] Quite strikingly, Robert Bailey (Interview) suggested some kind of government regulation to give brand innovators protection to prevent their new products from being copied, so that they could recoup investments.

[3] 'Let's not be naive about it, some of these issues about passing off or lookalikes, are not a retailer issue. It's another brand competition issue. Anybody can get in there. Once you have produced a brand, and established that brand in the consumer's mind, you can achieve a certain a level sale' (Bailey, Interview).

[4] Interviews at Heinz and Campbell's insisted on these major organisational differences for branded and own-label manufacturers. It is a frequent charge levelled at supermarkets by branded manufacturers that they do not do consumer research, in the way they themselves do. From their perspective this is almost a sin. But they fail to see things from the perspective of the retailers, who realise they do not need to generate demand in the same way, and certainly not for individual products.

[5] 'We should have ketchup as the same product all the way round the world' (Bailey, Interview) 'You get the reputation by producing quality products consistently over a very long period of time. That's what Campbell's and Heinz have done. That's how you build your brand reputation. The reputation has been there for a hundred years' (Woods, Interview).

[6] 'It was a revolution in outlook because it implied that the retailer should assume responsibilities, and discharge functions, which were not normally regarded as his; it was a revolution in method because it required that the retailer should become an active partner in the process of production and this in turn meant creating an entirely novel and unique form of relationship with the manufacturer' (Rees, 1969, 122).

[7] 'The reality today is that it is becoming increasingly hard for food brands to justify the levels of fundamental research which you would argue today that you need to drive true innovation. The exceptional rewards are not there. The reality is that they [retailers] are stunting innovation' (Bailey, Interview).

[8] For example, 'Virtually every scotch egg that you see anywhere will have come from Dorset Chilled Foods' (Jan McLoughlin, Interview). It is worth recalling how Van Heiningen Brothers have a similar monopoly position for fresh herbs, see p.105–6

[9] Its name does, however, border on self-parody.

[10] The strategies of control by Sainsbury and M&S towards Riverside differ, each retailer having a different 'personality' and culture to which, correspondingly, Riverside has to adapt, internally assuming different responsibilities and attitudes to the different retailers.

[11] So alien is this type of relationship that a leading authority in food innovation strongly recommended against it, in an earlier study of Pennine Foods, (Trail and Harmson , 1997, 201–11, see especially 211)

[12] It could not but strike the interviewer that a parallel existed, almost equally surreal, with Pennine Foods and Crystal Peaks springing suddenly into view on leaving Sheffield's industrial wastelands.

[13] 'We use it [reverse osmosis] now for the tomato and basil soup, for example, which is all reverse osmosis. With some of our pasta products, if you just took a plain pasta, and just use the reverse osmosis as a sauce, and put in a bit of olive oil, a bit of fresh basil in, and just dressed it. It's just perfect.' (Stanley, Interview)

[14] 'We don't have to market the products heavily, and therefore we don't have the development costs on that side of the thing. We don't do TV advertising or anything like that. That's a problem the branded people have in order to establish a product in the market. They have to put a lot of money in up front. And they don't have guaranteed shelf-space like us either. So it is very hard for them ever to contemplate doing the sort of range of things we do.' (Stanley, Interview)

[15] Here the focus is on chilled and convenience food which have burgeoned over the last 15 years, and which exemplify the distinctiveness of own-label innovation. Woolven et al., (1996), suggests four successive generations of own-label: generics; cheap economy quasi-brands; imitative 'me too' own-label; and value-added, market-segmenting own-label. Also Woolven, Interview, 1997.

[16] 'That is the big challenge for us. It is to buy into the advent of all the chefs on TV. People are exposed a lot more to new types of food, to new raw materials, things like that. They are more likely to take a chance I think. If you put something on the shelves now, it is not so much of a risky buy for them. They say, I've heard of Thai food, I know what that is. I know what coconut milk is, because I've seen Rick Stein doing it.' (Stanley, Interview).

[17] There is thus a parallel within the new configuration to Dorrance's education in the classic French restaurant kitchens, but now with a totally different purpose and product outcome (see p. 169).

[18] This view supports the argument made by Warde (1997) against Mennel's (1985) idea that there is both increased variety and diminishing social contrast. What is visible in own-label food is both increased variety and, especially through loyalty card and other information, increasing social contrasts based on inequalities of disposable income, household composition, ethnic and generational difference.

[19] Branding and own-label are, of course, not restricted to food, and it is not being argued here that identical processes are occurring in clothing, cars,

banking or other commodity markets. The argument here, rather, is that it is a particular reconfiguration of the production-distribution-retail-consumption configuration that has led to the social patterning of food in UK supermarkets.

[20] 'Temporality' here refers to the social organisation of time into durations, cycles, synchronies, sequences and limits. In this perspective, chronometric time is a further social organisation of measuring time according to a common standard, rather than an instrument for analysing different social organisations of temporal orders and disorders (see Harvey, 1999c)

[21] M&S experimented with outlets delivering an 'ultra-fresh' food category, with lead times between factory and store-shelf set at a maximum of three to our hours. This required continuous 24-hour working regimes and extreme time flexibility for the workforce.

9. Growing New Routes

> We have moved to a time of instant gratification – the consumer wants something and he wants it now.
> (John Cole, Managing Director, Hays Logistics, *Financial Times*, 28 September 1999)

> Everybody wants the stuff in the supermarket. They want to be able to go to the supermarket any minute of the day, any day of the week, and to get just what they want. But they don't want big lorries, or any of the means of getting it there. (Wigmore, Interview)

HIDDEN CHANGES

There is public awareness that supermarket shelves are stacked with fresh fruit and vegetables coming from all over the world, and of the 'breakdown of the seasons'. But there is probably less appreciation of what a massive transformation has occurred to make that 'instant gratification' possible. In the last chapter, changing temporalities of consumption were linked to changing working times and changing temporal organisation of production for new convenience foods. Here, the tomato's routes are traced, how they have changed in space and how new temporalities of 'freshness' are linked to a complete revolution in getting the tomato from grower to consumer, which in turn affects all who work along those routes.

This change could be described as a transformation of 'tomato logistics', but perhaps the more interesting way of putting it is to realise that 'logistics' as a military term has become more widely used only with the development of a new industrial organisation of distribution. Logistics has replaced the previous organisation of distribution, transportation and wholesale markets. It focuses attention on how the whole operation of getting things from A to B is itself a critical and *productive* activity,[1] open to rapid innovation and technological change. Transportation of an object *in a certain time frame* is an integral and essential part of turning it into a commodity for many commodities,[2] including certainly the tomato. A new breed of logistics

201

companies is now dedicated to trading and competing in the spatiality and temporality of products.

Once again, the supermarkets as the visible front of this change hold a key position in a new distribution configuration. As late as the 1960s, the dominant configuration for distributing fresh produce to consumers had been the wholesale market as its central hub. Everything fresh (including tonnes of tomatoes) passed through wholesale markets. By the mid-1990s, next to none of the produce appearing in supermarkets did, and apart from supplying the residual small independent retailer, wholesale markets had fundamentally converted their role into supplying the catering trade (Shaw et al., 1994; Allen, 1998, and Allen, Atkinson, Fowler, Interviews). In the space of a couple of decades, a form of organisation that had taken centuries to develop was largely swept away or marginalised. *Tomatoes had developed new routes*.

THE WHOLESALE MARKET CONFIGURATION

A wholesale market is a very particular type of socio-economic institution. In some ways it can be seen as a market *par excellence* because it is only a place for buying and selling. In the market itself, none of the buyers are prospective consumers, not even intermediary consumers buying inputs to be consumed in production. The buyers are buying in order to sell (either directly as retailers, their agents, or indirectly as secondary wholesalers who in turn sell on to retailers). Equally, none of the sellers are producers: they are traders, and do nothing but trade. So on either side of the trade, the trading parties are buying[3] only in order to sell, and the market is an institution whose function is trade and trade alone.

But this portrayal of the market is one-sided and creates the economist's illusion of frictionless exchange without regard to physical goods, and in particular without regard to transformations of location. For, in addition to being places for buying and selling, wholesale markets have a primary function in the physical distribution of goods. Moreover, as we shall see, demand for distribution (as opposed to for goods) has changed and will continue to change in significant ways, depending on modes of transport, aggregations of population and patterns of consumption. As well as a coordination of supply and demand mediated by price, a physical coordination of distribution is required in order for tomatoes to reach every single retail outlet in the United Kingdom from the island of Guernsey (Chapter 3). Wholesale markets played that role, creating 'reservoirs of supply' (Runciman, 1957). The vision is one of specially constructed spaces being filled and emptied, the engineering and location of reservoirs being quite subordinate to the economic function of buying and selling.

The physical distribution structure was established partly as a function of densities of population and partly in relation to transport infrastructure. All but Birmingham of the major wholesale markets were situated at ports, and London as a central hub of road and rail communications achieved a dominant position for distribution.[4] It is significant that the major wholesale markets were built and developed in the conurbations of the industrial revolution, Manchester in 1846, Liverpool in 1859, Glasgow in 1871 and Birmingham in 1883. They thus only came into existence, distinguishing themselves clearly from the markets and fairs typical of earlier periods, with the new demands of an extensively urbanised population.

As a distinctive institutional intermediary between direct producers and retailers and as a distribution infrastructure, wholesale markets as we know them today are recent constructions. They emerged as distinctive socio-economic institutions only after several centuries (Davis, 1965; Jefferys, 1954; Phillips, 1992). Covent Garden Market, the first known UK commercial venue for the arrival of the strange tomato from the New World,[5] provides the 'long-duration' perspective on both emergence and decline. It became the central and dominant hub of the wholesaling configuration in the UK.

To appreciate that markets are the outcomes of processes of insitutionalisation and de-institutionalisation, Covent Garden underwent four major 'configurational' phases in its history. First it was a conduit for selling local agricultural surplus from monastic (convent) gardens (1200–1530). Then it became the outlet for 'market gardeners' whose professional roles of producers, distributors and retailers were as yet undifferentiated (1530–1700). A third configurational phase occurred when growers ceased to sell their own produce, as outlying areas of London such as the Lea Valley[6] became centres of commercial agriculture supplying the capital. At this point, Covent Garden was a retail market, selling directly to the surrounding aristocratic households (1680–1830/50). A fourth major configurational phase occurred with the development of industrial urban populations, national rail networks, and thus greatly increased volumes of produce travelling at higher speed over greater distance. This was the period when Covent Garden gradually ceased to be a retail market, and became the wholesale hub for distributing producers' goods on to retailers. At the same time, permanent shops were replacing street markets. By the turn of the century, the presence of a major wholesale market in the centre of residential London, distributing international and national produce, was becoming a scandal of congestion and pollution, earning Covent Garden the sobriquet of 'Mud Salad Market'.[7]

Royal Commissions came and went, until finally the Runciman Committee was established in 1957, recommending a modernisation and relocation that would take another 17 years to accomplish (Allen, 1998). The Committee's Report represents both the apogee of the wholesale market configuration and its death–knell.

The Runciman Committee Report provides an excellent reference point in this history of the institution of markets and routes. It represents the culmination of the wholesale market and the channels through which tomatoes flowed for the central part of the twentieth century. Figure 9.1 indicates the extent of the dominance of wholesale markets as *the* tomato conduit of the time. Only 8 per cent went to retailers direct. Moreover, it seems that only 27 per cent of the smallest growers used this channel, probably on a local basis. All the remainder went to wholesalers, either by direct sales (10 per cent of output, 15 per cent of growers) or on commission to the major and minor local wholesale markets (83 per cent of output, 59 per cent of growers). Sale on commission was thus the dominant form of trading in wholesale markets and, by contrast, was a form incompatible with the retail trade.

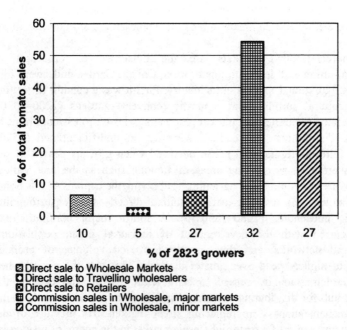

Figure 9.1 Tomato sales to different outlets, 1955
Source: Runciman Committee, 1957. From Table 5, Appendix II, 157

WHOLESALE MARKETS AS AN INSTITUTED MARKET FORM

Earlier, some of the broad distinguishing features of wholesale markets were outlined, and here some of the key features will be examined in order to establish how the nature of the trading affected the nature of the goods traded, and in particular tomatoes. The doubling up of the functions of a price-forming market and of logistical distribution was the fundamental structural feature of wholesale markets. Wholesale markets were the essential point of concentration in a flow of goods from a highly dispersed large number of producers to a highly dispersed large number of retailers: the flow can be seen as dispersion–concentration–dispersion. Given the dispersion at both ends of producers *and* retailers, there was no route either for distribution or for price-setting other than through a process of concentration in wholesale markets. The ratios given to describe this *raison d'être* of wholesale markets drawn from the Runciman Committee (1957, 7, 19) are represented in Diagram 9.1.

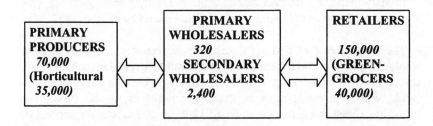

Diagram 9.1 Concentration in wholesale markets

The concentration phase is in fact much greater, for the 320 primary wholesale traders, the first point of concentration, are themselves grouped into 38 wholesale markets across the country, and of these 16 dominant ones take the overwhelming volume of produce, the three London markets outstripping all by a large margin. The distinction between primary and secondary wholesale reflects this initial concentration, as the secondary wholesalers purchase their produce from the primary wholesalers in order to redistribute it to retailers serving smaller populations at a local level more distant from major conurbations. Where growers are themselves quite geographically clustered as in Guernsey (Chapter 3), there can also be some upstream concentration, in that case through the Guernsey Tomato Marketing Board. The produce of some 1000 small growers was gathered and centrally distributed to a 'panel' of wholesale traders in all the mainland markets.

This logistical process of concentration for subsequent distribution to retailers was the basis of price formation at wholesale markets:

> There is ... at the markets a concentration of buyers and sellers dealing in a wide range of commodities and conscious of movements in supply and demand. It is the interplay between them that enables a general market price to be established. (Runciman Committee, 1957, 39)

Covent Garden, as the most important primary market, played a critical role in price formation for the whole country, with its turnover in 1955 of £70 million being seven times greater than Manchester, Birmingham, Glasgow or Liverpool.[8] Runciman noted that market intelligence was increasingly developed by use of the telephone, and with rapid transport by road enhancing distribution by rail. A *national* price-setting framework for wholesale markets consequently obtained, with goods able to swiftly respond if prices were out of line in any one wholesale market:

> Primary markets, with their functions of price-setting and equalising, [are] an essential part of the present system. (Runciman Committee, 1957, 41)

The whole fabric of trading is built into the architecture of these major wholesale markets, with central 'buyers' walks' stretching sometimes to several hundred metres long. The traders display produce on either side of the 'walk' without a single price on show. For tomatoes, in the 1950s, they would have been stacked in the standard 12 lb 'chip' baskets. Buyers test the market to see what deals are on offer with different traders in a truly 'atomistic' model. Each one is ignorant of deals any other buyer might have struck and is reliant at most on historic prices, these being published *post hoc* on a daily basis.

The second most significant 'instituted' aspect of trading and price formation in wholesale markets is that traders sold on commission for the vast bulk of their produce as Figure 9.1 shows, until quite recently.[9] This is truly the institution of the middleman, traders not acting on their own account. It has a number of significant ramifications. Commission trading arose in Covent Garden with the emergence of the specialised wholesaler (Webber, 1969),[10] and is the common form amongst European wholesale markets (Allen, Interview) as well as being formally enshrined in a regulatory framework by the Horticultural Produce (Sales on Commission) Act of 1926. It establishes a producer's market because traders sell on the growers' behalf, and merely get a commission on all sales, the rate of which itself is regulated, varying between 7.5 and 10 per cent.

The grower has got to be satisfied that he going to get a reasonable return, and that he doesn't see the wholesaler as taking too much ... I think it was done to protect the grower. It also helped the wholesaler, because he didn't need too much capital investment. His risk was also that much less. (Allen, Interview)

The regulations required registration of sales in quantities and prices, and rapid settling of accounts. But in turn, this legal framework was one in which trust *between trader and grower* could be sustained. In a market based on sale by commission, this is the trust relationship which is pivotal and privileged above all others:

Commission selling requires trust. You don't actually give the chap money at the time. The grower doesn't go away grasping his money. He leaves his stuff on a credit basis ... You have got to think that there are market firms going back three generations. You know, my grandfather dealt with that farmer's grandfather. You have got to have very close relations, and possibly they were social friends as well. You have those sort of relations in the past, which have tended to persist. There is a terrific lot of trust. (Allen, Interview)

The conditions for equivalent trust relationship between trader and retailer, let alone at one remove between retailer and grower, are precluded. Within this trading configuration, market-clearing on a daily basis, with a focus on volume of trade rather than quality or added value in products, was a categorical imperative. Two views of leading market traders in Manchester Smithfield and New Covent Garden express this perspective:

There is always a market for anything. At a price, you can sell anything, and there will be buyers who will take it. And you will make a profit. (Atkinson, Interview)

Actually what happens is, when I buy the product today, it's for tomorrow. When I get on the phone tomorrow, I buy for the next day ... We have very few long-term contracts. I can't think of one, actually.' (Fowler, Interview)

Operating as a spot market, and clearing on a daily basis, leads to a trading business focused on revenue flows rather than capital – a further significant aspect of commission trading. The salesman is 'put on a pedestal' (Allen, Interview) for his ability to cut deals.[11] The endemic short-termism implied in these trading patterns left and still leaves little room for investment in modernisation, developing integrated chill-chains, packaging systems, let alone a transport delivery service to retail outlets.

But even to describe wholesale markets in this way risks judging them in the light of subsequent developments. It has to be remembered that their existence was predicated on the dispersion–concentration–dispersion patterns. Retailers were made up of a myriad of small independent retailers who themselves, by virtue of scale, were limited in both the kind of delivery systems they could sustain and the variety of produce they could stock. Nonetheless, it is clear that under this configuration there was an absence of integration along the length of the value chain. In going from grower to consumer, the product passed through a series of discrete phases. A grower went to the trader, and handed over the produce for the trader to sell. Apart from getting a reasonable return for produce, for the grower that was the end of the story. Once in the hands of the trader, all that the trader was concerned with was selling, at the best price on the day, whatever the quality and to whoever would offer it. Once sold, for traders that too was the end of the story. There are already two discrete phases. In many instances, there would be more equally discrete phases in a series: the grower might take his produce to an intermediary marketing board or body,[12] the primary wholesaler might sell produce to a secondary wholesaler. In this case there would be at least four distinct 'breaks' in the flow of produce to market:

> Growers grew what they grew best, and brought it to market, and accepted they would get what the market would bear. Buyers would come into the market and see what there was and what they could buy. It was a very different world from the one we live in now. It is probably why they don't fill a major bill in the modern world. (Allen, Interview)

All these characteristics of the wholesale market configuration interlock:

- The logistical pattern of dispersion–concentration–dispersion;
- Centralised price–setting;
- Producer-oriented commission trading;
- The clearing imperative of a daily spot market;
- Short-termism of trading;
- The indifference of trading to the quality of what is traded (any quality finds its price);
- The flow from grower to consumer broken in a series of discrete phases.

These interlocking characteristics define the routes which along which produce flowed; and thereby also the links between price, quality, market and product. Particular tomatoes are grown for particular routes. There are two key aspects to tomato variety in this respect: variability of standards of any given variety, and the variety itself or ranges of varieties. It is clear that in both aspects, the routes were an important, if not the only, determinant of what tomatoes were available for consumption. There were grading systems in place. For example, in the one operated by the Guernsey Tomato Marketing Board, there were seven or eight grades:

> The top grade was known as pink and white, because you put pink and white paper in the chip basket. This had a star on it, you stamped a star on the side of the basket. The next grade was the yellow paper, and that was the diamond, which were slightly smaller, but these were round, and yet the blue was the very smallest, but round again. Then you had the roughs. They were misshapen and lined with white paper. And domestics which might have marks on them, that sort of thing. (Moffat, Interview)

This was a grading system which allowed full variability in the standard of the product, on the assumption that anything could find its price on the wholesale market. Whatever quality standard, it could be sold. Conversely for retailers, widely dispersed and serving very localised markets, there was no overall market imperative at the retail end to ensure uniform quality across independent outlets. Secondly, the tomato variety itself had to be able to withstand a distribution system in which the product was handled many times, in variable conditions, and over a long period from vine to retail display. Whatever its flavour, it had to be a variety that was durable. So tomatoes were bred for durability, to 'survive' the wholesale supply system. Again to pick up the Guernsey story:

> The Potentate was the main variety of tomato. They were big and rough producing tomatoes. They were a variety that would be able to sit on your shelf for a couple of weeks. (le Garff, Interview)

THE SUPERMARKET DISTRIBUTION CONFIGURATION

From the late 1960s, key tomato growers, such as the Van Heiningen Brothers or Alan Parker of Wight Salads, made strategic decisions to supply supermarkets directly, partly out of dissatisfaction with the way wholesale markets undervalued quality. For their part, supermarkets operated under an entirely different imperative from small independent greengrocers. They needed to establish uniformity of quality for any one variety of tomato across the entire network of their retail outlets. They established and specified to great detail both varieties of tomato, cultivation techniques, grading and packaging. Growers in Guernsey who resisted or failed to adapt to the new role of retailers in supply chain management, fell by the wayside.

As a consequence the wholesale configuration just described was swept away within a couple of decades, and supermarkets who now account for over 80 per cent of the fresh tomato retail market, source over 90 per cent of their produce directly. Wholesale markets have switched much of their business to an expanding catering section responding to the increase in consumers eating out, for which there are still a multitude of dispersed small independent outlets (Allen, 1998 and Interview; Shaw et al., 1994; Atkinson, Interview).[13] However, Trust House Forte and other hotel and restaurant chains are already beginning to use their concentrated buyer power also to bypass the wholesale route. Insofar as Covent Garden and Manchester Smithfield continue to supply small greengrocers, apart from a few in extremely select areas, the tomatoes are the supermarket rejects, grown by those 'contingent' tomato growers who have not made it into the network of direct suppliers (Chapter 5).

By sweeping away a major price-making market, and a whole intermediary stage from grower to retailer, the new configuration also swept away a whole distribution system. It is one thing to get rid of an intermediary market. It is quite another developing a distribution system for making sure that tomatoes, with new standards of freshness, packaging and quality, find their way into every supermarket outlet in the country. One of the key changes was the emergence in the mid-1980s of centralised buying for supermarkets (Wrigley and Lowe; Foord et al., 1996, and Woolven, Coombs, Bailey, Interviews). Individual stores in a multiple chain no longer bought independently. Rapidly, a network of Combined Distribution Centres, or Regional Distribution Centres developed across the country, so that instead of the London-dominated wholesale markets, each supermarket chain developed their own network. The RDCs are strategically located in relation to motorways and, in particular, junctions between motorways, instead of the London-dominated rail network.

Table 9.1 indicates the basic bones of the new configuration. This table for 1997 shows that between the major multiples there were 97 Regional Distribution Centres, of which 39 were directly owned and controlled by the supermarket, whilst the majority, 48, were outsourced to logistics companies. Compared with the network of wholesale markets, these RDCs represent in one respect a far more decentralised network system of distribution points than the previous wholesale markets. Yet in another, each retailer network is centrally controlled by the dozen major retailing multiples. None had less than 88 per cent of their distribution under the absolute and central control of their multiple's headquarters. Given that Tesco, Sainsbury, Asda and Safeway account for over 50 per cent of the total market, the control of the majority of produce has been concentrated in the hands of just four players, compared with the 150,000 of the previous configuration. The contrast could scarcely be more extreme.

	Number of stores	Number of RDCs	Inhouse RDCs	Outsourced RDCs	% central distribution
Tesco	568	20	11	9	97%
Sainsbury	385	18	5	13	95%
Somerfield	600	16	8	8	90%
Safeway	483	13	4	9	95%
Co-operative	494	12	4	8	95%
Asda	209	11	4	7	88%
Iceland	751	7	3	4	100%

Table 9.1 Regional Distribution Centres, 1997
Source: adapted from Distribution Review, 1997, Institute of Grocery Distribution.

However, just as with own-label food manufacturers in the last chapter, companies involved in supermarket logistics are major players in their own right. One of the largest, Exel, is a global operator, with its main operations in the UK but extending its logistical capacity across Europe (Bence, 1997; Fernie and Penman, 1994). With an annual turnover of £2.5 billion in 1999, employing 38,588 people, it is certainly a major player. Likewise Wincanton, part of the Unigate Group with a turnover of over £3 billion in 1999, had 52 warehouses nationwide, 15,000 employees and handled £25 billion goods annually. ADL is also a global operator, a US transnational corporation.

Moreover, there is a very similar type of matrix to the one already discussed in relation to own-label food manufacturers. Although each RDC is a dedicated warehouse for a given supermarket chain, many of the same logistics companies have all of the main supermarket chains as clients, and conversely, many of the supermarket chains have many of the main logistics companies as their distributors. So, in spite of the critical role that logistics plays in the competitivity of the supermarkets, they may be co-developing their logistics network with the same companies used by their competitors. Wincanton runs Asda's Washington (Tyne and Wear) RDC opened in 1993, a massive warehousing system covering 120,000 square feet; but Wincanton is providing similarly innovative logistic solutions with Tesco and Safeway, for example. Table 9.2 for 1997 shows some of the complex matrix between supermarkets and logistics companies.[14]

	Tesco	Sainsbury	Safeway	Somerfield	Asda	Co-operative
Exel	2	3	2	1		
Wincanton	Yes	2	Yes	4	1	4
ADL	3	1			2	2
Christian Salvesen	Yes	3	1	Yes	1	
TDG Harris			Yes	4		

Table 9.2 Supermarkets and logistics companies
Source: adapted from *Distribution Review*, and interviews. Institute of Grocery Distribution (1997b)

Thus, from the available information, Wincanton had RDCs with each of the six major retailers figured in the table, and conversely both Tesco and Sainsbury had RDCs outsourced to each of four main logistics companies, as well as their own in-house operations. So again the concentration in control and ownership in the logistics of produce supply stands in sharp contrast to the wholesale markets, seen as centres of distribution, especially if compared to the number of traders in those markets, relatively small independent operators, numbering a couple of thousand overall.

THE LOGISTICAL REVOLUTION

To the shopper going into a small independent greengrocer or a large supermarket superstore, the visible side of the revolution in retailing is quite evident. But the invisible side, the transformation of the distribution system and the creation of national logistical networks for each of the major multiples, is equally remarkable. Not only have new ways of getting tomatoes to consumers changed beyond recognition, creating the 'integrated supply chain', but new workforces, hidden from sight, yet nonetheless crucial to the whole operation, work to the accelerated rhythms and schedules regulating the flow of produce, fresh, ambient and non-perishable. New technologies and organisations have been the subject of intensive and continuing innovation. Entering this hidden world of the new retailing, the new routes sprouted by new tomatoes become apparent.

Alan Parker's tomatoes first encountered on the Isle of Wight (Chapter 5) reappeared in transit at a loading bay in a Safeway Regional Distribution Centre in Bristol which serves 57 supermarket stores in the South-West.

S.B.[15] They've all been scanned and labelled. They're ready to be picked now.

Q. Do you hold them here at all?
S.B. No. They come in today, and go out tonight, fresh each day. (Bailey, Interview)

This short interchange exemplifies the revolution in logistics. Within *one* or at most two days tomatoes get from grower to a retailer's outlets *everywhere* in the UK. What applies to one product line does so to every other fresh or chilled product line, several thousand different items for every supermarket store in the country. But there is more to it than that. This process is going on 24 hours of every day of the year. The overriding feature of the system is 'constant flow'. The engineering of the speed and regulation of this flow is what constitutes 'logistics':

> That's the logistics, the logistics is the arranging and organising all these different commodities to be in at a certain place, to be picked at a certain time, and to be delivered at a certain time. (Green, Interview)

People who work to constant flow have to adjust to constant flow, and they talk about traditional times when there were 'days' and 'nights', and activity followed a different temporal scansion:

> Now, it is just constant, round the clock. (Beynon, Interview)

There is constant flow, 24 hours a day, 365 days a year, a flow of products matched by a flow of human labour. It makes a forceful first impression. But the underlying logistics is strictly awesome. This new configuration can be looked at in three aspects: centralisation and organisation of flows; temporalities of products and labour; network capacity and out-sourcing to dedicated logistics companies. Moreover, the systems have undergone, and are undergoing, constant change and innovation on a major scale over the past two decades.

Centralisation and organisation of the RDC networks

In the new retail-orchestrated configuration, HQ-centralised internet control both for transactions and information integrates RDCs to a network of regional stores. Although these new logistical systems could not work without intra-business and business-to-business e-commerce,[16] *equally* the internet and software systems could not operate without the integrated control of the whole supply chain by retailers. The power of the retailers over the producers, distributors, transport and retail outlets and the integration of the distribution networks co-evolved with the software and internet systems which are necessary for that integration. The power and the technology go together. Thus, as Cooper et al. (1994) have argued, the UK supermarkets are unique both in having the degree of power over the markets and supply chains, and in establishing networks of specialised logistics operations to directly control the flow of products from suppliers to retail outlets. Where the power does not exist, whether in the USA or in continental Europe, integrated logistical systems do or did not exist either, and hence centralised internet command and control is absent too.

One of the key aspects of these systems is that they apply to the total flow of products. The distribution centres are 'combined' distribution centres, incorporating fresh, chilled, frozen and ambient-temperature goods. Clearly, as freshness is a qualitative part of the commodity being sold, the flow of fresh produce is the most time-critical. Nonetheless the imperative to increase stock flow and reduce inventories coincides with the production of 'freshness' through fast distribution, particularly as slow distribution increases wastage and loss of value in the overall value stream:

> Even a tin of beans and things like that, they don't hold several weeks stock. It's days – because obviously you get the money cashflow from that. The name of the game is that if you get it on 30-day terms from the supplier ... you could have had it in, sold it and got the money before you've even paid the supplier and you've got a positive cash flow. (Bailey, Interview)

The average superstore requires 20,000 to 50,000 product lines, of which 3000 to 6000 may be fresh or chill produce, to be constantly replenished. For the average-sized contemporary RDC that in turn means between 500,000 and 1 million cases to come in and go out every week, and between 1000 and 2000 lorry loads per day. All of this movement is controlled centrally, for each of the retailer's RDCs by centralised ordering and logistical planning. 'It's driven by the system' is the constant refrain of an operations manager in the Safeway RDC at Bristol.

The 'system', broadly speaking common to most retailers, with slight variations on software and planning systems, is a continuously repeated cycle Diagram 9.2

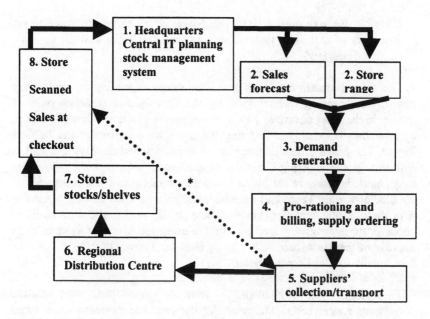

Note: *For discussion of this two-way arrow see p.217
Diagram 9.2 The integrated logistics system

In this 'system', headquarters receives directly all the information coming from every store in terms of sales of products from checkouts (1), as they are bar-scanned through. There are product category planners at headquarters that then generate sales forecasts, and plan the range of products sold for each of the stores (2). As will be seen, this can mean taking historic seasonal trends or exceptional events into account, in order to generate a model of overall demand. Once 'demand' is established by the model (3), orders for supplies (in our case, quantities of tomatoes of different varieties) are automatically transmitted to suppliers through Electronic Data Interchange (EDI), and transport is ordered for picking up the produce (5). The produce is then taken to the RDCs and from there distributed between each of the stores in its region (6) according to the pre-programmed central specification. Once in the stores, which have now ceased to warehouse or backroom their own stock beyond immediate requirements, the products go straight onto the shelves, and out through the checkouts (8), thence re-starting the cycle. This whole process is continuous:

> You can see the sort of cyclical type of thing it is. Let's take it from demand generation. From a store's demand, basically this all feeds back into it. Something from a cream cake to a sandwich which only has 2 days

life on it, we wait until 4.30 till we decide which stores are going to get quantities of that. The system captures that data right through the day. (Bailey, Interview)

The central system can, with few if any gaps depending on the current state of the scanning technologies, log the flow at each scanning point in transit. In the most advanced RDCs, for example, goods are first scanned in by laser bar-code readers. Ordering for stores by computer at the RDC is logged. The raised orders then appear on wrist-mounted displays attached to high-tech gloves showing quantities of each good to be picked. With index finger barcode scanners, the picker scans the goods out to await collection. At the time of writing Tesco and Sainsbury had either trialled or were operating with these £1000 scanning gloves. Once in the trucks, the movement of goods is subsequently tracked by satellite using the Mercator system, as in the case of the Rotherham RDC run by Exel for Tesco. Other RDCs use the functionally similar Logique system:

> Exel Logistics at Rotherham … have developed their own satellite tracking system called Mercator. All the trucks at Rotherham are fitted with it, and they have been for eighteen months. They had a new fleet of Renaults, and they use the satellite tracking. (Wigmore, Interview)

As a centralised network system, each organisational node in the chain can log in to their own particular phase of the flow: a store or RDC has no control over the range and quantity of products coming into the warehouse or store, but can log into the system to find out what produce in what quantities are to be expected at any time of the day. Thus, a manager in an RDC is involved only in the inward and outward flows of goods:

> We've got to access the system daily. You're looking at what's coming in. We do labour planning. We model, or track volume and trends, whether it's trending up in a period or whatever. (Bailey, Interview)

Whilst clearly there is little need for a given RDC or retail store to know anything beyond what is necessary for its own particular operations, the centre can access all of the system.

An integrated system of control such as this thus links the different economic agents together in a single network. In so doing it establishes new connections between eclipses and eclairs, tomatoes and heatwaves, soft drinks and school holidays, pizzas and World Cups. For the total eclipse of the sun in 1999, HQ modelled increased demand for éclairs in the South-West to follow the influx of people. The relevant RDC logged into its system to see the trend peaking for this period, and transport was arranged to hit a six-hour window from midnight to 6 am, to avoid traffic congestion for all produce trucks. At headquarters, a Category Demand Planner will be shadowing events:

> Sales forecasting is looking at the rolling average, over the year how things are doing, trending how products are trading, for every branch, product, for a period of four weeks, last week, this week, and two weeks forward. So it's doing models on how things are turning out ... The Category Demand Planner is the person who will manually tweek the system, to say, hang fire, we've got the World Cup. So we're going to sell more pizza and tinned beer, and more ready meals, curries, and things like that. Or, there's tremendous sunshine forecast this weekend, so I'm going to drive the BBQ lines in. (Bailey, Interview)

This whole process, quite impossible under the old configuration, is aimed to maximise the matching of supply and demand under an organisation which is

> dynamic to sale. That's the key to it. It's a case of putting it in when there's a sale there. That's the objective. (S. Bailey, Interview)

The integration of the successive phases from supplier to end consumer allows for almost instantaneous responses, with a mere 12-hour window to respond to trends as they emerge at the checkout to be transmitted back to purchase orders, resulting, where possible, in a switch of supplies. To facilitate this further, Safeway allows internet access to the system for some of its core suppliers so that they can monitor the sales of their own particular products at the electronic point of sale in the supermarket checkout (the dotted two-way arrow in Diagram 9.2):

> Basically they can see how their products are performing in our stores which is obviously commercially sensitive information. But what it does for the joint relationship between us as a retailer and them as a supplier is that they can predict what our order is going to be before we place the order. It's quite revolutionary really.' (Bailey, Interview)

This kind of feedback loop between supply and demand, as an aspect of the configuration, is used equally for demand creation, as when there is a promotional attempt to boost sales and volumes:

> Say they put tomatoes on 'buy-one-get-one-free'. Suppliers can look at that and see just how the promotion is going.... (Bailey, Interview)

Open access for suppliers to 'the system' enabling them to tap into sales of their produce at checkouts implies a very high trust level with the core suppliers, such as the tomato growers described earlier (Chapter 5). Growers become 'demand sensitive' in an entirely new fashion under this kind of trading relationship.

The objective of the system, so far depicted largely in terms of information flows, also relates to flows of goods, which in turn requires people to shift them. The IT innovation of the centralised network has involved also 'soft innovation' (Tether and Metcalfe, 2000), critical for accelerating the flow of goods. Tether et al. have shown that simply by altering the organisation of the flow of aircraft (by grouping small, medium, large) Heathrow's throughput was substantially enhanced. The flow of goods through RDCs bears some resemblances to air-traffic movements and in their case, too, changes in the physical organisation of the flow has resulted in major acceleration of the flow. Thus, pickers used to be assigned to 'pick by store', taking goods off racks where they had been stacked after being loaded in from the suppliers, each picker collecting all the product lines for the particular store. Now the system used is to take each line of produce (tomatoes, yoghurt, eclairs, pizzas) directly from the loading-in area to each store's loading-out area, pickers thus being assigned to 'pick by line', some picking only tomatoes, others yoghurt, and so on:

> With line pick, it comes in, it's scanned, the product's labelled up, it goes round the line into marshalling areas where a picker picks it. Then from midnight to night it starts a loading operation, taking the product out. So you are actually gaining a day's life on the product by line-picking it. In terms of minimising distress and wastage in stores, the gain is massive. (Bailey, Interview)

Tesco were the first to introduce the system (Fernie and Penman 1994 and Pointer,[17] Wigmore, Interviews), which is now widely used in many of the other RDC networks, once the IT systems were developed to accommodate the new physical flow systems.

An RDC operations manager plugs into 'the system' to find out the volume of product coming through the store. Labour and the organisation of the labour process then has to be engaged to maintain the continuous flow of goods in, goods out. This imposes a number of constraints and demands, which, depending on the strength of previously established patterns, and on power relations between management and unions, result in different organisation of the labour process, in terms of flexibility in division of labour, flexibility in the use of core and peripheral labour, and flexibility in the temporalities of working.

In order to match flow of labour with flow of products, the optimal solution has been to abolish pre-existing divisions of labour. For Sainsbury's newest RDCs 'a warehouseman is a warehouseman is a warehouseman' (Pointer, Interview). Likewise at Safeway's Droitwich RDC, run by Exel, there is just one category of warehouse operative on the warehouse floor. At Safeway Bristol, an in-house operation, there are six different categories, each distinct pool of labour restricting management's ability to shift labour to match product flow: cleaners, checkers-in, pickers (out), marshallers, fork-lift drivers and loaders. Moreover, recruitment to each of these is by seniority, with fork-lift drivers being the most preferred, followed by checkers.

Generally speaking, internal flexibility of the workforce is deployed as a means of matching flows more than using temporary or casual agency workers, mainly because of the requirements for combined accuracy and speed of picking.[18] However, at the more 'flexible' workplaces, use of temporary contract workers generally on repeat contracts, and agency casual workers, also often the same frequently called-on casuals, is the normal way of dealing with the marginal extra fluctuations in product-flow. Adrian Wigmore, Convenor Steward for Sainsbury's Exel RDC at Yate, near Bristol described this operation:

> Your core labour covers your core volume. But it's never that. It's always up and down ... If the average core volume is 780,000 pieces [cases] a week, we would man up to that level. That would be 360 warehousemen, 100 drivers, 6 shunters. And you end up with your core figure. We very, very rarely run at that core figure. If we are 780,000 we're usually running at 840,000. So there are an extra 60,000 pieces that have to be manned by casual labour. So they take on temporary staff for most of it, and then the last bit of the overflow is done by agency.' (Wigmore, Interview)

Temporalities of labour and product flow

Absolutely central to maintaining the continuous flow, 24 hours a day, 365 days a week, is the social organisation of time, the temporalities of labour matching the temporalities of product flow. In the last chapter, the new temporalities of product life, of reactivity to fashion and to rapid fluctuations in production were analysed. Here, in this sphere of the overall supermarket operation, there are also distinctive organisations of time and, as with the varied flexibility of divisions of labour, depending on circumstance there are also varied flexibilities of temporality to meet the imperatives of continuous flows of products.

Here again, the analogy with air-traffic movements is striking in terms of both language and logistics. The terms used are those of 'time windows' or 'slots':

> Every vehicle has got a slot to hit. Say I order you tomatoes, and I want it there at that slot in the morning. That's the time you have got to get it there for me. (Painter, Interview)

> Say half past eight would be the target time, and the window would be from quarter past eight till a quarter to nine. If you get there earlier than quarter past eight, the depot are fined, and if you get there later than quarter to nine, the depot get fined. (Wigmore, Interview)

The key time, which dictates all the time upstream, is the window or slot at the supermarket store: it is front-end driven. Penalty systems are motivated by store-shelf availability and by the 'dynamic to sale' principle. As everything that comes in to the store goes straight out onto display, timing is of the essence. Again, from the point of view of earlier distribution systems, this is quite revolutionary. In the old serially organised wholesale market configuration, at each stage product arrived only when it arrived, then waited to go on to the next stage: the timing of frequently interrupted flow was determined by the previous phase.

To match this new temporality of distribution, the most 'adapted' of labour temporalities are the variable-shift, annualised hours system worked, for example, at the Safeway Droitwich RDC or at Sainsbury's Exel RDC in Yate.[19] The variable-shift system replaces the old temporalities of the standard working day and overtime: the notion of overtime and premium rates associated with it is seen as a relic of earlier rhythms of working. The new temporal order is one of 'flexing up' and 'flexing down' to match the flow of products:

> They've got a flexing agreement. You can either be flexed up two hours, or flexed down two hours. If I'm working an eight-hour shift, and we need to get the work out, you can flex up two hours and cover that work. (Painter, Interview)

The variations in working time can be quite extreme between one day and the next, matching the peaks of product flow over the 24-hour period, with variability for each of the three 8-hour shifts:

> We do a minimum 6 and a half hour day, and a maximum 12 and a half. And it's all based on nine and a half hours.' (Wigmore, Interview)

Changes in working time, moreover, are unpredictable and immediate. At Safeway Droitwich RDC, for example

'If it's a day when they've got problems, they can go to their staff and say, well, you've got to stop for another hour. And that doesn't cost them overtime.' *Simon Bailey*

These systems of flexing up and flexing down are sustained by 'annualised hours' contracts, where hours are 'banked' in periods where hours are extended, to match times when hours are shorter, so giving an average working time over the whole year of a 40-hour week. As a continuous flow system, it does not recognise weekends, bank holidays, or Christmas Day, all time being treated the same. De-recognition of these 'special' days is reinforced by the absence of premium rates or rights to alternative and additional leave. Annualisation thus enshrines the new temporal order, in which every day of the year is subject to possible variation, when all that is left of the normal working week, important nevertheless, is the annual average working week.

One event at one RDC reflects the temporal imperative of the new order, where everything must keep on flowing to fill those supermarket shelves.

Perpetuum mobile

A shunter had been moving a lorry, trying to bring together his trailers. He was under time pressure, and to save a few seconds had not put the hand-brake on. Many other drivers also saved a few seconds by similarly leaving their hand-brakes off, without consequence. But on this occasion, the vehicle shot forward, gained momentum. The shunter tried to jump into the cab, but failed. He was crushed to death.

The area around the accident was cordoned off. The rest of the workforce was expected to carry on working normally, and did so. In many other work-places, building sites or docks for example, it is usual for some notice to be taken of a fatality. People stop work out of respect. But here the implacable logic of continuous flow, the absolute requirement to keep the supermarket shelves full, could not be relaxed.

The following morning, the widow came to the depot to see the manager. She walked past the scene of the accident. Nobody had had time, made time, to clear away the glass, clean the spilt blood. Such was the normality of their perpetual motion.

As part of the temporal regime of an RDC, there is continual monitoring of the time it takes people to shift cases of tomatoes, pizzas, yoghurts, cornflakes. This is linked to productivity payments. In the Safeway Bristol RDC, they operate a Taylorist system called MTMX (Motion, Travel, Movement, times variable distance, 'X'), developed from a video of how long it takes to label, pick, turn, travel, deposit a case from one place to another:

> It's all broken down into an elemental level. The co-ordinates of each pick point are measured. So it [the scanner] knows how far you are travelling to each assignment. A picker will go along and pick up a set of labels on a pallet, and he'll know that he's got 11 and a half minutes to do that product, do that pallet. (Bailey, Interview)

In other RDCs, where there is flexibility and a generic workforce, a simpler system of monitoring the throughput of cases per hour is used. But here too, it is a question of the checker checked. Every time a scanner scans, the person who scans is also scanned:

> Each picker's got an ID number. They're keyed into the system. (Bailey, Interview)

Network capacity and outsourcing to logistics companies

However, this principle of 'checkers-checked' occurs at every level of an RDC network, enabling headquarters to monitor performance continuously. The significance of this leads directly to a consideration of the final aspect of the new logistics configuration, network capacity and the strange matrix of retailers and logistics companies presented in Table 9.2. Performance of each RDC is measured for fresh produce, chilled, ambient and non-perishable, with each operation manager being presented with information on how other RDCs are performing within their area:

> They're constantly monitoring how we're performing. They're constantly doing all the stats, working out the running cost of the depot. What are we producing? What is our productivity? (Bailey, Interview)

This leads to a form of orchestrated competition between different RDCs, between the in-house RDCs and the contracted-out RDCs, and between different contracted-out RDCs. Thus, for example, if an RDC is performing well in terms of cases per hour for fresh produce – the speed it gets tomatoes to the supermarket – it will be 'rewarded' by being given more produce to handle:

> Sainsbury is saying to Wincanton and Exel, we want you to achieve these targets, and if you don't achieve them we'll penalise you, give you penalties, or even threaten you with losing the contract or renewing the contract. (Green, Interview)

But in talking of 'orchestrated competition', the key point is that the retailers are seeking to maximise the efficiency of the entire network, and not, or at least not necessarily, to replace one competitor with another. They are creating a kind of internal quasi-market within the network. So, for example, Safeway will play one RDC off against another *but at the same time* will bring together all their RDC operations managers from each of the different companies to share best practice. Putative competitors are 'constrained to co-operate' in order to spread new technologies and new methods of organising continuous flow across the whole network. It makes no sense to the retailer for one RDC to achieve sustained competitive advantage over another, for example, by having exclusivity over picking by line with its attendant information systems. Thus the role of the supermarkets in relation to their third-party logistics operators involves a high level of direction, much as with the growers or own-label producer. Often the third-party companies operate on an 'open book' basis of accounting:

> The way Safeways look at it is, come on we'll work together on this. We'll treat it as an open book, we'll pay you a management fee, providing you hit the performance targets. But the book is open for everyone to see, so we'll know how much you're paying the staff. The input from Safeway from the central logistics team into how they run their distribution centres is massive. They're virtually run by us. (Bailey, Interview)

The 'virtually' here could be seen to refer not only to the fact that the whole network is under the central control of the IT system run by headquarters, which integrates different third-party logistics companies and in-house operations together. It also involves the rules, targets, prescriptions on organisation and best practice laid down by the supermarket. As with the own-label manufacturers, rather than view this as 'quasi-vertical integration', it should be seen as a distinct form of inter-firm coordination in its own right, especially as the configuration involves the cross-cutting matrix of both major retailers and major logistics companies.

Consequently, although there may be benefits from orchestrated competition and cooperation between the different in-house and third-party logistic operations, there remains an unanswered question as to why major retailers are engaged with several of the same major logistics companies in the way that they are. It is clear that there is also a strategic logic related to the critical nature of the continuous flow, and the need to create a flexible network capacity. In the past, over the last decade, Safeway had a strategy of obtaining that flexibility through breaking down traditional working patterns, as well as breaking down union power. There used to be a national agreement, the Provincial Council Agreement, covering all their Distribution Centres. Systematically this has been dismantled, by cutting off the flow of produce going through an RDC, mothballing it for a period, and then reopening it using a third-party logistics company.[20]

This negative process of dismantling traditional operations in order to obtain internal flexibility within the RDCs, however, also has led to a series of rationalisations of the network itself as an overall system, in order to develop a capacity to switch routes rapidly, bypassing any given RDC should the temporary need arise, whilst maintaining the overall requirement to keep all stores supplied:

> If you look at the sort of mix of party operators we have, you've got quite a suite of them as well. You've got Salvesen, TDG Harris, Wincanton, Exel. It's all monitored. Obviously in case one of them came into difficulties, you don't put all your eggs in one basket. You can through the networking and the links in the suppliers. We can move product.
>
> If you had a fire in the depot or something went horribly wrong with industrial relations and they were all at the gate on strike, obviously it's going to impact on you immediately. But very quickly you could react to it. The network can very quickly pick that up, within 24 hours you could be back on track. (Bailey, Interview)

One of the aspects of a highly time-constrained, continuous flow system such as are controlled by UK supermarkets is that they are also potentially vulnerable to disruption, as is evident from the effects of air-traffic control disputes or software breakdowns in the analogous logistical system of air-traffic movements. By creating sufficient network capacity, distributed between different operators, and combining both in-house expertise and knowledge with a suite of out-sourced third-party operators, the overall logistical strategy minimises risks of similar disruption in supermarket supplies.[21] These two aspects together, orchestrated competition and cooperation (under constraint) to increase performance and efficiency, and diversified ownership and control to minimise risk, lead to a powerful and flexible network logistical operation.

CONCLUSION

The past two to three decades has seen a remarkable transformation in the routes the tomato has taken to get to the consumer, and of course, major changes of this order involved the whole range of fresh, chilled and other products, some of which have been discussed earlier. Nonetheless, these new routes have forged links between consumer, retailer and supplier where none existed before. Under the old wholesale–small independent greengrocer configuration, the links were broken at several stages. In the new configuration, it has become possible for a tomato grower to log into the internet and find out how their promotion of cherry tomatoes on the vine are doing at the store check-out in the latest promotion. In earlier chapters, it was shown how supermarkets laid down production protocols, enabled investment in new production technologies, and stimulated the production of new varieties and new seasonalities. In this chapter, it can be seen how a new distribution configuration is essential to those retailer–producer relations. They enable the construction of a new concept of quality, and changed the parameters of freshness with their capacity to distribute from anywhere to anywhere in the country in a 24-hour period. Entirely new hidden workforces, numbering hundreds of thousands, and occupying key strategic positions, work to the new temporalities of a continuous flow of product from first supplier to end consumer. Retail, distribution, production, and consumption hang together, and the processes of reconfiguration involve all aspects of that quartet.

The economic institutions of wholesale markets were linked to different kinds of production regimes, with different imperatives and different tomatoes, or tomato products. There is a continuing process of de-institutionalisation and re-institutionalisation, with the current networks of RDCs, supermarket stores and tomato growers setting down routes to market. Old pricing mechanisms, old modes of competition, are supplanted by new ones. Open book accounting down a supply and distribution chain leads to new modes of price formation and new conflicts over who captures the added values along the route. Distinctive inter-firm relationships of constraint and cooperation are developed, and these in turn are structured in distinctive ways, as in the matrix of logistical companies and retailers or in the matrix of own-label manufacturers and retailers. These two matrices each rest on different and distinctive emergent structural imperatives, the former closely related to the logics of continuous flow and risk minimisation, the latter to the production of variety, market segmentation and novelty.

NOTES

[1] It is interesting that even in contemporary management literature, logistics is seen in terms of a cost reduction and waste elimination process, as if, in classical political economy, transformations of location are costs on production unlike transformations of matter. Thus McLaughlin et al. (1998) suggested that $30 billion of 'waste' could be eliminated by efficient logistics in US grocery distribution.

[2] There are of course certain commodities that require consumers to move to them rather than the other way round, and others that can be 'consumed at a distance'.

[3] This is not strictly accurate in that until recently sellers normally have not bought produce in order to sell, but sell on a commission basis. This is highly significant, for reasons to be spelt out below.

[4] In 1957, Runciman observed that produce in Scotland could go via London back to other parts of Scotland more easily than going directly. The Strathclyde Report (Shaw et al., 1994, Pt II, Table 2.3) demonstrates the continuing and disproportionate domination of London's three fruit and vegetable wholesale markets (New Covent Garden, New Spitalfields, Western International) even as wholesale markets faced decline, with 38 per cent of the whole of the UK wholesale fruit and vegetable trade passing through them.

[5] From Samuel Hartlib's *Legacy of Husbandry*, 1655, Webber noted that 'Tomatoes were available, but besides being large and ugly, were suspected of causing cancer as well as being aphrodisiacal' (Webber, 1969, 29).

[6] The Lea Valley attracted Huguenot migration bringing horticultural skills during this period, so laying the foundation for the glasshouses we encountered earlier (Chapter 5), and had developed a canal and river distribution network.

[7] The Fabian Society (1891) and Punch joined unlikely forces in calling for reform and relocation.

[8] 'Provincial wholesalers know that they cannot for long keep prices out of line with those ruling at Covent Garden, allowance being made for costs of transportation.' (Runciman Committee, 1957, 41).

[9] Some big traders, such as C&C at New Covent Garden or J.B. Brown at Manchester Smithfield, now purchase some of their produce directly from the growers, to sell on as a higher risk but higher profit opportunity trading mode.

[10] Colin Allen, the ex-General Manager of New Covent Garden, speculates that commission trading had its origin in times when growers were very local to wholesale markets and would bring their produce to a trader daily for sale (Allen, Interview).

[11] 'They really glorify on this salesmanship. It's largely price salesmanship. It is not salesmanship on the basis of selling in a constructive way' (Allen, Interview).

[12] 'Whatever the grower had to do would be the absolute minimum ... He would just grow the tomatoes, and pack them, and send them ... It would all   be under his name and number and he would be paid. We would pay his   carriage, and would pay his box maker, and give him what was left, which was everything' (le Garff, Interview).

[13] 'From the point of view of the future life of wholesale markets, providing largely the catering trade, the great advantage is that although there are these massive chain restaurants like Harvester, nevertheless there is a terrific demand for new restaurants. So it seems to me, there will always be a lot of small individual restaurants' (Allen, Interview).

[14] The information for the table is incomplete and therefore illustrative, and understates the degree of matrix connections, as Wincanton has by 2000 added Tesco, Safeway and Somerfield to its clients, for example, and Christian Salvesen also supplies Tesco and Somerfield, including Tesco's new internet home delivery.

[15] Simon Bailey is Operations Manager for chilled foods at this RDC.

[16] 'Because you've got to do it down to product detail level, it's just too much than any human could ever do. It's got to be done by a system' (Bailey, Interview).

[17] 'The perishable will come in at one side of the depot. They will pick by line, straight out the other door, because there's a lorry waiting over this side to take it. It's a Just In Time system. That's what they want.'

[18] 'If one of our blokes pick 1000 pieces a night, an agency bloke might pick 400.'(Wigmore, Interview). As for 'picking accuracy. If you are only in for a night, you only dedicated for a night. So they [agency casuals] are not dedicated at all' (Painter, Interview).

[19] The in-house Safeway RDC in Bristol still operates on a standard time and overtime basis, and also recognises and pays premiums for weekends, bank holidays and Christmas. But it is seen by management as archaic. 'It's crazy that we are still paying allowances for weekend working and that sort of thing. Bank Holidays cost the depot a fortune ... Running an industry on that basis is crazy in this day and age. I'm sure it will change in time' (Bailey, Interview).

[20] Wakefield, Welwyn Garden City, Aylsford and Warrington RDCs are examples of this strategy.

[21] The fuel blockade in August 2000 demonstrated total vulnerability only when *all* RDCs were affected simultaneously, taking big capital (supermarkets and petrol distributors) as much as the government by surprise.

10. Supermarket Tomato

Whether in creating new ecosystems in glasshouses, stimulating new plant varieties, sourcing from all over the globe, adopting and then abandoning genetic modification, defining nature, setting pizza fashions, or reaching new peaks of freshness through IT-controlled distribution systems, the influence of UK supermarkets has been pervasive throughout the current configuration of production and distribution. In a sense, the story of the tomato culminates on the supermarket shelf, through to the check-out, and from shopping basket to kitchen table. Nonetheless, the transformations in production and distribution have been achieved within those areas: seed manufacturers alone can produce new seed varieties, beneficial pest or bumble-bee producers, not supermarkets, innovate and develop complex programmes of reproduction and techniques to make these insects work most efficiently. Growers affirm that supermarkets never invented anything – other than the systems for selling. Even within logistics, which has been more integrated within supermarkets' own operations, many of the technologies on which the new systems rely, such as temperature controls and sensing, satellite tracking, moveable bulkheads, laser scanners and bar-coding, stock-control software, involve a complex matrix of producers and a distributed process of innovation.

Thus rather than seeing supermarkets as creators of new 'demand' to which producers and logistics companies respond or, conversely, reducing supermarkets to the role of mere outlets for the 'supply' of new products, major changes can be seen as reconfigurations of the *relations* between supply and demand. Changes within each of the parts of the configuration affect relations with the other parts. These relations have the characteristic of asymmetries of power and mutual dependency. Manufacturers depend on retailers, but under changing power relations; likewise retailers and consumers. In turn, there is a distinction between 'powers to do' and 'powers to control'. Control cannot impose a 'power to do', and a 'power to do' does not necessarily accrue control. What retail organisations can do, how they organise their specific economic activity, has fundamentally changed. Partly through increasing concentration, their power to control has undoubtedly both been enhanced and extended. But also, perhaps more significantly, new forms of exercising control and new *qualities* of economic power have been developed. This chapter therefore finally examines this facet of the configurational transformation, and the change in relations of asymmetric power and mutual dependency between retailers and consumers. It is not a study of tomato consumption as such,[1] therefore, but of tomato consumption as mediated by changing relations between consumers and retailers.

Firstly, major structural changes in the configuration of UK retailing over the course of the twentieth century will be explored, an account of 'two revolutions'. This provides the broad contextual background for a detailed exploration of local tomato retailing geographies in Manchester, as exemplifying the contemporary relations between retailers and consumers. Finally, the new product vehicles for tomato consumption, especially ready-made and convenience foods, will be explored for their significance in the current configuration.

CHANGES IN RETAILER–CONSUMER CONFIGURATION IN THE TWENTIETH CENTURY

Much of the story of the twentieth century has been written in terms of major industrial change, the rise of mass production and, it is argued, its surpassal by 'post-Fordism'. Our account of food production and manufacture sits uncomfortably with the established narratives, and one of the key missing elements has been the successive revolutions in retailing. Figure 10.1 below provides a dramatic picture. It presents a simple tale of the rise of the supermarket and the demise of the independent grocery shops over the course of a century.

However, this picture is seriously misleading in two major respects, the historical status of the small independent shop and the continuity of the march of progress of the supermarkets. It suggests that independent shops were the dominant and universal form established by a nation of shopkeepers from a long-distant past. In particular, the high street greengrocer, as an outlet for the tomato or any other fruit and vegetable, does *not* have a history trailing back into the nineteenth century and beyond. It was as much a novelty as the emergence of multiple retail chains. Greengrocery shops began to replace traditional retail street markets and fairs only towards the end of the nineteenth century, well after the development of distinctive wholesale markets.

As Davis (1965) remarks of the turn of the century:

Fruit and vegetables – especially potatoes – were all getting more popular, yet even in London they had made little headway into fixed shops, while elsewhere greengrocers' shops were practically unknown (ibid., 253).

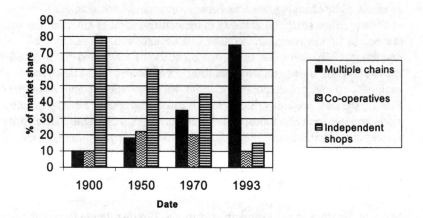

Figure 10.1. The historic rise of supermarket chains, 1900– 93
Source: Adapted from Woolven, et al. 1996

Thus, the growth of fixed shops for these goods was as much a late nineteenth- and twentieth-century phenomenon as the growth of multiple retail chains. Nineteenth-century fixed shops had largely been responding to middle- and upper-class demand, whilst markets and itinerant traders serviced urban and rural working classes (Jefferys, 1954, 3–4). Thus, according to Inland Revenue figures, the number of fixed shops nearly doubled from 1869 to 1911, from 177,000 to 310,000. The decisive changes took place in the last quarter of the nineteenth century, resulting from a combination of increasing levels of urbanisation, integration of distribution through rail transport, and a new and concentrated wage-dependent economy with increasing levels of real income.

The period 1875–1914 witnessed a transformation of the distributive trades comparable in many ways to the revolutionary changes that had taken place in the industrial structure of the country in the previous century' (Jefferys, 1954, 6)

This therefore points to the second illusion presented by Figure 10.1. There have really been two quite different revolutionary changes in configuration masked by the one graph in growth of multiple retail chains. Broadly speaking, the first took place beginning in the 1870s, whilst the second occurred roughly a century later. The first responded to a quite distinctive and novel 'social organisation of demand', which developed earlier and more radically than any other contemporary political economy, resulting in a quite distinctive 'instituted' basis of UK retailing in the inter-war period. This was to constitute an essential historical precondition for the subsequent distinctiveness of UK supermarkets today.

THE FIRST UK RETAILING REVOLUTION

The Co-operative Societies led the way in the first retail revolution, pioneering both new mass-production techniques in their Wholesale Societies but also new retailing operations. Each outlet was a separate Society for its co-operative staff and shopping members. Dedicated to providing low-cost, no credit, cash-only shopping to the working class, the Co-operative Societies had dramatic growth in co-operative members and turnover, as Table 10.1 illustrates, whilst the number of branches grew from 400 in 1862 to 1455 in 1903.

	1863	1881	1901	1914
Members	100,000	547,000	1,707,000	3,053,000
Turnover*	£2.5 m	£15 m	£50 m	£88 m

* At constant prices

Table 10.1 The early growth of the Co-operative Society
Source: Jefferys, 1954, 7, 17)

The Co-operative Society movement, however, was part of a much wider revolution in retailing. The growth of multiple chains in general was quite spectacular, at first many of the firms emerging in relation to colonial trade in tea as many of their names suggest,[2] and furnishing the working classes with the drink that had become associated with urban proletarianisation (Mintz, 1986). The number of branches of firms having more than ten outlets grew from 4671 in 1890 to 19,852 in 1910, 35,894 in 1920, and 44,487 in 1939. But during this same period, there was also a growth in the really big chains, with 500 or more outlets, some resulting from expansion but many from mergers and acquisitions.[3] The significance of this process of concentration is that it signalled a growth of a nationally integrated retail market, long before any other country in the world. Figure 10.2 demonstrates this process, with the conspicuous decline of the local chains with under 50 branches, and the equally notable increase in share of total number of branches for the multiples with extended networks embracing 500 branches or more.

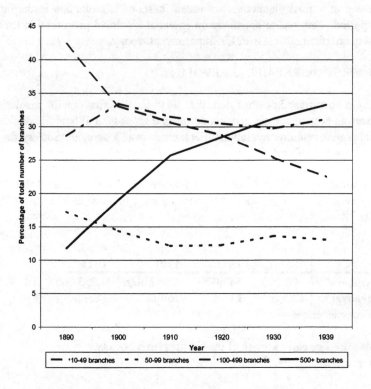

Figure 10.2. The growth of nationally integrated retail chains
Source: Adapted from Jefferys, 1954, Table 16, p .65.

By 1939, therefore, national or large regional-scale retail operators accounted for 70 per cent of all the branches of multiple outlets, providing the essential platform for the second revolution in retailing that occurred post-war. Marketing Boards for milk, potatoes and bacon, the nationalisation and hence integration of electricity supply under the Central Electricity Generating Board, all contributed to the formation of a national consumer market during the inter-war years to an extent largely unparalleled in other economies. It is significant, therefore, that even in 1960 the concentration of market share by the major retailers in the UK was more than three times higher than that of any other European country, and nearly double that of Switzerland (11 per cent) and the Netherlands (8 per cent), (Jefferys and Knee, 1962, Table 13, 65).

This first revolution involved the creation of multiple chains of retailers concentrating on selling a small range of goods at economy prices. That was the distinctive mark of this phenomenon. Thus, at the end of the First World War, 40 per cent of these newly emergent multiple chains were specialist 'provision' retail outlets, where 75 per cent of their turnover was in six items or less. By 1939, only 25 per cent were specialist to this degree, and by 1950, a mere 10 per cent.

> The rising working-class demand ... in the second half of the nineteenth century, for both food and goods other than food was still limited to a fairly short list of essentials. The demand was characterised not by a desire for variety, for selection and for range of commodities but by an acceptance of standardisation and an emphasis on cheapness and reliability.... (Jefferys, 1954, 32–3)

The picture for retailing at this time, which contrasts with the subsequent revolution in retailing, is of an almost dual market. The multiples were dedicated to working-class consumption and demand, whilst small shops and department stores provided specialist and high-value wares, covering wide catchment areas requiring consumers' own transport or delivery. Broadly, there was a division both in type of outlet and in product range and value between urban working-class oriented multiple chains, and middle-class and higher-class retail outlets. Both advertising and shop display accentuated these differences. In terms of tomatoes, this central period was that of the standard fresh tomato delivered through the wholesale marketing system on the one hand, and the mass-produced processed tomato (cans, ketchup, soups) on the other.

THE SECOND RETAILING REVOLUTION

In describing the second retailing transformation as a revolution to match the first, it should be stressed that there were already changes occurring prior to the 'take-off', which laid the ground for the change. If the first revolution involved a distinctive 'social organisation of demand', so too did the second, with slum clearance and major urban restructuring, increased mobility and transport infrastructure, the expansion of car ownership, and changing occupational structures figuring amongst the many preconditions. Other more direct changes, such as the development of self-service, were major innovations which not only changed the respective role of shopper and retailer, but also involved standardisation of packaging, pricing and quality essential to the subsequent technology of bar-scanning, loyalty cards and Electronic Point of Sale data. These changes were seen as quite novel and revolutionary in their own terms as late as the 1970s, and the new stores were still denoted 'self-service' (Institute of Grocery Distribution, 1977; Beaumont and Wilcock, 1979).

The most visible aspect of the second revolution has been the emergence of the (out-of-town) superstore, retail outlets of more than 2300 square metres (see Figure 10.3). Tesco stores had increased their average size by nearly 2½ times between the early 1980s and the early 1990s, with new stores all being built over 4250 square metres (Wrigley, 1998). The Competition Commission (2000), in defining the UK food shopping market, settled on 1400 square metres as the minimum size for a store meeting the core shopping needs and behaviours of consumers. The growth of large stores was quite dramatic until the planning permission restrictions of the middle and late 1990s,[4] and has been seen by Wrigley as partly resulting from lax accounting regimes on sunk capital (Wrigley, in Wrigley and Lowe, 1994).

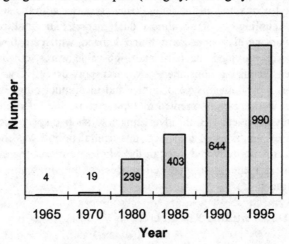

Figure 10.3. The growth of the food superstore in the UK: 1965–95
Source: Woolven et al, 1996

There are a number of features underlying this transformation of the nature of the retail outlet. Firstly, there has been a consolidation and concentration of market share so that by 1990 by the leading five supermarkets had 60 per cent of the market share for groceries. Between 1991 and 1996, the total food market grew from £63 billion to £82 billion, and within that total the share of the top three grew from 28.5 per cent to 35.2 per cent (Woolven et al., 1996).[5] Tesco, Sainsbury and Asda, by virtue of their leading position, effectively dominate the market, the key focus of interest being the competition between them over market share, especially since Tesco overtook Sainsbury as market leader in 1994–95, and has since consolidated its position by establishing 'clear blue water' from its rival (*Financial Times*, 1 June 2000). It is currently one of the largest employers in the UK with 163,401 employees.[6] With the acquisition of Asda by Wal-Mart, and the opening of the first superstore in Bristol under the Asda Wal-Mart banner (*Guardian*, 25 July 2000)[7] a further realignment is foreshadowed in the structure of UK supermarket retailing.

It was argued that in the 'first retail revolution', a distinctive, almost dual market was formed between the multiple chains with limited ranges of goods targeting a relatively homogeneous urban working class at low prices, and retail outlets, both small shops and department stores, with high-value specialist and quality goods for the middle and upper classes. In the second revolution, there are two intersecting aspects of change to the 'social organisation of demand' brought about by the dominance of the Big Three, and the rise of the superstore. The first aspect relates to the structuring of demand through different types of large retailer targeting *or shaping* different types of demand. The second and related aspect is the creation of the 'catchment area' and of the once-weekly one-stop shop, the effect produced by the scale of the superstore in shaping demand. These two aspects of the superstore retail economy are not at all the same, and indeed can conflict with each other. On the one hand, some retailers seek to respond to the full range of demand, adjusting the range to each particular location. By contrast, discounters aggregate demand nationally across all their stores irrespective of particularities of location. Finally 'top-niche' or 'bottom-slice' retailers locate in their socio-economically appropriate districts or urban centres. On the other hand, irrespective of which type of retailer, a superstore 'captures' the demand of the area in which they are located by scaling up the size of the store, and reducing the numbers of stores in any one area. Concomitantly, this supports a shopping style of less frequent visits and bulk shopping, which has become the norm for consumers' shopping behaviour.

Taking the first of these aspects, UK supermarkets can be grouped by distinguishing between 'full-range' (product and price), top-niche, bottom-tranche, and discounters, into which category Asda is now moving particularly following its takeover (Table 10.2). They were clearly distinguished both in store size (a ratio of 8:1 from biggest average to smallest) and in range of product lines on offer (a ratio of 15:1 from the biggest range to the smallest).

	Company	Number of stores	Average size sq.ft	Product range	% own label
Full range	Tesco[8]	568	23,600	34,820	48
	Sainsbury	385	21,300	21,300	56
	Safeway	483	22,700	20,000	33
Discount	Asda (Asda Wal-Mart)	209	40,400	38,000	41
Top niche	Waitrose (Marks & Spencer)[9]	115	15,514	13,000	50
Bottom tranche	Budgen	114	7,056	6,000	17
	Co-operative	494	5,799	8,000	14
	Iceland	751	4,818	2,500	50

Table 10.2. The stratification of demand by retailer type
Source: Woolven et al. (1996)

Historically, the UK has seen a very low level of penetration of the discount model of grocery retailing, such as that promoted by Wal-Mart, with Aldi, Netto; or Lidl making little impact (Sparks, 2000; Freathy and Sparks, 2000). The discounters only accounted collectively for 9 per cent of the market in 1997, compared with 27 per cent in Germany. The UK is distinctive in only having the one category of 'supermarket' whereas France and Germany distinguish between 'supermarkets' and 'hypermarkets'. In considering the structure of outlets, it is the *combination* of different types of outlets that characterise different national systems of retailing. In many ways, the top-niche, full-range, and bottom-tranche have lived in peaceful coexistence, not substantially contesting each other's distinctive markets. The emergence of a Wal-Mart-owned Asda, however, and the renewal of price wars (Wrigley, 1998), suggests an attempt of the discount model of retailing to present a more serious challenge to full-range retailing than heretofore. In the UK the dominant players, Tesco and Sainsbury, have exemplified and indeed jointly dominated the full-range type of outlet. Moreover, in recent developments, partly because of planning restrictions, partly because of the shrinking of available catchment locations, but also partly because of the possibilities of expansion provided by the platform of their distribution systems, Tesco, Sainsbury and Safeway are both looking to re-enter the central urban spaces with neighbourhood, convenience, 'Metro' or other variable formats. Again, these are complementary to, rather than substitutes for or competitors of, the superstore, and they aim to capture a different type of demand.

Turning to the 'scale effect' of the superstore, exemplified by the full-range supermarkets with their catchment areas, they present a very different social shaping of demand than the highstreet-based multiple chains that they superseded. The central principle of the catchment area versus the highstreet is, in Wrigley's words, that there is 'negligible catchment-area competition from rival stores of the same vintage' (Wingley, 1998, 122; Harvey 1999a; Competition Commission, 2000). The scale of the store and relative low geographical density of equivalent alternatives creates the infrastructure both for the catchment area embracing a particular socio-economically characterised population, *and* the habit of less-frequent shopping. The Competition Commission survey of 1999 exemplifies both these dimensions (Competition Commission, 2000). Seventy per cent of shoppers carried out a main shop on a weekly basis and a further 14 per cent even less frequently. Only 16 per cent shopped more frequently than once a week. Over 50 per cent used the same supermarket always and a further 26 per cent almost always. Only 5 per cent did not have a regular supermarket, and 1 per cent relied on local shops for their main food shopping. Although not an indication of the absence of alternatives, fully 85 per cent of shoppers had shopped in the same store for at least a year for all their main food shopping. This provides a strong indication of the power of the scale effect in transforming the relations between consumers and retailers, creating a store with a catchment population as a regular clientele. Without wishing to overstate the case, the consumer–retailer relation has monopsonistic parallels with the retailer–manufacturer (own-label), and retailer–logistics relationships of previous chapters.

However, within this framework there are distinct retailing strategies. Discounting retail outlets do operate in catchment areas, but with a competition strategy focused on quantity and price, rather than product and price differentiation. They can be said to focus on economies of scale across the aggregate demand of all their stores irrespective of location. In contrast, the 'full-range stores' undertake what they describe as 'health checks' of their location in order to obtain a socio-economic profile of their diverse catchment populations. In general terms, the United Kingdom has been characterised since the early 1980s as having one of the highest levels of income inequalities, and certainly the fastest growth of inequality, as measured by Gini coefficients amongst most–developed and many less–developed national economies (Rowntree, 1995; Goodman and Webb, 1994). The UK also has one of the highest levels of real disposable income as a percentage of total income (European Commission, 1995). This unique combination of high inequality and high levels of personal disposable income in the UK presented supermarkets with the opportunity to maximise product and price range, from economy low-price, value-for-money, lines, to distinctive marques, organic and speciality high-value-added products. Within the general, macro-economic features of demand, the superstores' 'health checks' allow them to adjust their product and price ranges of a given store to the particular socio-economic characteristics of each catchment area. They do so using a particular framework of consumer stratification, a way of coding the catchment population (see Table 10.3). The significant aspect of this stratification is that it is *consumer* rather than occupational stratification. It focuses on disposable incomes, which may vary during the life cycle, and on type of housing. It stresses the difference between the up-and-coming, high–income, but possibly high income-committed groups paying mortgages and with families, and the affluent greys, whose mortgage costs can be discounted along with family responsibilities. At the opposite end, it locates those with least income in public housing, in ethnic minority areas.

The 'health-checks' which map the particular demand configuration of a given catchment area are then, of course, supplemented by the check-out information derived from loyalty cards, and Electronic Point of Sale data. The kinds of adjustments to demand which have already been noted for the distribution system as necessary to predict the effects of World Cups or eclipses are also essential for tracing and anticipating demand from within the catchment area – in order to make sure that the appropriate range of pizzas or tomatoes is available. The essence of the 'one-stop' shop in its catchment area is to maximise its adjustments and reinforce the loyalty of its customers in order to exploit the catchment effect to the full, and prevent 'disloyalty'.

Tables 10.4 and 10.5 show the importance of loyalty, that is, the regularity and exclusiveness of the exchanges (monopsony) with one retail outlet sustained by the catchment area of consumers. Table 10.4 shows how many shoppers are loyal to the different types of stores described above, clearly demonstrating that the large full-range stores are those with the most monopsonistic exchange relations between store and consumer. By contrast, a top-of-the-range niche supermarket, or a bottom-tranche supermarket, proves much less of a 'one-stop' exclusive shop for a given customer. Table 10.5 shows just how important that loyalty is to the 'full-range' store's turnover, with 70 per cent of turnover being purchased by the 'loyal customers', and only 8 per cent by the outright 'disloyal' ones.

Class category	Stratifications	% Population 1997
Thriving	1. Wealthy achievers 2. Affluent greys 3. Prosperous pensioners	20.37
Expanding	4. Affluent executives, family 5. Well-off workers, family	10.89
Rising	6. Affluent urbanites 7. Prosperous professionals 8. Middle executives	8.31
Settling	9. Comfortable middle–agers, home–owning 10. Skilled workers, home–owning	24.5
Aspiring	11. New home–owners, settled 12. White–collar + Upper multi-ethnic areas	13.88
Striving	13. Older people 14. Council estate, with income 15. Council estate, without some income 16. Council estate, with little income 17. People in multi-ethnic, low income areas	21.37

Table 10.3 Supermarket consumer-class society
Source: CACI Acorn Profile, Institute of Grocery Distribution (1997a).

	Loyal	In between	Disloyal
Sainsbury	38	23	39
Tesco	37	24	39
Asda	32	24	44
Safeway	29	21	50
Morrison	26	26	48
Somerfield	20	16	64
Kwiksave	15	26	59
Waitrose	14	18	68
Co-op	14	18	68

Table 10.4 Percentage of shoppers according to loyalty
Source: *Adapted from Woolven et al. 1996*

	Loyal	In between	Disloyal
Sainsbury	70	22	8
Tesco	69	23	8
Asda	65	25	10
Safeway	60	28	12
Morrison	53	28	14
Somerfield	54	26	20
Kwiksave	39	40	21
Waitrose	45	34	21
Co-op	43	33	21

Table 10.5. The loyalty yield. Percentage of turnover purchased by degree of loyalty of shoppers
Source: Adapted from Woolven et al. 1996

The loyalty card system can be seen to enshrine a new form of trading relation between the retailing store and the final consumer. At each check-out transaction using a retailer-specific swipe card, the retailer gathers a range of information listed in the box below, to continuously upgrade its socio-economic profiling of its 'captive' population, and monitor trends in demand. As an information technology innovation, the loyalty card thus consolidates a form of monopsonistic linkage between end consumer and retailer in a new and distinctive relationship of power asymmetry and mutual dependence. It is part of the process of institution of a particular kind of market relation between seller and buyer. It ramifies the asymmetry of information that is present in most market transactions, in a way which makes the loyalty card very much a one-way ticket: 'loyalty' describes the relation of the shopper to the store, whereas market information describes the relation of the store to the shopper. The multiple ends up knowing more about shoppers' shopping habits than they probably know themselves. When buying a chill-fresh Thai chicken and lemon grass convenience meal with accompaniments, or a bunch of 'Gourmet' tomatoes on the vine, or hand-crafted pizzadella, the shopper is not just buying a product, but buying into a trading relationship and transformed consumption pattern as well.

Taking the two aspects of the 'social organisation of demand' together, the structure of the retail outlets and the scale effect, it is therefore clear that the second revolution in retailing has reconfigured the relationship between retailer and consumer. The dominant mode of retailing, the full-range one-stop shop, encompasses a broad socio-economic spectrum and it correspondingly delivers a broad spectrum of quality and price. This dominant mode is complemented by the low-cost, narrow-range, bottom-of-the-market stores and by the high-quality, high-price top-of-the-market stores. Of course, shoppers (or consumers) do not group themselves, or socially organise their lives, as 'full-range people', or 'niche eaters', and it is right to stress that the structures of retailing do not dictate consumption unilaterally. Nonetheless, the relationship between consumer and retailer has changed under the new configuration, and there is much to suggest that the retailer now enjoys enhanced asymmetry of power, both in information and in exclusivity of trading. Conversely, the shopper is presented with a product range unimaginable under previous retailing regimes.

THE LOYALTY CARD

Demand information

- Name, address, DoB, household size, children's DoB, cars, pets
- Average spend
- Visit frequency
- Time of visit
- Proportion of own-label to branded goods
- Impulse buying
- Sensitivity to promotions

The financial 'lock-in'

- Banking and credit card
- Direct financial transfer (Eftpos)
- Interest earned on 'dead money'
- Internal store 'currency' – bonus points
- Cash card

LOCAL SOUNDINGS: A MANCHESTER TOMATO LANDSCAPE

The fresh tomato demonstrates this new configuration of the retailer–consumer relationship to perfect effect. Although only a local case study of how tomatoes are distributed and priced in different locations and in different retail outlets in Manchester, the 'tomato landscape' has remarkably clear contours.[10] It is possible to read the socio-economic characteristics of the surrounding area from the range and quality of tomatoes that are available in the stores sited in them. The broad picture is summarised in Table 10.6, where a similarity can be seen between full-range stores located in affluent city suburbs, contrasting sharply with bottom-niche, and price-driven or discount stores located in poor inner-city districts. A socio-economic characterisation of the locations of these retail outlets, based on 1991 Census ward-level data, is presented in column three of Table 10.6.

Thus, the top-of-the-range shops and the top-of-the-range socio-economic characteristics, the affluent commuter suburb of Handforth and the middle-class, professional and predominantly white population of Didsbury, had the highest ratios of car ownership (between 34 and 44 per cent of population) of the seven wards analysed. Both wards had the lowest number of households without access to cars and the lowest rates of unemployment (4.2 per cent, 4.7 per cent and 7.6 per cent respectively). Handforth had the highest rate of employment, full-and part-time. They also had the highest rates of home-ownership.

Given these characteristics and the presence of the two leading full-range and one top-niche supermarkets (Tesco, Sainsbury and Marks & Spencer), the catchment population was blessed with an appropriate range of available tomatoes. Entering the Tesco store in Handforth Dene, tomatoes were prominently on display. The range and global sourcing, with countries of origin clearly flagged, reflected the extent of supply-chain control worldwide, with exclusive supply-chain relations in Zimbabwe, Zambia, Thailand, Kenya, Mexico and Israel, for example. Most organic produce on display was sourced from abroad, the only exception being cabbage. The 'Tom and Jerry' pack of cherry tomatoes for kids developed by Wight Salads was on display, along with all the other varieties with different culinary designations (Table 10.7).

Store	Location/Type	Social profile	Number of Fresh Tomato Product Lines	Global Sourcing
TESCO	Handforth Dene/ Superstore	Thriving/expanding Affluent, commuter 'village', outer suburb. White, homeowners, families. Professionals/ Executives/ Wealthy Retired - 'Stockbroker belt'	16 total inc. 2 organic	7 from UK 4 from Netherlands + Spain and Belgium
M&S	Handforth Dene/, prestige outlet	As above	16 total inc. 2 organic	8 from UK 3 Israel 2 France/ 2 Belgium 1 Netherlands
SAINSBURY	Handforth Dean/ Superstore	As above	13 total inc. 3 organic	6 from UK 4 from Netherlands 2 from It, 1 Portugal
TESCO	Didsbury/ medium store	'Expanding/Rising' Leafy suburban 'Village' on the City-fringe. Victorian/Edwardian family houses, & converted flats. Very high house prices. White, home-owner, families. Younger Executives/Professionals	16 total inc. 3 organic	7 from the UK 4 from Netherlands 1 from Spain, Belgium Mexico, Israel
SAINSBURY	Fallowfield / Superstore	'Rising/ Striving' High crime area of smaller Victorian terraces, majority rented. Massive and dominant student population. Recent apartment blocks for professionals. White, single (student), + Asian.	13 total inc. 3 organic	6 from UK 4 from Netherlands 2 from Italy 1 Portugal

To be continued

KWIKSAVE	Levenshulme – discount	'Striving/Settling' Decaying Victorian suburb. Mixed tenure - mixed social base. White/Irish/Asian	4 (no organic)	UK/Netherlands/Spain
High St Grocer 1	Levenshulme – Independant	See above	3 Total No organic	UK Blackpool
High Street Grocer 2	Levenshulme – Independant	See above	3 Total No organic	UK/Holland
ASDA	Longsight/ supermarket	'Striving' Decaying Victorian working class, mixed tenure, terraces. Predominantly Asian/Irish (black) families (+ students).	8 Total No organic	4 from UK 3 from Netherlands 1 from Spain
NETTO	Longsight/ supermarket.	See above	4 Total No Organic	2 Netherlands 1UK and 1 Spain
M&S	City Centre/ convenience food store	City centre + striving residential New professional inner city accommodation	15 Total inc. 1 organic	8 from UK 2 from Belgium 2 from France Israel, Portugal Netherlands
TESCO	City centre/Metro convenience store	See above	6 lines total inc. 1 organic	3 from UK 1 from Spain, Netherlands Israel

Table 10.6 : Tomatoes and the socio-economic profile of retail outlets

Product Line	Country of Origin
Classic finest	Belgium
Vine ripened	Netherlands
Cherry vine ripened	*England*
Three colour midi plum pack	Netherlands
Red midi plum pack	Netherlands
Baby plums	Spain
Flavour top round	*Britain*
Tom and Jerry	*Britain*
Loose cherries	*Britain*
Cherries pack	Spain
Round family pack	*Britain*
Loose round	*Britain*
Large slicing pack	Netherlands
Super sweet plum	*Britain*
Organic round (Soil Assoc. standard)	Netherlands
Organic cherry pack	Mexico

Table 10.7 Fresh tomato product lines at Handforth Dene Tesco, June 1999.

There was also a full range of tomato-based products. Apart from their pizza range own-label fresh tomato and basil soup, pasta sources, salsina-passata tomato base, and a variety of tinned tomatoes including premier-quality cans co-branded with Cirio, testified to the tomato's contemporary versatility.

The Marks & Spencer store in Handforth had its expected range of high-quality chilled ready meals (from Pennine Foods), along with luxury and treat items in its delicatessen ranges. Its fresh tomatoes provided a particular social distinction by a stress on special varieties with fanciful and high-flown names – Jester, Nectar, Rosa-on-the-vine, Sweetheart plum, Delice, and Santa Baby Plum. Sainsbury's superstore in Handforth was on a similar scale to Tesco and had a very similar range of product, the distinguishing feature being new niche varieties imported from Italy (Vittoria-vine and cherry-vine), so breaking relatively new ground in sourcing fresh tomatoes from that country. Further into the centre of Manchester, their Didsbury branch was one of the older generation of stores, smaller and with much more restricted parking space. However, as was common policy, the entrance and fresh vegetable section maintained the same levels of variety, including cherry tomatoes from Israel and 'Super Sweet' mini-cherries from Mexico.

A brand new Sainsbury superstore in Fallowfield was strategically located to capture a wide catchment area with few competitor rivals as close to the centre in that sector of the city, and with very good communications and parking. With a high student population yet to be induced into supermarket loyalties, the style was modernistic both in architecture and in the cosmopolitanism of its product range.

Less than two miles away, in the crumbling inner-city neighbourhood of Levenshulme, KwikSave stands in complete contrast. Surrounded with barbed wire, with a minimum of parking area, there was no fresh produce in the entrance. The greengrocery operation was even outsourced to a small local operator who obtained produce from Manchester Smithfield, the wholesale market. Both their smaller size and their policy of 'stack it high and sell it cheap' precluded the kind of investment in supply-chain development or distribution systems made by the 'full-range' supermarket chains. This store offered only four product lines – one of them beef, another cherry – apart from the standard commodity tomato, and no organic. They scarcely differentiated themselves, either in quality or in range, from the two small independent greengrocers further in towards the centre, each of which stocked three tomato lines, whose country of origin is unspecified. They too obtained their produce from Manchester Smithfield wholesale market.

Longsight was a decaying Victorian inner-city area, with low home-ownership (37 per cent), low car–ownership (65 per cent without cars) and a relatively high ethnic minority population (35 per cent). Netto as a discounter in Longsight was typically small-scale and with limited overall product range, offering only four product lines in tomatoes, and had very little of any produce under its own label. But even Asda, inbetween a discounter (before its acquisition by Wal-Mart) and a 'full-range' supermarket, had a markedly more restricted spectrum of produce and price than the two dominant retailers. Agressively marketing on the 'Asda price', with their slogan 'Rollback – now ever lower, forever', they were clearly targeting a price-sensitive clientele. There was no organic produce here, and of the eight fresh tomato lines, four were sourced from within the UK, none through dedicated suppliers, only through intermediaries such as Geest or English Village Salads, or The Greenery International from the Netherlands.

Moving in to the city centre, there has been a considerable urban revival, especially as a financial, cultural and leisure centre. Typically, the inner-city

Tesco Metro, or the Marks & Spencer store reconstructed after the IRA bombing, represented styles of outlet mainly for an urban professional class at work. The customer to these city-centre shops was quite different from the once-a-week, one-stop shopper in a car. In the Tesco Metro, £6 is the average spend for any given customer (Ward et al., 1998), whilst in Marks & Spencer, the sandwich counter with special check-outs captured the lunchtime purchaser with combinations of the standard BLT and a multitude of novelty sandwiches in a variety of specialty breads and rolls. Marks & Spencer did, however, also cater for the main shopping of the inner-city professional classes living in the refurbished, high-price, mill and dock buildings. They boasted 15 fresh tomato lines, compared with the six in the adjacent Tesco Metro.

This mapping of a tomato landscape revealed the distinctive ways that production meets consumption, through the structure of retail outlets and the catchment scale effect. Clearly, such a sketch traces a limited picture of how demand was socially organised in distinctive ways by the combination of the distinctive characteristics of different types of retail outlet operating within the UK. Full-range and discount, small independent greengrocer, top-niche and bottom-tranche outlets displayed different ranges of tomatoes in different socio-economic environments. This shaping of demand was by no means a permanently instituted style or structure. It was a landscape characteristic of the UK at this particular historical time.

Viewed historically, the changing nature and combination of different retailing outlets can be seen to articulate and organise demand for food. However, it would be mistaken to take the structure of market segmentation or product differentiation organised in this manner as a proxy for consumption. It is incorrect to simply infer a social hierarchy of consumption from a social hierarchy of retail outlets or a hierarchy of pizzas, tomatoes or whatever. There is a complex and changing 'relationality': consumers of commodities can only buy them in ways that have been socially organised and in given pricing hierarchies, but social structuration of consumers is certainly constructed not only by or through their shopping baskets. It may be that retailers stratify purchasers by their relative disposable incomes and propensities to purchase food according to their scales from thriving to striving. But Warde and others, for example, have powerfully argued that there are continuing enduring social norms,[11] based on class, as defined by occupation, that code and underpin consumption 'choice' (Warde, 1997; Warde and Tomlinson, 1995; Warde and Martens, 2000; Tomlinson and McMeekin, 2002).[12] So there is a relationality between forms of organisation of hierarchy between and within retail outlets on the one hand, and forms of organisation and distinction between and within consumers on the other.

Neither is independent of the other, but equally, how and on what basis each is articulated is also specific to each pole of the relation.

NEW FOODS, CHANGING VEHICLES OF CONSUMPTION

There is a great danger, however, when dealing with issues of social division between different categories of shoppers or consumers, or indeed social class, in viewing these hierarchies or divisions statically. The constant theme of this book is one of transformation, of the continually changing shape, variety and form of the tomato, some more radical than others. Chilled foods, sandwiches, convenience meals, as well as the array of fresh tomatoes just described in a Tesco or Marks & Spencer are a testimony to constant innovation. These are the really dynamic areas of expansion in new food consumption. Between 1993 and 1998, the sales in chilled ready meals grew by 50 per cent, from £340 million to £507 million in 1993 prices:

> Such a performance is rarely, if ever, achieved in food markets other than those with a much shorter history. (Mintel, 1998)

Of this growth, moreover, the most rapid has been in 'ethnic' foods (Indian, Chinese, South-East Asian) and Italian dishes, each of which have grown by 70 per cent in the period 1993–97. The growth of this new market in chilled ready meals, moreover, was led from the top, by Marks & Spencer, and percolated down during that period. Table 10.8 demonstrates this gradual erosion of the leading innovator, as the market is developed across a broader band of retail outlets.

Pizzas and the sandwich have been two of the main vehicles gathering momentum for new tomato foods. The pizza market has been growing rapidly and is expected to expand from £178 million to £205 million from 1999 to 2002, whilst pasta and sauces are expected to grow on current trends by nearly 50 per cent over the same period (*Retail Intelligence*, cited in *Eurofood*, February 2000),[13] with own-label accounting for over 80 per cent of the market (Taylor Nelson Sofres, 2002). The sandwich market in particular has grown enormously, now standing at £3.26 billion,[14] with astonishing growth rates of 13 per cent per annum over several years, with 2.2 billion sandwich packs sold each year. An NOP survey found that young working adults, aged 25–34, figured as the group of most frequent purchasers (*Checkout*, June 1999). Fillings have become more exotic, and product differentiation and price spectrum have been rapidly established similar to other food ranges.

Hazlewood Foods (see Chapter 8) claim to be the world's largest sandwich-maker, and following their strategy of continuous innovation and novelty seeking, have just produced the 'conewich', a cone-shaped sandwich contained in a paper cone, with six fillings, including egg and bacon with tomato and chives. But alongside these 'fun' concepts, more exotic sandwiches are found in their Connoisseur range, with fillings such as chargrilled pheasant, roasted leeks, capsicum, and pepperberry chutney in a malted bloomer (*Grocer*, July 1999).

	1993	1995	1997
Marks & Spencer	46	45	40
Sainsbury	24	20	25
Tesco	14	14	17
Asda	na	4	5
Safeway	5	5	4
Waitrose	6	5	3
Other own label	2	2	2
Branded	3	5	5

Table 10.8. Market share in chilled ready meals as peer cent of market, 1993–97.
Source: Mintel 1998

In the big picture, the working and middle class of the time of the first retailing revolution was very different from that of the second. Moreover, changes in one pole, say the production, distribution and retailing of convenience ready meals or sandwiches, can be seen to be related to changes in demand and consumption of those very same commodities. Tesco, as one of the largest, if not the largest private sector employer, also runs 24-hour working *and* shopping, and along with other UK supermarkets, uses flexible labour in more flexible ways than European retailing counterparts (Baret, Lehndorff and Sparks 2000). There is a 'societal effect', it is argued, with the particular characteristics of UK labour markets, in terms of part-time and working time regulation (Gadret and Lehndorff, 2000; Baret, Lehndorff, and Ribault, 2000), leading to conditions which, in turn, can be seen to transform the character of food consumption. To take one small illustrative example, the erosion of the institution of the lunch hour amongst office workers is itself an important stimulant to the sandwich culture:

with eating lunch at the desk common among office workers – 70 per cent now often do this – and longer hours resulting in snacking on the journey home. (The *Grocer*, July, 1999)

In terms of the macro-shaping of demand and consumption, therefore, the new forms assumed by tomatoes in convenience ready meals, pizzas or sandwiches reflect both changing characteristics of hierarchy and new modes of consumption. The contemporary sandwich, for example, can be seen to result from *either* a process of commodification (when household labour is replaced by the sandwich factory), *or* commodity switching (when a sit-down commercial outlet is replaced by a sandwich eaten whilst working) *or* commodification and switching (as when purchased sandwiches replace school meals):

Time pressed working mothers are seeking nutritious tempting snacks for children's lunch boxes. (The *Grocer*, July 1999)[15]

It is clear that new structures both in production and consumption are being formed as class relations and occupational stratifications are being restructured, and that these also are connected to other major shifts in the social organisation of consumption by changing temporalities of work, leisure and household activity. The creation of distinction between an economy pizza and a handcrafted or Classico range, or between a Connoisseur malted bloomer and standard BLT triangular 'wedge' signifies both different forms of socio-hierarchical coding and different modalities of consumption. Social codes and distinctions are embodied in these foods, and strategies of product differentiation within product categories are a central feature influencing the foods we eat. Of course there have always been differences in what different classes and groups of people eat. What is new is the way these differences are organised and articulated, and what is important is that such differences are always subject to major and continuous restructuring.

CONCLUSION

This chapter has focused on two poles of a relationship, retail outlets and consumers, whilst exploring tomato transformations. It has been argued that there have been two major restructurations of that relationship. The changes have been massive and have been preceded and complemented by many less discontinuous or radical shifts. But the changes have also been seen to be quite specifically rooted in UK society and economy. In terms of the emergence of major patterns of retailing and the structuring of consumption, the approach and analysis has exemplified the 'instituted economic process' approach. These are historical and located events. The distinctiveness of the second revolution in UK retailing and food consumption was predicated on, and emanated from, the distinctive realities of the first. There are particular societal trajectories for instituting economic relations pivoting on the market exchange of shopping, through which economies of retailing are sustained and expand. The tomato itself, naturally but a small refracting mirror of all these changes, nonetheless demonstrates precisely how it too is a socio-economic institution whose own transformations were embodiments of major historical transformations. It takes on shapes, travels different routes, assumes a place in a spectrum of prices, becomes integrated into new modes of eating food, and acquires different liveries encoding different social norms, as part of a process of continuous institution and de-institution. Of course, the tomato is not alone in this. Indeed, it is well accompanied by all the other foods we eat, commodities we buy.

NOTES

[1] This creates a break between shopping and consumption, and brings the tomato narrative to a precipitate end at this point. That there is a significant further domain of consumption practices and household economies is fully consistent with the perspective of this book, but falls outside its scope.

[2] The Star Tea Company of London, the International Tea Company, Thomas Lipton (who owned their own tea plantations), the Newcastle Tea Company, the Globe Tea Company of Manchester, the Home and Colonial.

[3] Union Cold Storage merged with leading firms in frozen goods to make a group with over 2000 outlets nationwide; Home and Colonial amalgamated with Lipton's, the Maypole Dairy Company and the Star Tea Company, to create a national network with over 3000 outlets.

[4] Department of Environment, *6 Town Centres and Retail Development*, 1993, 1996.

[5] The Competition Commission (2000), in their defined market of one-stop stores of greater than 1400 square metres, Tesco, Sainsbury, Asda, Safeway and Morrison had 84 per cent of the total market for groceries between them in 1999.

[6] Many of these are part time (Freathy and Sparks, 2000), and in Full Time Equivalents their employees number 104,930 (July 2000, Tesco Company Facts Homepage). It is a curiosity that on their general consumer homepage (www.tesco.com) the most prominent feature heading their design is a bunch of tomatoes on the vine.

[7] At 63,000 square feet the store is bigger than a football pitch, has 60 checkouts, and sells 45 varieties of baked beans, aggressively discounting at prices up to 60 per cent lower than rivals.

[8] The July 2000 figures provided by Tesco for their different store formats are 225 superstores, 200 supermarkets, 48 neighbourhood stores, 42 Metro stores and 21 Express stores.

[9] Marks & Spencer have a more department store format, and comparable figures were not available. It can be assumed, however, that their style of operation is quite similar to that of Waitrose.

[10] The case study, entailing visits to all retail outlets areas of South Manchester, was undertaken in June 1999.

[11] Such embedded norms are conceived as a form of social 'habitus' as conceptualised by Bordieu, with the supporting concept of the intergenerational transmission of 'cultural capital'. The argument is the basis of a critique of a major thesis advanced by one of most significant contributions to the study of food consumption in the Elias tradition by Mennel (1985) arguing for more variety and less *social*, more individuated, difference.

[12] 'The capacity to display rank in a social hierarchy by consuming in accordance with the criteria of a symbolic representation of that hierarchy confirms the powerful and multi-faceted link between class and consumption. Distinction persists.' (Warde, 1997, 175) Similar arguments apply equally to consumption within the household as eating out (Warde and Martens, 2000).

[13] This picture of retail sales is mirrored by eating out, where pizza tops the list with 166 million pizza meals bought in 2000 (Taylor Nelson Sofres, 2002).

[14] Figures from Sandwich Trak data, provided by Promar International for the British Sandwich Association (*Caterer and Hotel Keeper*, February 2000)

[15] In a feature article on chilled snacks, Hardcastle argues that chilled snacks and sandwiches, and novelties like the conewich, are evidence of 'a plethora of innovations meeting modern lifestyles more effectively'.

11. Tomato Variations or *Plus C'est la Même Chose, Plus ça Change*

Adam and Eve fell into temptation when they ate the tomato of the tree of knowledge. They did this, that is, if one takes the European view of celestial botany. For most of its nations, the tomato was such an exotic fruit that it deserved a noble title. The French call it the *pomme d'amour*, the Italians the *pomo d'oro* – the golden apple – and the Croats the *paradis*. Ridiculous, perhaps, but whatever Eden's fruit may have been it was not an apple... (Steve Jones, 2000, *Almost Like a Whale. The Origin of the Species Updated*)

VARIATION AND DIFFERENTIATION

Biologists have sought to trace the emergence of species as a process of genetic variation. In a quest for understanding how one species becomes discontinuous with another, the tomato has provided a useful tool (Jones, 2000, 242–4). The wild variety of tomato is sexually dimorphic with male and female plants, and crosses only with members of its own kind. The cultivated tomato now has become self-fertile as a result, it appears, of a mutation in one single gene. Although in interaction with other genes, this gene controls pollen and flower form and so lays the basis for ensuring successful sexual reproduction between members of its own kind and unsuccessful crossing with 'outsiders'. Despite the best attempts of the United States Department of Agriculture to cross wild with cultivated tomatoes, the shift in this gene therefore led to the cultivated tomato becoming a different *species* from the wild kind: sexually dimorphic and self-fertile versions generally do not get on together, reproductively speaking.

This book's analysis begins where biologists leave off, the period when processes of evolution have been accompanied by the very different processes of historical and social change. But there is a similar interest in how processes of variation and difference have occurred and become established in the bio-socio-economic histories of the tomato. The tomato ketchup tomato, for example, has undergone constant change from the moment of its commercial inception, despite the similarities and

253

standardisation of twentieth-century ketchup. But so too have its bottle container and its consumption use. Yet, throughout its own changes, the ketchup tomato has resolutely maintained a bio-socio-economic institutional difference from fresh or other processed varieties. There are dedicated varieties for dedicated purposes. Moreover, the science and technologies of hybridisation – the means for creating new varieties – have themselves been revolutionised during the same period. Barriers between bio-socio-economic varieties have thus been formed and reformed even when everything inside and outside them has been continuously altering.

As with dogs, cats, corn and cattle, different hybrid breeds of tomato are socio-economic institutions. Processes of bio-variation and differentiation are intimately connected with changing cultures and techniques of production, as well as new markets and cultures of consumption. People have changed along with the tomatoes they eat. Indeed, in intricate and indirect ways, changes in one are related to changes in the other. The constantly varying ways in which people produce, process, distribute and purchase tomatoes are linked to altered patterns of consumption, schedules of leisure and household organisation. Different socio-economic constructions of what constitutes 'fresh' in Californian mechanically harvested, North European glasshouse or Southern Mediterranean sun-ripened tomatoes have led to further variations, with new varieties of all shapes, colours and vines appearing in different places in different seasons. Likewise, new cuisines and new modes of delivery of food in chill-chains have emerged with new technologies of processing combined with new and dedicated hybrids.

There are contrary forces pulling towards global standardisation (ketchup again) and local or regional differentiation (socially distinct classes of pizza for UK supermarkets). Clashes between such forces can be articulated through different strategies of supermarket retailing: the construction of the global retailer selling super-brands at discount prices (Wal-Mart) or powerful nationally-oriented supermarkets controlling distinctive supply bases, whether for manufactured or fresh produce. These are different ways of being 'global': the former establishing a pattern of trading between global players to provide standard global commodities, the latter extending distinctive tentacles of control across the world to supply distinctive (and counterseasonal) products to distinctive local or national markets. The outcome of such clashes is more likely to produce further variation than a scenario in which one model leads to the extinction of all others.

Genetic engineering, far from creating a global genetically modified tomato based on a globally common science of genetics, has rather opened up a huge new field of possible variation. One type of genetically modified tomato (the Flavr Savr) appeared on one side of the Atlantic in one regulatory and production set of circumstances, whilst another appeared in the United

Kingdom (as processed purée but similarly genetically modified tomato). These early processes of variation have subsequently witnessed significant turbulence, with conflicts between different regulatory regimes being sharpened by clashes between different consumer worlds, divergent levels of trust in science, interventions by commercial organisations (banks, finance capital and supermarkets) and political pressure groups. The development of new types of Nutrient Dense tomatoes, or tomatoes that can be grown under different stress conditions, or super-ecological tomatoes, is being profoundly affected by the different forces present in this socio-economic turbulence. There is geographical specificity as to how these forces stack up. The power of transnational corporations, supermarkets, national science bases, Greenpeace, or governmental or supra-governmental regulation is unevenly distributed. The future direction of both science and technologies is being formed in this cauldron, and we could be witnessing a profound geopolitical shift in the centre of their gravity, from West to East, even from North to South.

With some confidence, it can be said that the direction taken now for the scientific and technological development of genetically modified tomatoes (as well as for other organisms) has been irreversibly altered. This highlights a quite different aspect to variation, variation in direction as much as in outcome. A focus on nutrient density or stress tolerance, and corresponding allocation decisions for funding of research, will mean that different aspects of gene functionality will be scientifically understood as well as a new orientation given to genetic engineering technologies and markets. At the same time, a different spectrum of sciences will be enrolled, dealing with epidemiology, diet and human physiology, blurring boundaries between food and pharmaceuticals. So even if a commonly accepted worldwide scientific understanding and a range of shared technologies emerges, which irreversibly supplant previous accepted understandings and technologies, nonetheless both the science and the technologies will be different than they might otherwise have been as a consequence of changes in direction. Even if the outcome is singular, it is a result of variation. A person can take only one route at a time resulting in a single destination. But the actual destination can be the result of many changes in direction, and the least plausible future for the genetically modified tomato is that the destination would be the same, no matter what routes are taken.

If variations in direction affect some of the fundamental aspects of the life of the human tomato, changes in direction are a widespread source of variation. The tango between Dutch producers and German discount retailers and consumers took both partners down a more and more extreme route of high yield, low price – and no taste. Until they both fell off the dance floor, the market collapsed, and everyone decided they did not like the watery

music anymore. New routes had to be sought, and the Dutch industry turned
to the United Kingdom example, where product differentiation, value-added,
and broad-spectrum pricing provided everything from the cheap and tasteless
to the chic and tangy. In a sense too, the 'horticultural route' can be seen as a
general direction taken, which became more and more oriented towards the
creation of a total ecology where every aspect of cultivation became the focus
of intense innovation: soil, pest control, atmosphere, seed, heat and light,
nutrient and water flows, information and traceability. In other cases, routes
taken have led to dead ends: the Guernsey industry, locked into a UK market,
went so far down an institutional route leading nowhere, that it could not be
reversed or diverted rapidly enough to prevent terminal collapse. So different
tomatoes take different trajectories, and variation in the direction of these
trajectories is as much a source of change as variation in type, breed or use.

It would be mistaken to think of the tomato as uniquely versatile, and it is
important to bear in mind that its relative prominence in North American or
European, and even Italian, diets is much more recent than might be assumed.
The ubiquitous tomato is essentially a twentieth-century phenomenon.
Nonetheless, the tomato is exemplary in the extent of its variation and
differentiation, in how many shapes and forms it has assumed, and in how
many different trajectories it has followed in different parts of the world.
From the time it became one of the pioneers of mass production for mass
consumption, its variations provide a distinctive reflection of the dynamics of
change in recent capitalism. As a 'simple', low-cost, low-status object, it may
only play a bit part in the mainstream core of socio-economic development.
But, nonetheless, it is in there.

And for that reason, perhaps, the more a tomato remains a tomato the more
it changes.

PROCESSES OF INSTITUTION

If variation was continuous, unceasing, and all was flux, there would be no
variety. Difference would constantly dissolve. For that reason, processes of
institution are constitutive of variety and variation. Analysis switches from
change in general to structural change, and to how things have relations to
other things that stabilise *and* destabilise. We can identify four processes of
variation: variation of form; differentiation of forms; direction or trajectory of
forms; and complex combinations of these. Sets of relations, practices and
objects cohere and become articulated with each other, and assume a
distinctive form, whether in modes of cultivation, in cuisines or in markets,
for example. Processes of institutionalisation and de-institutionalisation of
different forms of tomato thus present ways of looking at how socio-
economic variety is constituted. At the European level, patterns of trade,

cultivation, processing and consumption revealed profound levels of variety between different European countries, decades after migrations, mass holidays and European integration might have been expected to dissolve or soften differences. Italy and Spain stand as contrasted opposites: the one exports fresh and no processed tomatoes for Northern Europe, the other supplies almost exclusively processed, and until recently next to no fresh. Domestic consumption of fresh and processed in Northern and Southern Europe differs sharply. 'Fresh' in the North means eaten fresh in salads, whereas 'fresh' in the South also significantly refers to ingredients for subsequent cooking and processing in the household. National cuisines still predominate in consumption cultures for tomatoes, and to take the two extremes, Greeks eat nearly 20 times more tomatoes per head than the Dutch, even though the Netherlands is by far the dominant tomato-producing country in Northern Europe. There are sharp differences in consumption within Southern European countries, between Italy and Spain, or within Northern countries, between United Kingdom and the Netherlands.

These broad patterns can be seen in terms of how differences are instituted, some in distinctively economic ways, as with trade, others more socially and culturally, as with consumption patterns. Some of these differences might be long-standing, having roots in culture and climate, in landownership and productive systems. Dutch horticulture is a classic instance of a tradition, perhaps the most durable level of institutedness, stretching back at least into the seventeenth century and the epoch of 'tulipomania'. People, as bearers of skills and ways of living, are embodiments of instituted difference.

So, assuming a form and stabilising it is part of the process of instituting variety. But, as is clear from the example of the 'round Europe tomato', it is as much the relationship between different forms that makes them different as the way in which forms emerge in their own terms. The Netherlands' tomato production is overwhelmingly export oriented, as is that of Southern Spain. What makes them both different is their facing outward, contrasting with those countries whose relation to tomatoes is essentially one of consumption driven by imports, most notably Germany. Likewise even 'global cuisine', picking and mixing national or regional cuisines, relies on the latter retaining, even developing, their contrasts. It would lose appeal if all cuisines went through a universal blender. For supermarkets, too, product differentiation would be seriously impeded were differences obliterated between their Indian, Italian, Thai, Mexican, *etcetera*, enrolments of the tomato even if the outcome is distinctively UK supermarket-Italian, -Thai, -Mexican, etcetera. This is no more a philosophical point about 'the Other' than a Ricardian point about comparative advantage. Rather, the tomato demonstrates processes of institution of interrelated differences, and the ways in which these change over time.

Instituted differences are built on previous instituted differences, and this in turn can lead to increasing divergence between different varieties. So at one level, for a couple of decades at least the Northern European horticultural regime intensified its difference with Southern European open-field or polythene-protected production regimes. The most tangible economic aspect of this divergence was to be seen in yield per hectare, where the former increased by nine times whilst the latter only doubled over a 30-year period. From the point of view of innovation creating variation, however, the divergence was between a total ecology capital-intensive horticultural regime and an agrochemical regime, each driven by different innovation logics.

Another example relates to why UK supermarkets are so different from both continental European and US counterparts. Although the explanation is still far from complete, it is clear that UK supermarkets went through an early and more complete process of national market integration at the end of the nineteenth century, which then formed the basis of a further revolution and concentration of power resulting in their current unique *modus operandi*. They now pick the cream off the European tomato market, not because of some inherent comparative advantage, but as a result of these two phases of concentration of power and market integration building on each other.

Divergence based on initial instituted difference also characterises the different trajectories travelled by the UK and Dutch horticultural regimes, despite their high level of shared innovation and technologies. At the outset of the 1970s, the differences were perhaps less marked, and indeed there were many similarities between the Dutch and the Guernsey tomato industries. A critical difference even at that stage, however, was that the Dutch industry, being primarily export, faced a number of very diverse retail markets, with strong contrasts between their main market in Germany and their second-largest market in the United Kingdom. By contrast, UK growers only ever related to the UK market. That difference meant that under similar pressures of competition from Southern European tomato industries, both the Dutch and the UK industries had to change. The Dutch have concentrated on changing the nature of their common intermediating institutions (from the auction system to The Greenery International), and changing the organisation of growers' co-operatives feeding into it. The UK by contrast has developed a hierarchy of growers matching the hierarchy of supermarkets, along with the establishment of direct trading with supermarkets and a considerable concentration of production units. Comparing the outcomes, the divergence between the two models now is much sharper than 30 years ago, although built on more narrow, if significant, antecedent institutional differences.

There is another related way in which processes of institutionalisation reinforce varieties in form, when different processes of variation combine and reinforce each other in a complex instituted matrix. The bio-socio-economic variety of the 'Guernsey Tom' is perhaps the clearest example, partly because the island economy was dominated by tomato production for a while. A whole institutional fabric of the island revolved around the tomato. There is a temptation to think that a simple unpretentious object like a tomato would require a simple and uncomplicated society and economy to sustain it. Commonwealth preference, a favourable climate, good soil and South-facing slopes supported a conversion from grapes to tomatoes. The island State played a critical role, establishing a planning and development framework, and a Tomato Marketing Board which centralised distribution, giving it unrivalled price-bargaining power in relation to the then mainland wholesale market system on which it depended. This unified the product under a single grading system, and, at the same time, if temporarily, confirmed and sustained smallholding family cultivation and property relations. Scientific infrastructure and support was also created by the State. As a consequence of this complex institutional framework the 'Guernsey Tom' briefly became like nothing else on earth. But, this institutional complexity eventually became an impediment to change. As pillar after pillar was removed, the industry met a critical turning point and, unable to adapt to the disappearance of wholesale markets as the main tomato conduit, rapidly collapsed. Institutional support became institutional straightjacket.

The 'Guernsey Tom' manifests variety almost in an island 'test tube'. Different processes of institutionalisation constitutive of variety combined together: form stabilisation, interdependent differentiation, institutional trajectory and institutional complexity. In all the various forms assumed by tomatoes explored in this study, these four processes of instituted variety are present, whether pursuing the trajectory of the genetically modified tomato, the emergence of the Tesco pizza concasse or the development of the high-tech glasshouse fresh tomato. In each case, however, new forms of tomato emerged as a result of *transformation* of pre-existing forms, rather than an original moment of institution, of form appearing out of primordial (tomato) soup. A new form of tomato has always appeared as a variation of earlier variations rather than as an innovation out of nothing, or a moment of pure creation. The quest for an original form appears vain and unnecessary. Radical breaks and discontinuities, as much as incremental variation, are different possibilities of trans-formation. Hence, the concept of variation is intimately linked to a concept of structural change, of one set of coherences between relations, practices and objects being transformed and superseded by another.

THE INSTITUTED 'ECONOMIC' TOMATO

This instituted view of the tomato as a process of generating variety argues against a tomato as subject to any universal economic laws, or even monolithically 'fundamental' laws of historical capitalism. If there were to be universal or global laws, these would have to be instituted globally. Whereas money or capital markets are probably more globally instituted than tomato markets (labour or product), they too are far from achieving a single, coherent instituted global form. It could also be argued that (at least, fresh) tomato markets, as product markets, are less globally instituted than other products such as cars. However, cars too are far from universal commodities in a homogeneous economic space.

For all that it is not subject to universal laws, the tomato *is* instituted as an 'economic' tomato. For the central decades of the twentieth century, for example, fresh tomatoes in the UK were subject to the specifically economic logic of wholesale markets. Particular instituted processes of atomistic price–setting, of sale on commission and daily spot markets constituted a relatively historically durable economic *modus operandi*. Demand was articulated with supply in this particular institutional framework, linked to other institutions like the Guernsey Tomato Growers Marketing Board. There was a stable pattern of distinctively economic coherence, coordinating a multiplicity of economic agents and ensuring flows of tomatoes were matched by flows of money and profit.

However, the economic 'laws' of supply and demand, of market clearing and price-setting, were instituted within this framework, and in turn these 'laws' disappeared when the wholesale markets disappeared as the principal tomato conduit. They were then replaced by the quite different 'laws' of the value chain, where price-setting was shifted downstream to the retail end-market, and where power asymmetries between different economic agents became critical in determining value apportionment.

Markets, whether end (retailer–consumer) or intermediary (wholesale, manufacturer–retailer), are premier instances of economic institutions, where processes of exchange and competition as well as supply and demand take particular forms. The Dutch clock auction system, so characteristic of an entrepôt, export-oriented industry, acted as a centralised intermediary for small-scale growers. In contrast to the replacement of intermediation by supply-chain arrangements in the UK, the Dutch currently have an instituted central brokerage agent, competing with various alternative forms of intermediation. Again, this institution of The Greenery International has retained its role as dominant tomato clearing house, for setting North European fresh tomato prices. But this economic *modus operandi* is far from stable or secure.

In addition to markets as organised exchange relations, relations of asymmetric power and mutual dependency between different classes of economic agent – consumers, retailers, manufacturers, growers – can also be seen to become instituted over quite long periods of time. The brand manufacturers that produced tomato ketchup or tomato soup were involved in a particular set of economic relations with their own suppliers, with retailers and with consumers. Supermarket own-label manufacturers, or manufacturers producing under own-label disguise, have entirely different 'instituted' economic relations with their supply base and with retailers, and are almost hidden from consumers. There is a strange 'monopsonistic matrix' in which a small number of manufacturers supply a small number of retailers on an exclusive one-to-one basis with new ranges of food, from pizzas to mozarella and tomato ciabatta rolls, chill-fresh tomato soups to Mediterranean tartes tatins. They differ critically in having relatively secure access to market under long-term trading relations with supermarkets. Likewise, UK supermarkets established a distinctive relationship with tomato growers, first in the UK and then, occasionally through UK grower intermediaries, with Spanish growers. A hierarchy of growers with relatively secure and long-term supply relations, frequently exclusive to a particular supermarket, matched the hierarchy of UK supermarkets. This in turn has been critical for capital accumulation, innovation and the development of high-technology, capital-intensive modes of cultivation.

If one looks at how consumers purchase tomatoes, and the instituted relationship between consumers and retailers, this too has undergone several dramatic changes over the course of the last century. As a relation between supply and final demand, it assumes particular instituted forms in different countries, at least partly depending on the very distinctive patterns and organisation of retail markets. The contrasts between US and UK retailing, say between Wal-Mart and Tesco or Sainsbury, and between these and discounters like Netto or Lidl, are quite marked. These contrasts are then expressed in tomato terms, whether in the range and differentiation of fresh tomatoes or in the hierarchies of economy, branded, own-label and niche-branded chilled foods. Price range and quality differentials as against economies of scale and low-cost standardisation may not be mutually exclusive types of retail market, but nonetheless there are strongly differentiated retail institutions along those different economic logics.

Within the UK, moreover, the history of the exchange relations between consumers and retailers has seen the emergence of the small permanent independent grocer replacing the once- or twice-weekly street markets, only for these to be progressively marginalised by the growth of multiple retail chains. Two retailing revolutions, the first creating multiple retail chains, the second making these into highly centralised economic organisations, completely altered relations of asymmetric power and mutual dependency between retailers and consumers. The emergence of the quasi-monopsonistic supermarket catchment area, of socio-economic profiling and of continuous demand monitoring at the check-out with the use of loyalty cards and other electronic information, has transformed both the exchange relation and the market knowledge relations between the two parties.

So, the tomato can be seen to be instituted *economically* by distinctive patterns of coherence involving production, distribution, exchange and consumption, and the relations between them. Competition, supply, demand, and price all operate within particular instituted economic logics, over periods of time and in distinct locations. Economic agents (whether these are firms of different economic functions or consumers with distinctive purchasing attributes) are also instituted in time and place with distinctive structural features and distinctive relations with other agents. In addition, economic scale is an instituted phenomenon. One cannot assume the global or the local. If one takes the fresh UK tomato, it is a distinctively national institution, unlike the Dutch tomato that has a Northern European zone of operations. But a single scale rarely defines tomatoes. Thus, at one scale the UK tomato growers compete with each other to obtain the privileged and preferred trading relations with top supermarkets, and at another they compete together under a common logo with Dutch tomato growers. At yet another scale, both Dutch and UK tomato growers combine together, share technologies and develop the product range specific to the Northern European horticultural regime in competition with Southern Europe. As a productive system, glasshouse production developed across the whole of Northern Europe as a distinctive system. How long this particular instituted productive system will compete and remain distinctive is uncertain, but at least for a period it has operated with its own cost and accumulation logic – where each tomato vine, computer-monitored and controlled, has a value structure quite different from open-field or semi-covered productive systems. So, the Northern European glasshouse tomato institutes a particular economic scale, overlaying nation-to-nation and intra-national economic scales. Clearly, these scales may be quite peculiar to different product markets – whether these are exotic fruits or automobiles.[1] And the differently instituted scales of different product markets might be quite different from money, capital or labour markets. The Northern European tomato is now price-benchmarked in Euros in the Dutch market rather than guilders, allowing price transparency between different European countries within the Euro-zone. But this only illustrates how economic scale is a complex made up of different intersecting scales. The case of the European tomato only illustrates how one component, however insignificant, contributes to this complex scale formation. The homogeneously global economic tomato remains a chimera, except in the certain political and academic economic rhetorics.

CONTINGENCY AND OVERDETERMINATION

If the tomato is instituted with distinct economic logics and causalities, and these cannot be taken as given, naturally occurring or universal, similarly other spheres of social life also have their distinctive patterns of stability and unity. Just as economic 'laws' cannot be taken as given, so too the formation of different logics and causalities have their own distinctive processes of institution, the state, law, force and coercion, civil society and culture. The instituted specificity of the economic sphere is only constituted in relation to the instituted specificities of other social domains. An instituted economic process analysis thus allows us to analyse *both* the specific economic aspects of a tomato's life *and* its interactions with other social domains. Indeed, boundaries between different domains can be more or less clearly instituted, can shift from society to society, and from historical period to historical period, so defining the shifting place of economy in society.

Moreover, if nature as such is not socially instituted, and is endowed with its own autonomous causality, human transactions with biological nature are instituted. These necessarily result in interactions between radically different causal domains. Likewise with climate. The laws of physics are autonomous of humans, but transactions with our physical environment, such as the burning of carbon fuels or deforestation, can induce significant interactions between two (or more) different causal domains.

For this reason, the 'instituted economic process' analysis developed around the tomato directly implies forms of explanation which involve interactions between different causal domains. In respect to a given causal domain, the effects of these interactions are contingent, outside its own internal patterns of coherence and logic, and therefore also overdetermined, subject to multiple causalities. In the case of the tomato, and other similar economic objects, two other causal domains, biology (human, other organic species and ecology) and climate can play a particularly significant role. The interactions of these multiple causalities are most manifest when something 'goes wrong', in terms of the laws (instituted or natural) of a given causal domain. BSE, as an outcome of an interaction between economic logic of intensified industrialised agriculture and the biological properties of the hitherto little-understood prion, is a recent notable example. That prions with their unique *biological* properties were not destroyed by stipulated sterilisation procedures subsequently had immense *economic* effects on meat markets and on regulatory frameworks.

For the tomato, therefore, these interactions with other spheres have been central to the analysis. Whether in terms of the total ecologies of the glasshouse system, or the bio-socio-economic varieties of tomato generated by the interactions between national cultural cuisines, economic processes and a cultivated biological species, multiple causal domains are necessarily intertwined. In simplistic terms, therefore, these interactions can be represented diagrammatically as shown in Diagram 11.1.

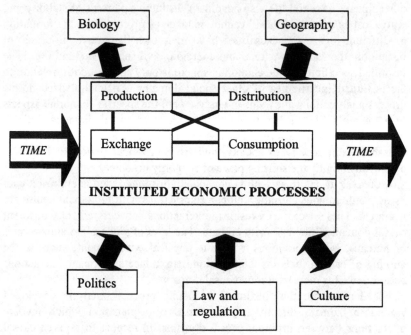

Diagram 11.1 Multiple casual domains

In this analysis of the human tomato, instituted economic process has been a central focus, looking then at significant interactions with other causal domains. But, equally, it would have been possible to rotate the diagram, and to take some other causal domain as the central focus. No assumption of primacy is attributed to the economic, although clearly many of the dynamics of change have been seen to be economic. The immense growth and development of the tomato in the social world has to take into account the specifically economic processes involved. In the case of the genetically modified tomato, however, at this point in its history, politics, the cultural construction of 'Nature', state and international regulation – and the *biology* of genetic modification – have all played significant roles in market formation and destruction. The equation between the 'natural', 'organic' and 'ecological' may be a conjunctural one involving supermarkets creating new product and price differentiation for organics, some green politics combining anti-corporatism or anti-globalisation and an anti-modernist conception of the ecological. But, in the United Kingdom at present, it is a contingent combination that carries institutional force. Any analysis of genetic modification that confined itself to innovation processes within the economic sphere alone would be woefully inadequate to the explanatory task.

The 'fabrication of nature' of glasshouse ecologies involves a rather different combination of some of the same causal domains. The outputs of these radically artificial ecologies are marketed as being super-'natural'. The use of biological pest controls is advertised as more 'natural' than the use of manufactured organic chemicals, in spite of the fact that bumble-bees, wasps and mites are commercially mass produced in ways that involve highly 'unnatural' reproductive rhythms and micro-environments. The organic movement stipulates use of 'natural' soil as a required substrate, along with the naturally occurring atmosphere (however unintentionally altered). So the Soil Association refuses to validate super-natural ecologies as organic, due to the total recycling of waste and water in hydroponic methods, and the modified atmospheres for absorption of carbon gases generated by electricity production. The opposition between 'nature' and 'culture' is at once a marketing device; a reprise of cultural polarities; an obfuscating and politically motivated confusion of organic with eco-sustainability; and an economic logic of competition between Northern glasshouse systems and open-field agrochemical cultivation systems. Yet, weighing these different causal interactions, it is clear that the logic of instituted *economic* processes has driven both the innovation and competition behind the development of 'fabricated nature', and the competition between supermarkets to be 'more natural than thou' with new organic ranges of tomatoes.

Contingency and overdetermination arising from the interaction of multiple causal domains are therefore the necessary counterpart to the institution of specifically economic processes. The notion of *specific* processes must not therefore be confused with *autonomous* processes. There is no such thing as an autonomous economic domain – a tomato or any other commodity as an autonomously economic object. Rather, a specific domain owes its specificity partly to its relations with other domains, and partly to its own internal logics, coherencies and causalities. It is important to understand what a tomato is economically, but to do so also entails understanding how that economic tomato is constituted in social, political and cultural frames as well.

CONFIGURATIONS AND CHANGE

Instituted economic processes are essentially 'open structured', and in two senses.[2] Firstly, they are open to, and often interconnected with, differently instituted economic processes, and these interconnections are always potentially destabilising. Secondly, as has just been argued, they are open to and also interconnected with other causal domains within which changes can occur, having major reciprocal impacts. To take but one example, it is more than possible that climate change will affect the relative economic viability of Northern European horticultural regimes and Southern European open-field systems in terms of the redistribution of heat and water.

Economic change and its dynamics therefore refers to the first of these two senses, and economic change is now considered separately in order to analytically elucidate what was meant earlier by structural change, without the added complication of dealing with multiple causal domains. To take the example of a particular instituted process of exchange (a market with relatively stabilised trading relations between a relatively stabilised set of economic agents), it is 'open structured' inasmuch as it does not form one coherent and total system that incorporates all other interconnected economic processes. A market can open out on other markets; is connected to patterns of distribution and logistics; relies on instituted patterns of demand; and provides a channel for commodities, which in turn are produced under instituted sets of conditions, in labour markets, employment relations, labour processes and so on. As argued above, its instituted characteristics are both specific but not autonomous. For that reason, its interconnectedness with other instituted economic processes, each with their specific characteristics, always contains a potential for emergent conflicts and tensions. If one or many of the interconnected economic processes change internally, previously normalised relations can be disrupted. This then can be seen as instability leading to possible variation from relatively exogenous change. But equally, markets themselves have dynamic processes, exchange relations between suppliers and buyers, which reflect power asymmetries and imbalances between them. Growth and/or concentration can intensify power imbalances within markets in ways that lead to relatively endogenous change within market institutions. The 'openness' and interrelatedness of instituted economic processes – their lack of autonomy – underlies notions of relative exogeneity and endogeneity. The source of change is neither absolutely 'inside' or 'outside', on the assumption that the specificity of an instituted process develops and emerges in relation to specificities of other instituted economic processes. Innovation processes,[3] such as the many we have analysed involving the tomato, also have this duality of relative endogeneity and exogeneity, especially when distributed between a number of diverse economic agents. In the case in point, markets develop only in relation to the organisation of production, distribution and consumption.

Continuing with market institutions as our example, the Dutch clock auction system or the Guernsey Tomato Marketing Board are thus both distinctive organisations, pricing and grading systems, which face both towards production and towards further markets, retail and wholesale. The great German water bomb scandal, which can be interpreted as an alteration in demand, presented a relatively exogenous destabilisation of the auction system. Yet, as argued, there was a dynamic in which high-yield low-cost production developed in relation to a strongly discount-oriented retailing system, so producing a cheaper and cheaper, more and more tasteless tomato. Conversely, the response to the crisis in establishing The Greenery International as a centralised brokering organisation to replace the clock auctions, revealed continuing and unresolved tensions between the power of the marketing organisation and the power of the growers' associations that owned it. Reorganisation of the trading institution through centralisation thus created conditions of relatively endogenous change within market-instituted processes. Overall, the change can be seen as a *combination* between relatively endogenous and exogenous sources of change. A similar analysis of the demise of the Guernsey tomato industry revealed an interaction between relatively exogenous and endogenous economic processes: the growth of UK supermarkets and the collapse of wholesale marketing, on the one hand, and the concentration and modernisation of growers combined with fundamental shifts in labour market conditions on the island, on the other.

CONFIGURATIONAL CHANGE

So far structural causality for economic change has been treated in relation to a given economic process, arguing that instituted economic processes, being open-structured, have both endogenous and exogenous dynamics for change. Much of the analysis of the tomato, however, has been in terms of configurations combining the different economic processes of production, distribution, exchange and use. This adds another level of analysis to the one just undertaken.

Although, for reasons just stated, any instituted economic process by virtue of being interconnected with others is always open to change, nonetheless there emerge relatively stable relations where interconnections are coherent and reproducible, between the four elemental economic processes. In capitalist economies, interconnected processes of production, distribution, exchange and use reproduce and grow. Consumption of commodities by end-consumers, with all the internal social structuring of use by different social classes, groups and categories, nonetheless is strongly interconnected with modes of exchange through retailing, which in turn is connected to different ways of instituting processes of distribution and production. When these interconnections themselves become instituted, reproduce and expand in distinctive ways over periods of historical time and space, it becomes possible to speak of instituted configurations of economic processes. It should be stressed that configurations too are open-structured combinations of instituted economic processes.

The emergence of Heinz tomato ketchup and Campbell's Condensed Tomato Soup were heralded as truly 'revolutionary' events because, as commodities, they were leading members of a number of similar foods which created mass standardised urban consumption on an unparalleled scale. However, what was significant about this change is that it was the outcome of a combination of distinct and specific changes in the spheres of production, consumption, distribution and retail. Mass standardised production involved the creation of a dedicated supply base of tomato growers, a relatively new form of relationship between primary and secondary producers under a particular asymmetry of power. The new tomato factories, amongst the first to introduce flow-line production processes, were strategically located on newly integrated transport networks, essential to economies of scale by extension of markets. Retail outlets also underwent dramatic change, with multiple chains competing with independent owner-keeper shops. The institution of brands through advertising became a central vehicle of consolidating a mass demand: consumers could ask for the identical thing wherever they went (repeat demand), imitate other consumers (multiply demand) or simply independently replicate demand, given standardisation plus branding. In turn, the new foods led to new styles of consumption that could not simply be unilaterally caused by the existence of such products. Ketchup and hamburgers became a combination that helped to form American national culinary identity, and condensed soup slotted in to new domestic modes of cooking and eating as an early convenience food.

Describing a configuration like this, however, is to see it through a *post facto* perspective. It all fits together – only too well. The different instituted parts of the eventual configuration, such as an integrated rail transport system or the growth of fast food outlets, clearly had their own dynamic and trajectory. The different interrelated instituted processes had different and uncoordinated trajectories, emerging at different times and developing at different speeds. There was no master plan. However, there was equally no 'hidden hand', an equilibrating aggregation of multitudinous independent acts, smoothing out friction to eventually arrive at a harmonious coordination between previously disarticulated processes.

For, on the one hand, the emergence of a configuration is a process of instituting new patterns of coordination (including new markets) which cannot therefore rely on already existing forms of coordination. On the other hand, the emergence of new instituted processes involves the disruption, dislocation and often destruction of the pre-existing configurations. In the case just described, for example, urban demand based on mass wage labour did not arise from a *tabula rasa*, but from the dislocation of previous modes of life, mass migration and the break-up of old channels of food provision and supply.

To demonstrate this double aspect of transformation and destruction, the emergence of the UK supermarket configuration, a central underlying condition for our 'tomato variations', was approached from four different angles. Firstly, relations between retailers and growers created parallel hierarchies between supermarkets and suppliers, developing long-term partnerships between the top-of-the-range core suppliers and the top of the range in quality and range in supermarket shelves. This relation underpinned multiple and interlocking technological innovations in the productive systems, whether in the UK and the Netherlands or in Almeria and Gran Canaria. But at the same time, the old productive organisation, and the old relations between growers and their access to market, were largely destroyed and replaced. In the case of Guernsey, there was no place for their tomato economy in the new configuration. In the case of the Netherlands, there are continuing tensions between the direct grower-to-retailer supply relations and the intermediated channels that have recently been developed.

Secondly, the relations between retailers and manufacturers and the emergence of own-label manufacturers involved a fundamental change in the structure of manufacturing firms with the development of compartmentalised and exclusive supply relations and partnership product development. A 'monopsonistic matrix' developed on the basis of these criss-crossing exclusive supply relations for particular ranges of products (chilled soups, pizzas, pasta sauces, and so on) between the leading retailers and a relatively small group of major own-label manufacturers. New asymmetric power relations between retailers and manufacturers characterised this matrix, in which, significantly, manufacturers under the own-label arrangement had secure access to market space. This in turn formed the basis for new instituted modes of innovation, with entirely different risk parameters to those of the super-branded goods manufacturers. Short product life and lead times, continuous variety, and the following and leading of food fashion, combined with radical innovations and new types of food within the chill-food market.

Thirdly, relations between retailers and the distribution system of goods, both fresh and manufactured, have been completely transformed with the emergence of highly centralised retailer-dedicated logistics systems. Earlier forms of intermediation, independent manufacturer deliveries and, in particular, wholesale markets have been circumvented and replaced. For the UK, wholesale markets had become a nationally integrated system, dominated by Covent Garden, with regional and sub-regional counterparts. As the main conduit for fresh fruit and vegetables the route was long and strenuous, requiring tough and durable tomatoes. This wholesale market system, and a separate transport delivery system, has been swept aside by each supermarket's logistical networks. A 'monopsonistic matrix' between a limited number of major logistics companies and different retail chains, with criss-crossing dedicated exclusive partnerships, resembles that between retailers and own-label manufacturers. Integrated ICT systems, to which core suppliers have access, drive a continuous flow system from the point of sale to point of supply. For tomatoes, this means that the parameters of 'freshness' have been changed beyond recognition, with produce getting from farm gate to supermarket shelf in under 48 hours.

And fourthly, the relation between retailers and consumers has been transformed. Superstores linked to the car as the final link in the distribution system developed into the weekly one-stop shop. Catchment areas surrounding superstores are profiled for socio-economic characteristics, electronic point-of-sale information tracks purchasing behaviour, and product differentiation is developed and stratified to match differential disposable incomes. In terms of asymmetric power, supermarkets can achieve both a quasi-monopsony within a catchment area, as well as building market knowledge of consumer characteristics to much higher levels. They certainly know more about individual shoppers' neighbours' shopping behaviour and possibly more about individual shoppers' behaviour than they do themselves. Demand is societally organised in a different way through this changed relationship, enabling more choice within outlets and less choice between them. Socially stratified pizzas match socially stratified consumers in different ways through these channels. Tomato landscapes reflect social landscapes, both in the location of retail outlets and what is found in them. Old shopping habits disappeared with old shopping outlets; old food and product ranges distributed across a multiplicity of retail outlets are replaced by new food types (ready meals, chill-fresh, chill-cooked, multi-ethnic, *etcetera*) flowing through a single check-out under one roof.

It was argued that one of the preconditions for this uniquely UK configuration had been a high level of concentration and national integration in the first 'retail revolution' for an exceptionally urbanised and geographically dense population at the turn of the twentieth century. But the current configuration involved uneven tensions, transformations and dynamics for each of the four relations. Transformations of one relation created strains for others, and resistance from relatively enduring institutions no doubt constrained and shaped the pattern of change. Covent Garden, after centuries of change and decades of recent growth to a point where it was bursting at the seams, moved location and modernised institutionally for an imagined future that, almost immediately, dissolved. As with tectonic shifts, release of pressure in one area intensifies pressure for structural change in others.

Thus the transformation and reconfiguration of each of these four relations was necessarily an uneven, contingent and higgeldy-piggeldy process of de-institutionalisation and re-institutionalisation. Given the instituted character of economic processes, their separation *and* interrelation, structural causality involves a dynamic of conflict and tension arising from a mixture of relatively endogenous change from within a process and relatively exogenous change through relationships between processes. Configurational economic change is focused on particular and strong interdependencies between the four processes of production, distribution, exchange and use.

CLASHES BETWEEN CONFIGURATIONS

From the example of the emergence of the UK supermarket configuration and its attendant 'tomato variations' it is clear that configurations are bounded in space and time. They are also open-structured configurations in much the same way as any of their component instituted processes. The UK supermarket configuration, for example, is open to invasion by an American-style discount retailing spearheaded by Wal-Mart, based on economies of scale obtained across its global operation with standardised goods, predominantly manufacturer-branded. In this case, two very different modes of interconnecting processes of production, distribution, retail and consumption are present in the same or overlapping economic spaces. At one level, the ensuing disturbance can be seen in terms of competition. But, inasmuch as the forms of competition of each configuration is different, they are more like ships that pass in the night: one competing on price on one type of range of goods, the other competing on segmented and price differentiation over a quite different range of goods, sustained by its own-label and dedicated and/or exclusive supply bases. At this level, the contest between configurations is one of structural conflict, of incompatible modes of doing business. The conflict between own-label and branded manufacturers is symptomatic of this kind of structural tension: they do not operate either in the same market or with the same relation to the market. Competition has yet to be normalised within a shared instituted organisation of inter-firm relations and markets, in the way, for example, that Sainsbury and Tesco do within a configuration.

The disruption and contest over GM markets in the UK is another example. Analytically setting aside the crucial 'overdetermined' and contingent causal interplay of non-economic processes, the Zeneca matrix of firms and institutions, and in particular the engagement of supermarkets in market formation for GM tomato purée, contrasted sharply with the Monsanto agribusiness orientation. It was argued that these biotechnology firms were operating within very different power asymmetries between seed manufacturers, farmers, food manufacturers and retailers. They also were involved in quite different relations between public science infrastructure, funding, and in-firm privately financed R&D. This difference in configurational relations contributed to the strategic decision in the UK for Zeneca and retailers to segregate and label GM tomato purée as well as to market it under supermarket own-label. In the US, Monsanto scarcely considered end-markets, and indeed probably viewed, even still view, segregation as potentially market destroying. This in turn produced a clash in configurations when non-segregated and unlabelled and segregated and labelled GM products entered the same markets. Although Zeneca and Monsanto were not even operating in the same or even overlapping markets, the economic disruption of market formation and subsequent capital restructuring of biotechnology companies into separate pharmaceutical and agri-food businesses, can be seen to be an effect of structural conflict between differently configured economic processes. Quite apart from the role of ecological politics, contradictory and underdeveloped regulatory systems, consumer resistance, food panics, and other significantly shaping factors, there were therefore also distinctively *economic* processes of disruption.

HISTORY CONTINUES

The tomato, both as probe and object in its own right, manifests both diversity and causes of diversity in contemporary capitalisms. Whether as a hybrid golden mini-plum, a GM tomato purée, or pizza concasse in own-label livery, the structural causality of instituted economic process generates both relatively stable patterns and continuous and ongoing variation and diversity. The tomato acquires a specifically instituted economic existence, but only in relation to other instituted processes, cultural and political, legal and social.

Even within instituted economic processes, no single central structural causal principle, such as between relations and forces of production, capital accumulation and realisation, or market equilibration, exercises its sway.[4] Contingency and overdetermination deter reductionism to any mono-causality, and even within the economic sphere there is a diversity of dynamic processes of growth and destruction. The reality of the tomato in capitalism is fundamentally diverse by virtue of processes of institution and structural causality. In this view, capitalism is a many-fissured reality, not an overwhelming monolothic totality, obeying universal, now global iron laws. The view of capitalism as a monolithic global totality is firstly incorrect, but secondly politically disarming. It sustains a rhetoric of globalisation and market forces beyond social and political control, an economy outside society, not instituted in society. In small tomato-shaped ways, it has been shown that forms of capital, productive organisation, innovation, markets and competition are diversely instituted in different societies in different historical periods, and on different scales. Processes of transformative change are destructuring and restructuring in ways that constantly create new points of tension and conflict alongside stability and smooth functioning. There is nothing permanent or everlasting about capitalism. It has an undecided future. And so does the tomato.

NOTES

1 The perennial controversies surrounding the price of cars in the United Kingdom compared with Europe, or more recently over the comparative price of fuel and road transport, demonstrate how wrong it is to assume that global markets for cars and petrol have been instituted even in cases where global producers dominate.
2 The term 'open-structured processes' is preferred to both 'structure' and 'system', both on account of the unit of analysis being one of processes, hence ongoing occurrences and activities, rather than entities or arrangements of parts and wholes, and in order to avoid implications of closed totalities, either architectural or functionalist.
3 The role of innovation processes in disturbing existing instituted processes and inducing new ones has been central to the analysis of the changing tomato. However, as has been argued, innovation has also been analysed as an instituted economic process, and is far from the neo-Schumpeterian view of endogenous innovation. Care has also been taken to avoid introducing innovation as a 'moment of agency' or voluntaristic creation into an otherwise consistently causal account of change. Although quite different from economic processes, even epistemological change can be readily analysed causally in terms of a dynamic relation between exogenous and endogenous processes, viewing conceptual processes as open-structured. Indeed, stripped of its biological universalism, Piagetan 'structural genesis' theory analyses change causally in terms of conflicting internal structured conceptual schema open to external resistances from other conceptual schema, or structural characteristics of the natural and social world (Piaget, 1967, 1970).
4 The fact that relations between wage labour and capital have not figured prominently in the account of the tomato does not imply a lack of

recognition of their central significance in the instituted economic processes of different capitalisms. What is clear, however, is that there are important processes of change within capitalism which are additional to those generated by that relationship or within labour process.

Bibliography

Afshar, H. and Barrientos, S. (eds.) (1999), *Women, Globalisation and Fragmentation in the Developing World*. Macmillan. London.

Alberts, R.C. (1973), *The Good Provider: H.J. Heinz and His 57 Varieties*. Houghton Muffin. Boston.

Allen, C. (1998), *Transplanting the Garden. The Story of the Relocation of Covent Garden Market*. Covent Garden Market Authority. London.

Appadurai, A. (ed.) (1986), *The Social Life of Things. Commodities in Cultural Perspective*. Cambridge University Press. Cambridge.

Appadurai, A. (1988), 'How to make a national cuisine: cookbooks in contemporary India', *Comparative Studies in Society and History*, 30, 3–24.

Appert, N. (1810), *Le Livre de Tous les Ménages au L'Art de Conserver Pendant Plusiers Années Toutes Les Substances Animal et Végetales*. Bureau Consultatif des Arts et Manufactures. Ministre de L'Intérieur. Paris.

Artusi, P. (1891), *La Scienza in cucina e l'arte di mangiar bene*. Einaudi. Florence.

Baret, C., Lehndorff, S. and Sparks, L. (eds.) (2000), *Flexible Working in Food Retailing. A Comparison between France, Germany, the United Kingdom and Japan*. Routledge. London.

Baret, C. with Lehndorff, S. and Ribault, T. (2000), 'Societal Constraints and strategic room for manoeuvre' In Baret et al. (eds.), *Flexible Working in Food Retailing. A Comparison between France, Germany, the United Kingdom and Japan*. Routledge. London.

Barrientos, S., Bee, A., Matear, A., and Vogel, I. (1999), *Women and Agribusiness. Working Miracles in the Chilean Fruit Export Sector*. Macmillan. London.

Barrientos, S. and Perrons, D. (1999), 'Gender and the Global Food Chain: A Comparative Study of Chile and the UK', in Afshar, H. and Barrientos, S. (eds.), *Women, Globalisation and Fragmentation in the Developing World*. Macmillan. London.

Beaumont, J. and Wilcock, G. (1979), *The Grocery Industry. Market Developments*. Institute of Grocery Distribution. Watford.

Beeton, I.M. (1861), *Book of Household Management*. S.O. Beeton. London

Bence, V. (1997), 'Internationalising a distribution brand. Exel Logistics' in Taylor, D. (ed.) *Global Cases in Logistics and Supply Chain Management*. International Thomson Business Press. London.

Benson, J. and Shaw, G. (eds.) (1992), *The Evolution of Retail Systems, 1800–1914*. Leicester University Press. Leicester.

Best, M. (1990), *The New Competition. Institutions of Industrial Restructuring*. Harvard University Press. Cambridge MA.

Beynon, H., Grimshaw, D., Rubery, J., and Ward, K. (2002), *Managing Employment Change. The New Realities of* Work. Oxford University Press. Oxford.

Bitting, A.W. (1912), *The Canning of Foods; a Description of the Methods Followed in Commercial Canning*. United States Department of Agriculture Bulletin, 151.

Bitting, A.W. (1937), *Appertizing, or the Art of canning: its history and development*. TradePressroom. San Francisco CA.

Bonanno, A., Busch, L., Friedland, W.H., Gouveia, L., and Mingione, E. (eds.) (1994), *From Columbus to ConAgra. The Globalisation of Agriculture and Food*. University of Kansas Press. Kansas.

Bradley, R. (1720), *The Gentleman and Gardeners Kalendar ... to which is added the design of a greenhouse*. Mears. London.

Bradley, R. (1728), *Dictionarium Botanicum, or a Botanical Dictionary for the use of the Curious in Husbandry and Gardening*. Woodward & Peele. London.

Briggs, R. (1788), *The English Art of Cookery, according to the present practice*. Robinson. London.

Burnett, J. (1985), *Plenty and Want. A Social History of Diet in England from 1815 to the Present Day*. Methuen. London.

Busch, L., Lacy, W.B., Burkhardt, J., and Lacy, L.R. (eds.) (1991), *Plants, Power and Profit. Social, Economic and Ethical Consequences of the new Biotechnologies*. Blackwell. Oxford.

Callon, M. (1986), 'Some elements of a sociology of translation: domestication of scallops and the fishermen of St Brieuc Bay' in Law, J. (ed.), *Power, Action, and Belief: A New Sociology of Knowledge*. Routledge. London.

Callon, M. ed. (1998), *The Laws of the Markets*. Introduction. Blackwell. Oxford. 1-57.

Callon, M. (1998), 'An essay on framing and overflowing: economic externalities revisited by sociology' in Callon, M. (ed), *The Laws of the Markets*. Blackwell. Oxford. 244-269

Camporesi, P. (1993), *The Magic Harvest. Food, Folklore and Society*. Polity. Cambridge.

Castles, F.R. and Macself A.J. (eds.) (1911), *Tomatoes: and how to grow them*. Collingridge. London.

Clarke, A. and Fujimura, J.H. (eds.) (1992), *The Right Tools for the Job. At Work in the Twentieth Century Life Sciences*. Princeton University Press. Princeton, NJ.

Coe, S. (1994), *America's First Cuisines*. University of Texas Press. Austin.

Coates, K.S. and Silburn, R.L. (1970), *Poverty: The Forgotten Englishmen*, Penguin. Harmondsworth.

Collins, D. (1994), *America's Favourite Food: The Story of Campbell Soup Company*. Harry Abrams. New York.

Competition Commission (2000), *Supermarkets. A Report on the Supply of Groceries from Multiple Stores in the United Kingdom*. 3 vols. HMSO. London.

Coombs, R., Harvey, M. and Tether, B. (2001), 'Analysing Distributed Innovation Processes'. ESRC Centre for Research in Innovation and Competition, Discussion Paper 43. http://les.man.ac.uk/cric/papers.htm

Coombs, R. and Metcalfe, S.J. (1998), 'Distributed capabilities and the governance of the firm.' ESRC Centre for Research in Innovation and Competition, Discussion Paper 16. http://les.man.ac.uk/cric/papers.htm

Coombs, R. and Metcalfe, S.J. (2000), 'Organizing for innovation: co-ordinating distributed innovation iapabilities' in Foss, N. and Mahnke, V. (eds.), *Competence, Governance, and Entrepreneurship*. Oxford University Press. Oxford.

Coombs, T. (1997), 'Marketing genetically modified foods.' Lecture to Future Foods '97. Auckland, New Zealand. (Head of Public Affairs. Safeway, UK)

Cooper, J., Browne, M. and Peters, M. (1994), *European Logistics. Markets, Management and Strategy*. 2nd edition. Blackwell. Oxford.

Corstjens, J. and Corstjens, M. (1996), *Store Wars: The Battle for Mindspace and Shelfspace*. Wiley. New York.

Dakers, J.S. and Macself A.J. (eds.) (1930), *Simple Greenhouse Management*. Collingridge. London.

Davis, D. (1965), *A History of Shopping*. Routledge & Kegan Paul. London.

Diamond, J. (1999), *Guns, Germs, and Steel. The Fates of Human Societies*, W.W. Norton. New York.

Dixon, J. (2000), 'Cooks, Chooks, and Culinary Cultures. A Cultural Economy Model for the Study of Commodity Systems', PhD thesis, Royal Melbourne Institute of Technology University, Melbourne.

Doel, C. (1996), 'Market development and organisational change: the case of the food industry' in Wrigley, N. and Lowe, M. (eds.), *Retailing,*

Consumption and Capital. Towards the New Retailing Geography. Longman. Harlow.

Dressler, R.L. (1953), *Botanic Museum Leaflets*. Harvard University, 6, December.

Drummond, J.C. and Wilbraham, A. (1939), *The Englishman's Food. A History of Five Centuries of English Diet*. Cape. London.

Duncan, J. (1841), *History of Guernsey, with occasional references to Jersey, Alderney and Sark*. Longman, Brown, Green & Longman. London.

Eco, U. (1989), 'Lowbrow Highbrow, Highbrow Lowbrow.' In Mahsun, C.A. (ed), *Pop Art. The Critical Dialogue*. UMI Books on Demand, Ann Arbor. London.

Encyclopaedia Britannica (1771). Bell & Macfarquhar. Edinburgh.

European Commission (1995), *Social Protection in Europe*. Brussels.

Fabian Society (1891), *The Scandal of London's Markets*. Fabian Tract, 36. London.

Farley, J. (1789), *The London Art of Cookery, and Housekeeper's Complete Assistant*. Scatcherd & Whitaker. London.

Featherstone, M. (1991), *Consumer Culture and Postmodernism*. Sage. London.

Fernie, J. and Penman, I. (1994), 'Supply chain management in grocery retailing: Exel Logistics' in Hughes, D. (ed) *Breaking with Tradition. Building Partnership and Alliances in the European Food Industry*. Wye College Press. Wye.

Fine, B., Heasman, M. and Wright, J. (1996), *Consumption in the Age of Affluence. The World of Food*. Routledge. London.

Fine, B., Heasman, M., and Wright, J. (1998), 'What we eat and why: social norms and systems of provision' in Murcott, A. (ed), *The Nation's Diet. The Social Science of Food Choice*. Longmann. London.

Foord, J., Bowlby, S. and Tillsley, C. (1996), 'The changing place of retailer-supplier relations in British retailing' in Wrigley, N. et al., (eds.), *Retailing, Consumption and Capital. Towards the New Retailing Geography*. Longman. Harlow.

Francatelli, C.E. (1841,1973), *Chef to Queen Victoria, The recipes of Charles Elmé Francatelli*. Ed. Curah., A.M. Kimber. London.

Freathy, P., and Sparks, L. (2000), 'The organisation of working time in large UK food retailing firms' in Baret et al. (eds.), *Flexible Working in Food Retailing. A Comparison between France, Germany, the United Kingdom and Japan*. Routledge. London.

Friedland, W.H. (1994), 'The new globalization: the case of fresh produce' in Bonanno, A., Busch, L., Friedland, W.H., Gouveia, L. and Mingione, E. (eds.), *From Columbus to Conagra. The Globalisation of Agriculture and Food*. University Press of Kansas. Austin.

Friedland, W.H. and Barton, A. (1975), *De-Stalking the Wily Tomato: A case study in social consequences in California Agricultural Research*. Research Monograph, 15. University of California, Davis.

Friedland, W.H. and Barton, A. (1976), 'The harvesting machine saved tomatoes for California.' *Society*, 13, 34–42.

Gadrey, J. and Lehndorff, S. with Ribault, T. (2000), 'A societal interpretation of the differences and similarities in working time practices' in Baret et al., (eds.), *Flexible Working in Food Retailing. A Comparison between France, Germany, the United Kingdom and Japan*. Routledge. London.

Garton, J. (1770), *The Practical Gardener, and Gentleman's Directory*. Saunders. Dublin.

Gerard, J. (1636), *The Herball Or Generall Historie of Plantes*. Adam Islip, Joice Norton and Richard Whitakers. London.

Gereffi, G. (1996), 'Global commodity chains: new forms of co-ordination and control among nations and firms in international industries', *Competition and Change*, 4, 427-39.

Gereffi, G. and Korzeniewicz, M. (1994), *Commodity Chains and Global Capitalism*. Praeger. Westport, CT.

Gillow, G. J. (1958), *A Short Survey of Horticulture in Guernsey*. Guernsey Press. Guernsey.

Girrard, P. J. (1966), *Peter Girrard's Guernsey. A Miscellany of Guernsey History and Its People*. Guernsey Press. Guernsey.

Glucksmann, M. (1990), *Women Assemble. Women Workers and the New Industries in Inter-war Britain*. Routledge. London.

Goodman, A. and Webb, S. (1994*), For Richer and Poorer: The changing distribution of income in the United Kingdom 1961–1991*. Institute of Fiscal Studies Commentary, 42. IFS. London.

Goody, J. (1982), *Cooking, Cuisine, and Class: A Study in Comparative Sociology*. Cambridge University Press. Cambridge.

Gould, W.A. (1992), *Tomato Production, Processing and Technology*. 3rd edition. CTI Publications. Baltimore, MD.

Granovetter, M. (1985), 'Economic action and social structure: the problem of embeddedness', *American Journal of Sociology*, 91, 3, 481–510

Granovetter, M. (1992a), 'The sociological and economic approaches to labour market analysis: a social structural view' in Granovetter, M., and Swedberg, R. (eds.), *The Sociology of Economic Life*. Edward Elgar. Cheltenham.

Granovetter, M. (1992b), 'Economic institutions as social constructions: a framework for analysis', *Acta Sociologica*, 35, 3–11.

Granovetter, M. and McGuire, P. (1998), 'The making of an industry: electricity in the United States' in Callon, M. (ed), *The Laws of the Markets*. Blackwell. Oxford.

Green, K. (1991), 'Shaping technologies and shaping markets: creating the demand for biotechnology.' *Technology Analysis and Strategic Management,* 3, 1, 57–76.

Grewe, R. (1987), 'The arrival of the tomato in Spain and Italy: early recipes'. *Journal of Gastronomy,* 3, 67–83.

Grierson, D. (1991), 'Controlling gene expression and fruit quality in transgenic tomatoes'. *Royal Agricultural Society of England Journal,* 127-132.

Grierson, D. (1996), 'Silent genes and everlasting fruits and vegetables'. *Nature Biotechnology,* 14, July, 828–9.

Grierson, D. (1997), 'The development of a product: from university research to commercial application'. BBSRC /Gatsby Charitable Foundation booklet.

Griffiths, P. (1967), *The History of the Indian Tea Industry.* Weidenfeld & Nicolson. London.

Guha, A. (1977), *Planter-Raj to Swaraj.* People's Publishing House. New Delhi.

Hallsworth, A.G. (1999), 'Wal-Mart in Canada or: in the Wal-Mart panopticon they never sleep'. Paper for the LCCS/IBG conference, November. London.

Hallsworth, A.G. and Taylor, M. (1996), ' "Buying" power – interpreting retail change in a circuits of power framework'. *Environment and Planning, A,* 28, 2125–2137.

Harvey, J.H. (1974), *Early Nurserymen.* Phillimore. London.

Harvey, M. (1998), 'UK Supermarkets: New products and labour market segmentation and the restructuring of the supply-demand matrix'. Paper to the International Labour Market Segmentation Working Party. Trento. Italy.

Harvey, M. (1999a), 'Innovation and Competition in UK supermarkets', *ESRC Centre for Research in Innovation and Competition,* Briefing Paper, 31. http://les.man.ac.uk/cric/ papers.htm

Harvey, M. (1999b), 'Cultivation and Comprehension: How genetic modification irreversibly alters the human engagement with nature'. *Sociology Research Online,* Rapid Response Issue, October.

Harvey, M. (1999c), 'Economies of time: a framework for analysing the restructuring of employment relations'. In Felstead, A.. and Jewson, N. (eds.), *Global Trends in Flexible Labour.* Macmillan. London.

Harvey, M. (2002), 'Markets, supermarkets and the macro-social shaping of demand. An instituted economic process account'. In McMeekin, A., Green, K., Tomlinson, M. and Walsh, V. (eds.), *Innovation by Demand: Interdisciplinary Approaches to the Study of Demand and its Role in Innovation.* Manchester University Press. Manchester.

Harvey, M., Beynon, H. and Quilley, S. (1999), 'Processes of variation: how capitalism has appropriated the tomato'. Paper to the CRIC

International Symposium, Approaches to Varieties of Capitalism, March.

Hill, J. (1755), *The Gardener's Pocket-Book, or a Country gentleman's recreation. Being the Kitchen, Fruit and Flower Garden*. London.

Hill, J.W. (1874), *Historical Directory of the Channel Islands, Guernsey*. Frederick Clark. London.

HMSO (1926), *Horticultural Produce (Sales on Commission) Act*. London.

Hodgson, G.M. (1997), 'The ubiquity of habits and rules'. *Cambridge Journal of Economics*, 21, 663–84.

Hogan, D.G. (1997), *Selling 'em by the Sack. White Castle and the Creation of American Food*. New York University Press. New York.

House of Lords (1998), *EC Regulation of Genetic Modification in Agriculture*. Select Committee on European Communities, Second Report. 15 December.

Hughes, D. (ed.) (1994), *Breaking with Tradition. Building Partnership and Alliances in the European Food Industry*. Wye College Press. Wye.

Hyam, E. (1954), 'The Tomato'. *National English Review*, 142:36, 36–40.

Institute of Grocery Distribution (1977a), *Developments in the Retail Trade*. Watford.

Institute of Grocery Distribution. (1997b), *Distribution Review*. Watford.

Jefferson, T. (1944), *Thomas Jefferson's Garden Book, 1766–1824*. Ed. E.M. Betts. American Philosophical Society. Philadelphia.

Jefferys, J.B. (1954), *Retail Trading in Britain. 1850–1950*. National Institute of Economic and Social Research, Economic and Social Studies, XII. Cambridge University Press. Cambridge.

Jefferys, J.B., and Knee, D. (1962), *Retailing in Europe. Present Structure and Future Trends*. Macmillan. London.

John, J. (1999), 'Housing as Deprivation', in *The plight of 'Unfree' Tea Workers*. Labour File, 5, 7–9, 20–7.

Johnson, J.W. (1829), *A History of English Gardening*. London.

Johnson, J.W. (1850), *The Cottage Gardener or Amateur and Cottager's Guide to Outdoor Gardening and Spade Cultivation*. London.

Johnston, J.J. (1976), 'The development of the food canning industry in Britain during the interwar period'. In Oddy, D. and Miller, D. (eds.), *The Making of the Modern British Diet*. Croom Helm. London.

Jones, S. (2000), *Almost Like a Whale. The Origin of the Species Updated*. Transworld Publishers. London.

Joseph Rowntree Foundation. (1995), *Inquiry into Income and Wealth*. York.

Justice, J. (1765), *The British Gardener's New Director*. 4th edition. Exshaw. Dublin.

Kimmelman, B.A. (1992), 'Organisms and interests in scientific research. R.A. Emerson's claims for the unique contributions of agricultural genetics'. In Clarke, A. and Fujimura, J.H. (eds.), *The Right Tools for the Job. At Work in the Twentieth Century Life Sciences.* Princeton University Press. Princeton, NJ.

Kopytoff, I. (1986), 'The cultural biography of things'. In Appadurai, A. (ed.), *The Social Life of Things. Commodities in Cultural Perspective.* Cambridge University Press. Cambridge.

Kozloff, M. (1997), '"Pop" culture, metaphysical disgust, and the new vulgarians'. In Madoff, S.H. (ed.), *Pop Art. A Critical History,* University of California Press. Berkeley.

Kurlansky, M. (1999), *Cod. A Biography of the Fish that Changed the World.* Vintage. London.

Kuspit, D. (1989), 'Pop art: A reactionary realism'. In Mahsun, C.A. (ed.), *Pop Art. The Critical Dialogue.* UMI Books on Demand. Ann Arbor. London.

Lash, S. and Urry, J. (1994), *Economies of Signs and* Space. Sage. London.

Latour, B. (aka Jim Johnson) (1995), 'Mixing humans and nonhumans together: The sociology of a door-closer'. In Star, S.L. (ed.), *Ecologies of Knowledge. Work and Politics in Science and Technology.* State University of New York Press. New York.

Law, J. and Callon, M. (1995), 'Engineering and sociology in a military aircraft project: A network analysis of technological change'. In Star, S.L. (ed.), *Ecologies of Knowledge. Work and Politics in Science and Technology.* State University of New York Press. New York.

Lehndorff, S. (1999), 'Striving for greater personnel flexibility: the retail trade and the segmentation of internal labour markets'. Paper to the International Working Party on Labour Market Segmentation, Bremen.

Letablier, M.T. and Delfosse, C. (1995), 'Genèse d'une convention de qualité. Cas des appelations fromagères'. In Allaire, G. and Boyer, R. (eds.), *La Grande Transformation de l'agriculture.* INRA, Economica. Paris.

Lindemann, J. (1993), 'Marketing transgenic food crops in the U.S.: regulatory issues'. In Yoder, J.I. (ed.), *Molecular Biology of Tomato: Fundamental Advances and Crop Improvement.* Technomic Publishing. Lancaster, PA.

Livingstone, M. (1990), *Pop Art. A Continuing History.* Thames & Hudson. London.

Loudon, J.C. (1831), *An Encyclopaedia of Agriculture.* London.

Luckwill, L.C. (1943), *The Genus Lycopersicum: An Historical, Biological and Taxonomic Survey of the Wild and Cultivated Tomatoes.* Aberdeen University Studies. Aberdeen.

MacKendry, M. (1973), *Seven Centuries of English Cooking.* Ed. A. Boxer. Wiedenfeld & Nicolson. London.

Madoff, S.H. (ed.) (1997), *Pop Art. A Critical History*. University of California Press. Berkeley.

Mahsun, C.A. (ed.) (1989), *Pop Art. The Critical Dialogue*. UMI Books on Demand. Ann Arbor. London.

Mandeville, B. (1970), *The Fable of the Bees*. Penguin Classics. London.

Manglesdorf, P.C., and Reeves, R.G. (1939) 'The Origin of Indian Corn and its Relatives'. *Texas Agricultural Experiment Station Bulletin*, 574. Texas.

Martineau, B. (2001), *First Fruit. The creation of the Flavr Savr Tomato and the Birth of Biotech Food*. McGraw-Hill. New York.

Mayer, S. and Rutovitz, J. (1996), 'Trojan tomatoes: genetically engineered for delayed softening or ripening'. Greenpeace draft report, unpublished.

McKelvey, M. (1996), *Evolutionary Innovations: The Business of Biotechnology*. Oxford University Press. Oxford.

McKelvey, M. (1997), 'Coevolution in Commercial Genetic Engineering'. *Industrial and Corporate Change*, 6: 3, 503-32.

McLaughlin, E.W., Perosio, D.J. and Park, J.L. (1998), 'Retail logistics and merchandising in the US. Current status and requirements in the year 2000. In Ziggers, G.W., Trienekens, J.H. and Zuurbier, P.J.P. (eds.), *Proceedings of the 3rd International Conference on Chain Management in Agri- and Food Business*. University of Wageningen. Wageningen.

Meader, J. (1771), *The Modern Gardener, or Universal Calendar*. Hawes. London.

Mennel, S. (1985), *All Manners of Food. Eating and Taste in England and France from the Middle Ages to the Present*. Blackwell. London.

Middleton, C.H. and Heath, A. (1937), *From Garden to Kitchen. Wherein the gardener learns how to grow vegetables and the housewife how to cook them*. Cassell. London.

Miller, P. (1748), *The Gardener's Dictionary: containing the methods of cultivating the garden, conservatory and vineyard*. 3rd edition. London.

Minguzzi, A. and Passaro, R. (1993), 'Considerazioni metodologiche sui modelli di competitività internazionale delle imprese'. *Dynamis*, 1:93. IDSE, Milan.

Mintel (1998), 'Chilled ready meals', *Marketing Intelligence*, May.

Mintz, S.W. (1986), *Sweetness and Power. The Place of Sugar in Modern History*. Penguin. London.

Mintz, S.W. (1996), *Tasting Food, Tasting Freedom. Excursions into Eating, Culture and the Past*. Beacon. Boston, MA.

Mitchell, A. P. (1964), *Modernisation of the Glass House Industry*. States of Guernsey Horticultural Committee Report

Mitchener, B. (1998), 'Tomato Wars. Safeway, Sainsbury say novel paste hits the spot in Britain'. *Wall Street Journal.*

Mittman, G. and Fuasto-Sterling, A. (1992) 'Whatever happened to *Planaria?* C.M.Child and the physiology of inheritance'. In Clarke, A. and Fujimura, J.H. (eds.), *The Right Tools for the Job. At Work in the Twentieth Century Life Sciences.* Princeton University Press. Princeton, NJ.

Moore, E. (ed.) (1880–5), *The Florist Pomologist and Suburban Gardener, A Pictorial Monthly Magazine.* London.

Murcott, A. (ed.) (1998), *The Nation's Diet. The Social Science of Food Choice.* Longman. London.

Nevins, D.J. and Jones, R.A. (eds.) (1987), *Tomato Biotechnology.* Proceedings of a symposium University of Davis, CA. New York, NY Liss.

Ogier, D. M. (1962), 'Reformation and society in Guernsey: c.1500 – c.1640'. University of Warwick, PhD thesis.

Ogier J.P. (1997), *Horticultural Profitability and Viability Report.* States of Guernsey Archive.

Ortega, B. (1999a), *In Sam We Trust: The Untold Story of Sam Walton and how Wal-Mart is Devouring the World.* Kogan Page. London.

Ortega, B. (1999b), 'The Wal-Marting of America' Rocky Mountain Peace and Justice Centre. Boulder, CO.

Owen, E. (1974), 'Glassing over difficulties'. *Financial Times,* 23rd August.

Philips, P. (1978) 'California Canneries'. MA Thesis. Mimeo. University of California, Davis, CA.

Phillips, H. (1822), *History of Cultivated Vegetables, comprising their botanical, medicinal, edible and chemical qualities, natural history and relation to art, science and commerce.* 2nd edition. 2 vols. London

Phillips, Lord (2000), *The BSE Inquiry: The Report.* HMSO. London.

Phillips, M. (1992), 'Fairs, markets, pedlars and small-scale shops'. In Benson, J. and Shaw, G. (eds.), *The Evolution of Retail Systems, 1800–1914.* Leicester University Press. Leicester.

Piaget, J. (1967), *Biologie et Connaissance. Essai sur les relations entre les régulations organiques et les processus cognitifs.* Gallimard. Paris.

Piaget, J. (1970), *Structuralism.* Basic Books. New York.

Pilcher, J.M. (1998), *Que vivan los tamales! Food and the Making of Mexican Identity.* University of New Mexico Press. Albuquerque.

Polanyi, K. (1944), *The Great Transformation. The Political and Economic Origins of Our Time.* Beacon. Boston, MA.

Polanyi, K. (1957), 'The economy as instituted process'. In Polanyi, K., Arensberg, C.M., and Pearson, H.W., (eds.), *Trade and Market in the Early Empires. Economies in History and Theory.* Free Press. New York.

Redenbaugh, K., Hiatt, W., Martineau, B., Kramer, M., Sheehy, R., Sanders, R., Houck, C. and Emlay, D. (1992), *Safety Assessment of Genetically Engineered Fruits and Vegetables. A Case Study of the Flavr Savr^{TM} Tomato*. CRC Press. Boca Raton, FA.

Rees, G. (1969), *St Michael. A History of Marks and Spencer*. Weidenfeld & Nicolson. London.

Rhodes, G. (1999), *New British Classics*. BBC Consumer Publishing. London.

Richards, A.A. (1945), *Tomato and Cucumber Culture*. Collingridge. London.

Rick, M.R. (1978), 'The tomato'. *Scientific American*, 239, 67–76.

Rifkin, J. (1998), 'Apocalypse When?' *New Scientist*, 31 October. 34–37.

Rifkin, J. (1999), *The Biotech Century. How Genetic Commerce will change the World*. Phoenix. London.

Rose, J.N. (1899), 'Notes on useful plants in Mexico', *Contributions to the US National Herbarium*. Vol. 5. Washington, D.C.

Runciman Committee (1957), *Report of the Committee on Horticultural Marketing*. HMSO. Parliamentary Papers. Cmnd 61.

Sabine, J. (1820), *Transactions of the Horticultural Society of London*. London.

Santich, B. (1995), *The Original Mediterranean Cuisine. Medieval Recipes for Today*. Wakefield Press. Kent Town, Australia.

Schuch, W. and Poole, N. (1993), 'The evolution of the regulation of genetically modified organisms in Europe'. In Yoder, J.I. (ed.), *Molecular Biology of Tomato: Fundamental Advances and Crop Improvement*. Technomic Publishing. Lancaster PA.

Sereni, E. (1974), *Storia del Paesaggio Agrario Italiano*, Laterza. Rome.

Sexton, L. (1988), 'Eating money in Papua New Guinea'. *Food and Foodways*, 3, 119-142.

Shaw, S.A., Gibbs, J. and Gray, V. (1994), *The Strathclyde Wholesale Markets Study Main Report*. University of Strathclyde. Fresh Produce Consortium.

Shephard, S. (2000), *Pickled, Potted and Canned. The Story of Food Preserving*. Headline. London.

Shewell-Cooper, W.E. (1979), *The Complete Greenhouse Gardiner*, Mayflower. London.

Smith, A.F. (1994), *The Tomato in America. Early History, Culture, and Cookery*. University of South Carolina Press. South Carolina.

Smith, A.F. (1996), *Pure Ketchup. A History of America's National Condiment*. University of South Carolina Press. South Carolina.

Sparks, L. (2000), 'The rise of the large format store'. In Baret, C., Lehndorff, S. and Sparks, L. (eds.), *Flexible Working in Food

Retailing. A Comparison between France, Germany, the United Kingdom and Japan. Routledge. London.

Spice, H.R. (1959), *Polythene Film in Horticulture*. Faber & Faber. London.

Star, S.L. (ed.) (1995), *Ecologies of Knowledge. Work and Politics in Science and Technology*. State University of New York Press. New York.

States Committee of Horticulture (1982), *Review of Guernsey Horticulture 1982 and Proposals for Support to 1993*. States of Guernsey Archive.

Stark, B.L. (1981), 'The rise of sedentary life'. In *Supplement to the Handbook of Middle American Indians*. Vol. 1, *Archaeology*, ed., J.A. Sabloff. University of Texas Press. Austin, TX.

Strasser, S. (1989), *Satisfaction Guaranteed. The Making of the American Mass Market*. Pantheon Books. New York.

Swedberg, R. (1998), *Max Weber and the Idea of Economic Sociology*, Princeton University Press. Princeton, NJ.

Sylvander, B. (1995), 'Conventions de qualité, concurrence et coopération. Cas du "label rouge" dans la filière Volailles'. In Allaire, G. and Boyer, R. (eds.), *La Grande Transformation de l'Agriculture*. INRA, Economica. Paris.

Tanksley, S.D. (1993),'Development and application of a molecular linkage map in tomato', in Yoder, J.I. (ed.), *Molecular Biology of Tomato: Fundamental Advances and Crop Improvement*. Technomic Publishing. Lancaster PA.

Taylor Nelson Sofres (2002), *Consumer Usage Panel*, http://www.tnsofres.com

Tedlow, R.S. (1990), *New and Improved: The Story of Mass Marketing in America*. Basic Books. New York.

Teitel, M. and Wilson, K.A. (2000), *Changing the Nature of Nature. What you need to know about genetically modified food*. Vision. London.

Tether, B.S. and Metcalfe, J.S. (2000), 'Horndal at Heathrow? Incremental innovation through procedural change at a congested airport.' In Metcalfe, J.S. and Miles, I. (eds.), *Innovation Systems in the Service Economy. Measurement and Case Study Analysis*. Kluwer Academic Publishers. London.

The Grocer, (1999) 'Focus on chilled-snacks', Sarah Hardcastle, 17 July, 37–40.

Thévenot, L. (1995), 'Des marchés aux normes'. In Allaire, G. and Boyer, R. (eds.), *La Grande Transformation de l'agriculture*. INRA, Economica. Paris.

Thomas, K. (1983), *Man and the Natural World: Changing Attitudes in England 1500–1800*. Allen Lane. London.

Tomato News. (2000), http:// www. tomate.org.

Tomlinson, M. and McMeekin, A. (2002), 'Social Routines and the consumption of food'. In McMeekin, A., Green, K., Tomlinson, M.

and Walsh, V., (eds.) *Innovation by Demand: Interdisciplinary Approaches to the Study of Demand and its Role in Innovation*. Manchester University Press. Manchester.

Torres, G. (1997), *The Force of Irony. Power in the Everyday Life of Mexican Tomato Growers*. Berg. Oxford.

Trail, B. and Harmsen, H. (1997), 'Pennine Foods: always prepared for a new ready meal'. In Trail, B., and Grunert, K.G. (eds), *Product and Process Innovation in the Food Industry*. Blackie Academic & Professional. London.

Trienekens, J.H. and Zuurbier, P.J.P. (eds.) (1996), *Proceedings of the 2nd International Conference on Chain Management in Agri- and Food Business*. University of Wageningen. Wageningen.

Tuper, F. B. (1976), *History of Guernsey and its Bailiwick*. 2nd Edition. Simkin Marshall & Co. London.

US Patent Serial No. 07/119,614. (1987), 'Tomatoes with reduced expression of polygalacturanase'.

Van der Vorst, J.G.A.L. (1996), 'Logistical Control Concepts in chain perspective – a framework to structure logistical control.' In Trienekens, J.H. and Zuurbier, P.J.P. (eds.), *Proceedings of the 2nd International Conference on Chain Management in Agri- and Food Business*. University of Wageningen. Wageningen.

Van Hoek, R.I. and Muntenden, J. (1996), 'Value-added logistics in the international agri- and food supply chain'. In Trienekens, J.H. and Zuurbier, P.J.P. (eds.), *Proceedings of the 2nd International Conference on Chain Management in Agri- and Food Business*. University of Wageningen. Wageningen.

Walton, J.K. (1992), *Fish and Chips and the English Working Class 1870–1940*. Leicester University Press. Leicester.

Ward, K., Grimshaw, D., Beynon, H. and Rubery, J. (1998), 'The management of employment change in the North West. Case Study of three Tesco Stores. Mimeo. Manchester.

Warde, A. (1997), *Consumption, Food and Taste. Culinary Antinomies and Commodity Culture*. Sage. London.

Warde, A. (1999), 'Convenience food: space and timing', *British Food Journal*, 101:7, 518–527.

Warde, A. and Martens, L. (2000), *Eating Out. Social Differentiation, Consumption and Pleasure*. Cambridge University Press. Cambridge.

Webber, R. (1969), *Covent Garden: Mud Salad Market*. Dent. London.

Webber, R. (1972), *Market Gardening. The History of Commercial Flower, Fruit and Vegetable Growing*. David & Charles. Newton Abbot.

Woolven, J., Harris, D., Dawson, J. and Marshall, D. (1996), *Food Industry Forces for Change*. Institute of Grocery Distribution. Watford.

Wrigley, N. (1998), 'How British Retailers have shaped food choice', in Murcott, A. (ed.), *The Nation's Diet. The Social Science of Food Choice*. Longman. London.

Wrigley, N. and Lowe, M. (eds.) (1996), *Retailing, Consumption and Capital. Towards the New Retailing Geography*. Longman. Harlow.

Yoder, J.I. (ed.) (1993), *Molecular Biology of Tomato: Fundamental Advances and Crop Improvement*. Technomic Publishing. Lancaster, PA.

Zabel, P., Van Wordragen, M., Weide, R., Liharska, T., Stam, P., and Koornneef, M. (1993), 'Integration of the classical and molecular linkage maps of tomato chromosome 6', in Yoder J.I. (ed.), *Molecular Biology of Tomato: Fundamental Advances and Crop Improvement*. Technomic Publishing. Lancaster PA.

Zuckerman, L. (1999), *The Potato*. Macmillan. London.

Appendix: list of interviews

Interviews were conducted between February 1998 and March 2000

TOMATO GROWERS

Agombar, Peter	Arreton Valley Nurseries, Marketing Manager	Isle of Wight
Blair, Douglas and Penny	Low Carr Nursery (organic)	Lancashire
Chadwick, Steve	Van Heyningen Brothers, Technical Director	Sussex
Hamilton, Kevin	Cantelo Nursery	Somerset
Harvey Chris	Buckland Garden Nurseries	Worcestershire
Higgs, Fred	Guernsey Growers Association	Isle of Wight
Jones, John and Caroline	Guy and Wright Nurseries Tomato Growers Association	Hertfordshire
Lewis, Arnold	Van Heyningen Brothers, Chairman	Sussex
Matthews, Michael	Styal Road Nurseries	Lancashire
Moffat, Fred	Guernsey Growers Association	Guernsey
Parish, Jim	Amateur, Three generations1870-1998	Powys
Parker, Alan	Arreton Valley Nurseries, President, Tomato Growers Association	Isle of Wight
Pearson, Philip	Woodhouse Nurseries	Lancashire
Rudd, Frank and Chris	Wood End, Stocks Lane	Lancashire
Turner, Alan	Cantelo Nursery	Bucks

OTHER GUERNSEY INTERVIEWS

Dickson, John	Economist Guernsey States	Guernsey
Daly, Harold	Kenilworth Nurseries Ex-Manager	Guernsey
Galliene, Fred	Horticultural Advisory Service, Ex-Advisor	Guernsey
Le Garff, Jim	Guernsey Tomato Marketing Board, Ex-Chairman	Guernsey
Ogier, John	Committee for Horticulture, Guernsey States	Guernsey

UK TOMATO INDUSTRY SUPPORT AND INFRASTRUCTURE

Baulcombe, Prof. David	John Innes Centre, Sainsbury Laboratory	Norfolk
Dennis, Prof. Colin	Campden and Chorleywood Gloucestershire Food Research Association, Director General	
Evans, Tom	Mineral Solutions, University of Manchester	Lancashire
Kierstan, Dr. Mark	Leatherhead Food Research, Association, Director	Surrey
Parker, Catherine	Tomato Growers Association, Secretary	Lincolnshire
Pool, Sarah	Horticultural Research Council	Kent
Quantick, Dr. Peter	Food Research Centre, Lincoln University	Lincolnshire
Shepherd, Prof. Richard	The Food Technology Centre, University of Plymouth	Devon
Walker, Dr. Steve	Campden and Chorleywood Gloucestershire, Food Research Association, Research Director	

SPECIALIST TECHNOLOGY AND BIOTECHNOLOGY COMPANIES

Addis, Chris	Priva, UK Director	UK
Greatrex, Dr. Richard	Novartis plc	Essex
Ives, Julian	Koppert, UK Sales Manager	UK
Schoones, Dr. Stephen	Novartis plc, Technical Services Manager	UK
Scopes, Dr. Nigel	Novartis plc, Technical Services Manager	UK

RETAILING INDUSTRY

Andrews, Paul	Safeway plc, Produce Manager	UK
Bayley, Gavin	Safeway plc, Technical Operations	UK
Coombs, Tony	Safeway plc, Public Relations	UK
Finlayson, Ian	Sainsbury plc, Technical Director	UK
Myers, Bill	Williams de Broë, Analyst	London
Woolven, Dr. Jon	Institute of Grocery Distribution, Research Director	UK

TOMATO PROCESSING

Bacon, Tracy	Riverside Bakery Development Manager	Nottingham
Bayley, Robert	Heinz plc Sales Director, Europe	UK
Charlton, Andy	Northern Foods Supply Auditor	Nottingham

Craig, Vince	Hazlewood Foods, Technical Director	Nottingham
Culbey, Neil	Heinz, plc, Technical Director	UK
Grainger, Mike	Riverside Bakery, Supply Manager	Nottingham
Kirwana, Esther	New Covent Garden Soups, Technical Director	London
McLoughlin, Jan	The Pizza Factory, Managing Director	Nottingham
Stanley, David	Pennine Foods, Technical Manager	Sheffield
Tomlins, Richard	BOC, Technical Director	UK
Woods, Dr Barry	Campbell's Soups, UK, QA Director, Europe	UK

GENETIC MODIFICATION

Bramley, Prof. Peter	Royal Holloway College University of London	Surrey
Grierson, Prof. Don	University of Nottingham	Nottingham
Bright, Dr. Simon	Zeneca Science Jealott's Hill Research Station, Technology Interaction Manager	Berkshire
Poole, Prof. Nigel	Zeneca plc Jealott's Hill Research Station, Communications Director	Berkshire
Schuch, Dr. Wolfgang	Zeneca Science Jealott's Hill Research Station, Chief Research Scientist	Berkshire

ENVIRONMENTALIST ORGANISATIONS

Harwood, Rob	Soil Association	London
Mayer, Sue	Genewatch	London
Riley, Pete	Friends of the Earth	London
Thomas, Jim	Greenpeace	London

MARKETS AND LOGISTICS

Allan, Colin	New Covent Garden, Ex-General Manager	London
Atkinson, Ken	J.B. Brown, Tomato Trader New Smithfield Market	Manchester
Bailey, Simon	Safeway Regional Distribution Centre, Operations Controller	Bristol
Beynon, Alun	South West Region TGWU, Full Time Officer	Bristol
Fowler, Peter	C & C, Market Trader New Covent Garden	London
Green, Malcolm,	South West Region TGWU, Regional Industrial Organiser	Bristol
Mellonie, Andy	Victoria Trading, Paddock Wood, Technical Manager	Kent
O'Driscoll, Tony	New Covent Garden, TGWU, Full Time Officer	London
Pointer, Gordon	South West Region TGWU, Education Officer	Bristol
Wigmore, Adrian	Exel Logistics, TGWU Convenor Steward Regional Distribution Centre	Bristol

THE NETHERLANDS

Amerlaan, Jan	Research Station for Floriculture And Glasshouse Vegetables	Naaldwijk
Barnet, Robin	The Greenery International, Import Manager	UK
van Haan, Margareet	The Greenery International, Marketing Director	Utrecht
Postma, Dr. Erik	De Ruiter Seeds, Technical and Research Director	Zoetermeer

Zuurbier, Dr. Peter   University of Wageningen   Wageningen

SPAIN

Muñoz, Nazario	AENOR (Asociacion Española de Normalizacion y Certificacion), Technical Manager	Madrid
Cox, Stephen	AGRIVERA (Agricultural Verification & Assessment, S.A.), General Director	Almeria

Index

Addis, C. 124, 129
advertising
  branded *versus* own-label products
    177
  and mass production 168–69
Agombar, P. 97, 125
agriculture, industrialisation of 41, 99
Alberts, R.C. 161, 162, 163, 165, 166
Allen, C. 202, 206, 207, 208, 210
Altimiras, J. 29
American Grocer 160, 166
Anderson, A. 172
Anderson, J. 34
Andes, tomatoes first domesticated in
    2–3, 26–27
antioxidants 142, 143, 144
aphrodisiac qualities 17, 28, 41
Appadurai, A. 6, 9
Appert, N. 36
art, tomato in 157–58
Artusi, P. 41
Asociacion Española d Normalizaçion y
    Certifacaçion (AENOR) 94–95
Atkinson, K. 207, 210
auction system (Dutch)
  Greenery International
    brand identity, establishing 91
    brokerage function 89–90
    category management function
      89–91, 106
    as intermediary in supply process
      86–87, 89
    market exigencies, responding to
      90–91
    organisations of supply, competing
      modes of 87–89
    seasonal continuity, aiming for
      91–92

tensions arising from formation of
    86–87
  UK multiples, conforming to
    standards of 91
grower associations 85–86
small holdings 79–80, 82
water bomb scandal 106, 255–56
  auction system 82–83, 260, 267
  Dutch supply, German demand, and
    'tasteless tomato' 83–84
automated feedback closed ecology
    110

Bailey, R. 175, 198
Bailey, S. 212–13, 214, 216, 217, 218,
    221, 222, 223, 224, 227
Baret, C. 249
Barnet, R. 82, 84, 88, 90, 92, 100, 128
Barrientos, S. 9
Barton, A. 12
Beaumont, J. 234
Beer, G. 38
Beeton, I.M. 34–35
Belgium 38
Bence, V. 211
Bennett, J.C. 35
Benyon, A. 195
benzoate wars 166–67
Beynon, H. 213
bio-socio-economic institution, tomato
    as 10–12, 68, 97–98, 253–54
biological institution, tomato as 16
biological pest control (BPC),
    development of 108, 117–18
Bitting, A.W. 36, 172
Blackpool tomatoes 39, 44
Blair, D. and P. 117
Bonanno, A. 13

295